T5-BAL-498

Studies in Christianity and Judaism / Études sur le christianisme et le judaïsme : 5

Studies in Christianity and Judaism / Études sur le christianisme et le judaïsme

Studies in Christianity and Judaism / Études sur le christianisme et le judaïsme publishes monographs on Christianity and Judaism in the last two centuries before the common era and the first six centuries of the common era, with a special interest in studies of their interrelationship or the cultural and social context in which they developed.

GENERAL EDITOR: *Peter Richardson* University of Toronto

EDITORIAL BOARD: *Paula Fredriksen* Boston University
John Gager Princeton University
Olivette Genest Université de Montréal
Paul-Hubert Poirier Université Laval
Adele Reinhartz McMaster University
Stephen G. Wilson Carleton University
Lyle Eslinger (*ex officio*) Canadian Society of Biblical Studies

STUDIES IN CHRISTIANITY
AND JUDAISM

Number 5

DANGEROUS FOOD

1 Corinthians 8-10 in Its Context

Peter D. Gooch

Published for the Canadian Corporation for Studies in Religion / Corporation Canadienne des Sciences Religieuses by Wilfrid Laurier University Press

1993

Canadian Cataloguing in Publication Data

Gooch, Peter David, 1954-
Dangerous food : I Corinthians 8-10 in its context

(Studies in Christianity and Judaism ; 5)
Includes bibliographical references and index.

ISBN 0-88920-219-2

1. Bible. N.T. Corinthians, 1st, VIII-X – Criticism, interpretation, etc. 2. Food – Religious aspects – Christianity. 3. Jewish Christians – History – Early church, ca. 30-600. I. Canadian Corporation for Studies in Religion. II. Title. III. Series.

BS2675.2.G66 1993 227′.206 C93-093980-8

© 1993 Canadian Corporation for Studies in Religion / Corporation Canadienne des Sciences Religieuses

Cover design by Jose Martucci, Design Communications

Dangerous Food: 1 Corinthians 8-10 in Its Context has been produced from a manuscript supplied in electronic form by the author.

All rights reserved. No part of this work covered by the copyrights hereon may be reproduced or used in any form or by any means—graphic, electronic or mechanical—without the prior written permission of the publisher. Any request for photocopying, recording, taping or reproducing in information storage and retrieval systems of any part of this book shall be directed in writing to the Canadian Reprography Collective, 214 King Street West, Suite 312, Toronto, Ontario M5V 3S6.

Order from:

Wilfrid Laurier University Press
Wilfrid Laurier University
Waterloo, Ontario, Canada N2L 3C5

BS
2675.2
.G670
1993

Printed in Canada

JESUIT - KRAUSS - McCORMICK - LIBRARY
1100 EAST 55th STREET
CHICAGO, ILLINOIS 60615

Contents

Figures

Fig. 1. Plan of the sanctuary of Demeter and Kore on Acrocorinth.

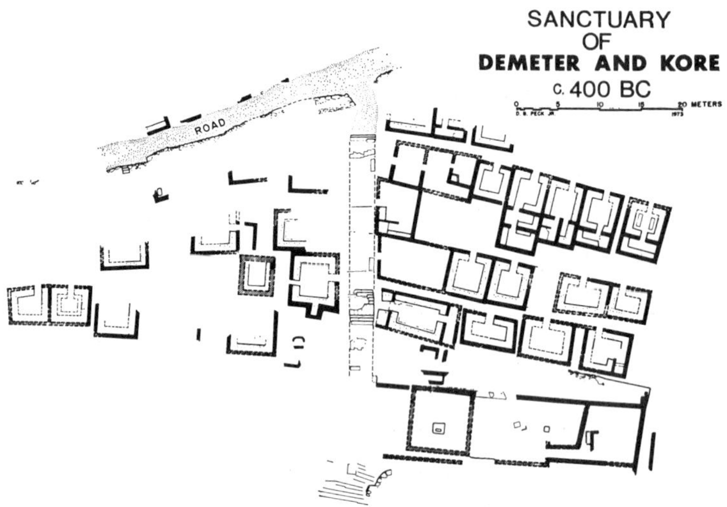

Source: Nancy Bookidis and Joan E. Fisher, "The Sanctuary of Demeter and Kore on Acrocorinth: Preliminary Report 5: 1971-1973," *Hesperia*, 43 (1974): 274. Courtesy of the American School of Classical Studies at Athens.

Fig. 2. Plan of a typical dining room in the sanctuary of Demeter and Kore on Acrocorinth.

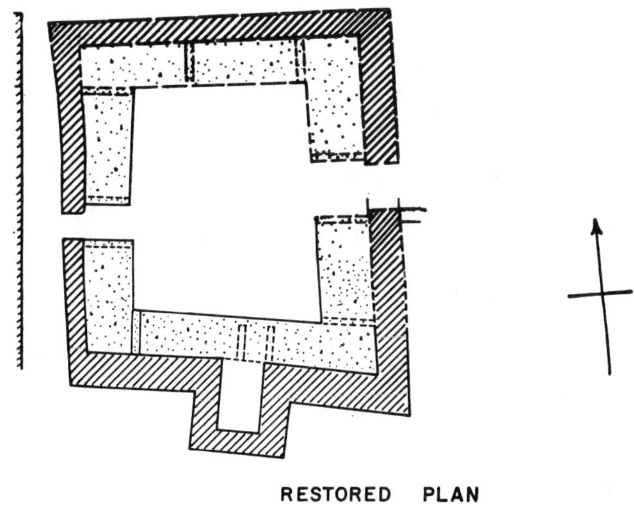

Source: Nancy Bookidis and Joan E. Fisher, "The Sanctuary of Demeter and Kore on Acrocorinth: Preliminary Report 4: 1969-1970," *Hesperia,* 41 (1972): 289, fig. 3. Courtesy of the American School of Classical Studies at Athens.

Fig. 3. Plan of Lerna, in Corinth. The shaded area to the east (right) of the colonnade is the precinct of the Asklepieion; the *abaton* of the Asklepieion was above the dining rooms.

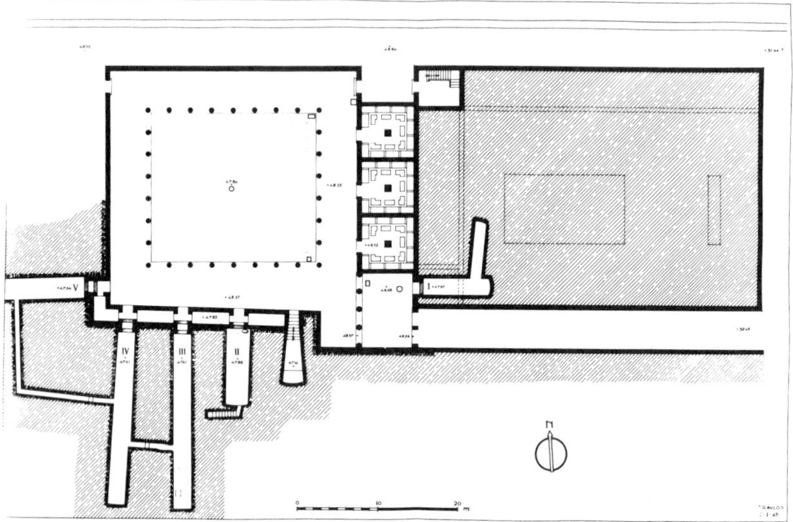

Source: Carl A. Roebuck, *Corinth: Results of Excavations Conducted by the American School of Classical Studies at Athens*, vol. 14: *The Asklepieion and Lerna* (Princeton, NJ: American School of Classical Studies at Athens, 1951), Plan C (partial reproduction). Courtesy of the American School of Classical Studies at Athens.

Fig. 4. Plan of the south dining room of Lerna, in Corinth.

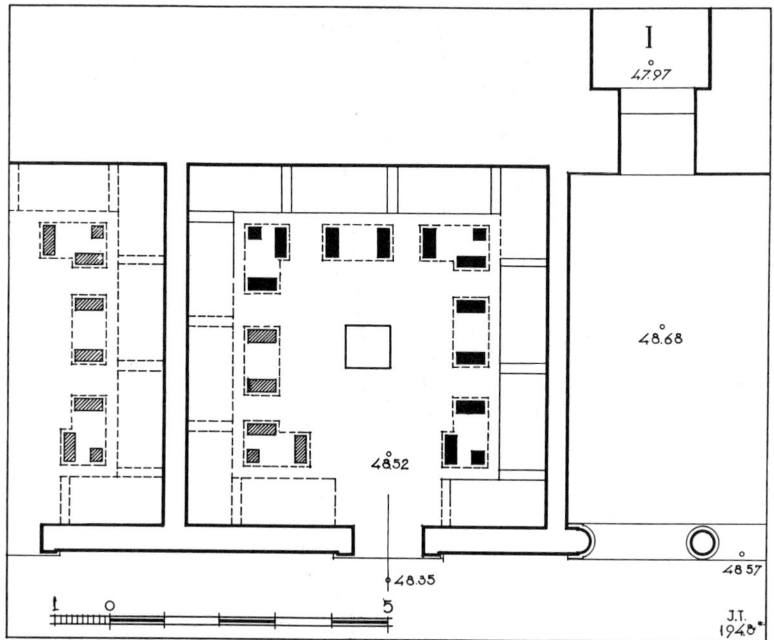

Source: Carl A. Roebuck, *Corinth: Results of Excavations Conducted by the American School of Classical Studies at Athens*, vol. 14: *The Asklepieion and Lerna* (Princeton, NJ: American School of Classical Studies at Athens, 1951), p. 52, fig. 13. Courtesy of the American School of Classical Studies at Athens.

Fig. 5. Plan of the Asklepieion near Troizen.

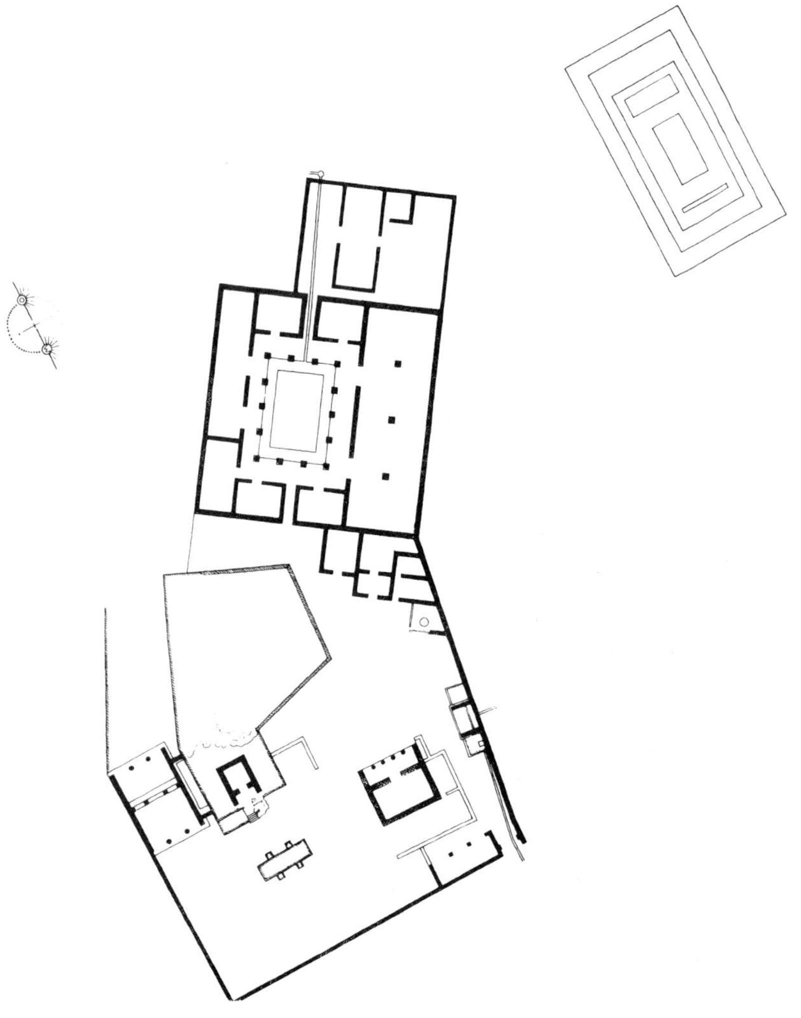

Source: Gabriel Welter, *Troizen und Kalaureia* (Berlin: Verlag Gebr. Mann, 1941), table 12.

Fig. 6. Plan of the banquet hall of the Asklepieion near Troizen.

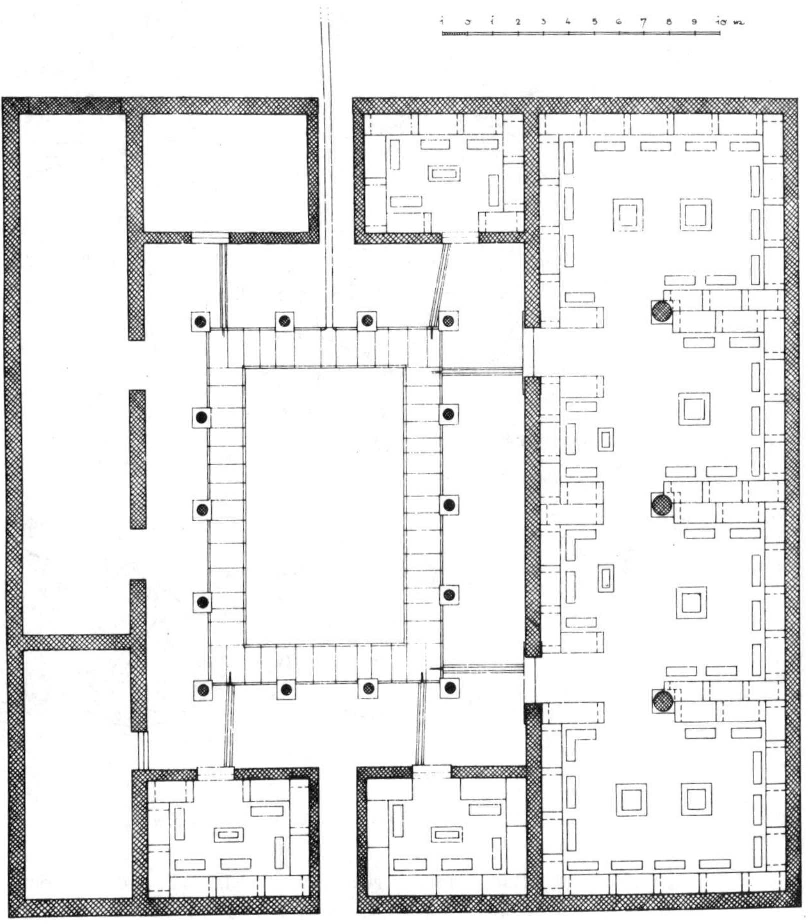

Source: Gabriel Welter, *Troizen und Kalaureia* (Berlin: Verlag Gebr. Mann, 1941), table 15.

Fig. 7. Plan of the Asklepieion near Epidauros.

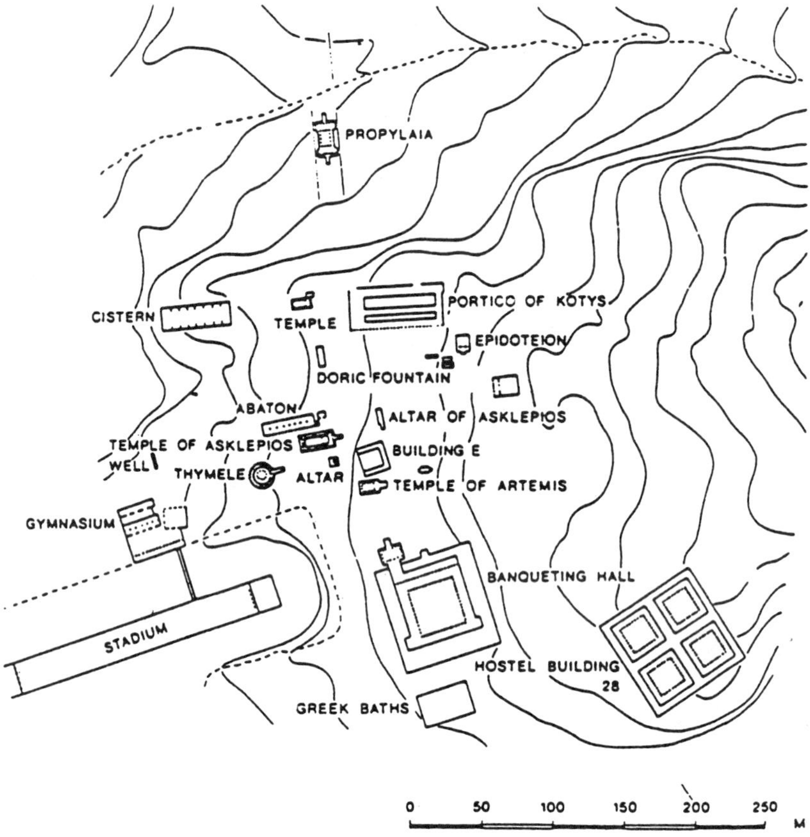

Source: R. A. Tomlinson, *Epidauros, Archaeological Sites*, ed. Malcolm Todd (London: Granada, 1983), p. 41, fig. 4. Courtesy of Paul Elek Books, an imprint of HarperCollins Publishers Ltd.

Fig. 8. Plan of the Asklepieion near Epidauros. The building numbered 26 is the banquet hall. The square plan enclosing the courtyard indicates walls in the Greek and Roman periods; note also the Roman theatral structure built within the courtyard of the Greek structure.

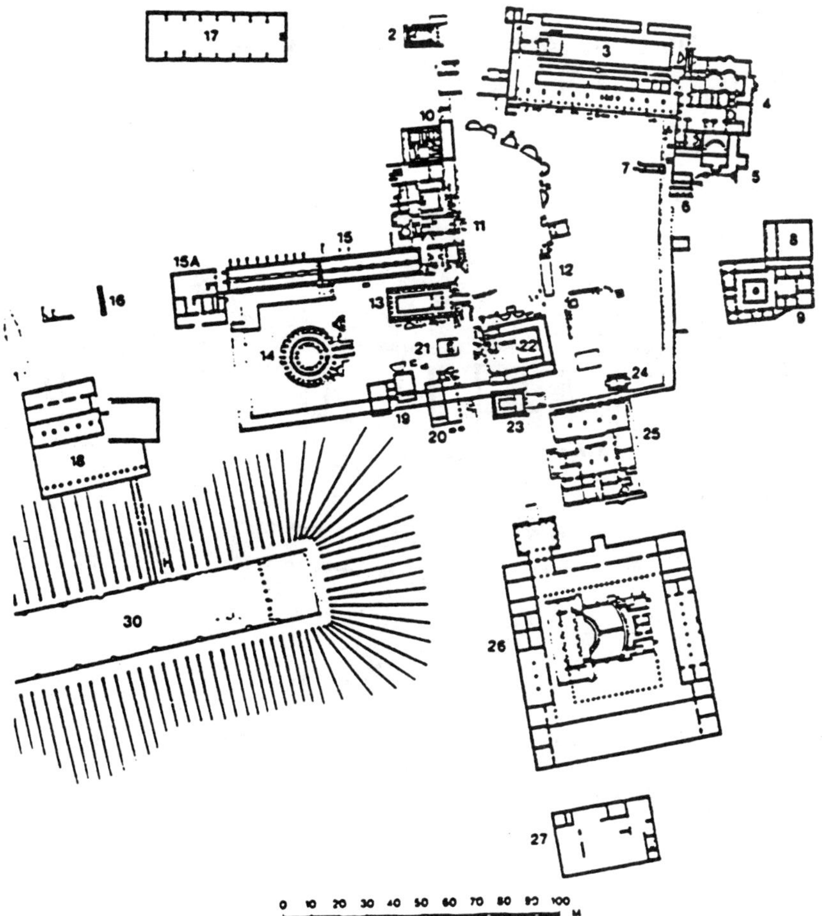

Source: R. A. Tomlinson, *Epidauros, Archaeological Sites*, ed. Malcolm Todd (London: Granada, 1983), p. 42, fig. 5. Courtesy of Paul Elek Books, an imprint of HarperCollins Publishers Ltd.

Fig. 9. Plan of the Asklepieion and adjacent dining rooms in Athens.

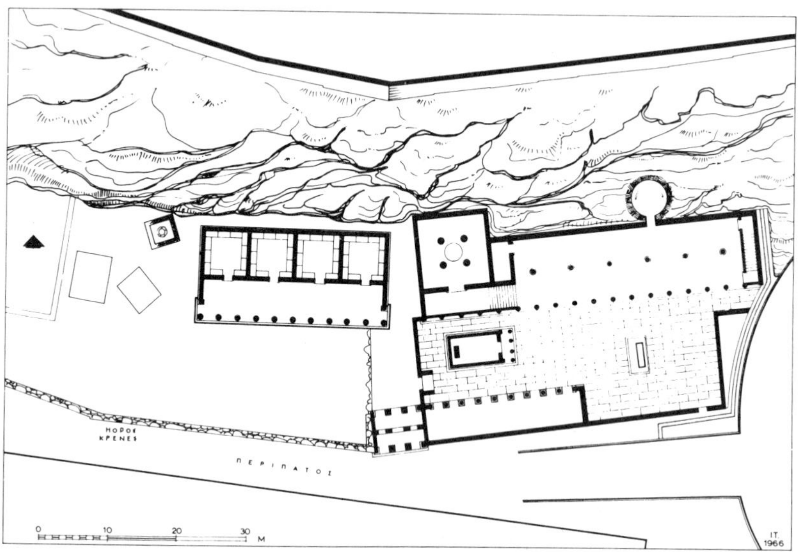

Source: John Travlos, "The Asklepieion," in *Pictorial Dictionary of Ancient Athens* (New York: Praeger, 1971), p. 129, fig. 171, an imprint of Greenwood Publishing Group, Inc., Westport, CT. Reprinted with permission.

Preface

Commentary on 1 Corinthians 8-10 shows a lack of scholarly concern over the concrete social contexts addressed by Paul: meals in temples (8:10), tables of demons (10:21), food sold in markets (10:25) and invitations from those outside the Christian group (10:27). Almost without exception, scholars are uninterested in the concrete social contexts which Paul's instructions addressed or are satisfied with superficial and ill-evidenced assumptions.

What follows is an extended attempt to read 1 Corinthians 8:1-11:1, Paul's response to the Corinthian Christians' query concerning food offered to idols, against the specific and concrete social context of the letter. This demands a reconstruction of the immediate occasion of the letter and the wider situation—that is, what food offered to idols was, and what it meant in that place at that time to eat or to avoid it. A reconstruction of what followed from Paul's writing of 1 Corinthians 8:1 to 11:1 is also attempted. My reconstruction runs against a well-entrenched scholarly consensus.

This investigation is "social-historical." This approach, as practised by scholars of the New Testament and of other historical data, is too diverse and inclusive to be in any true sense a method. Rather, scholars practising this approach employ several methods—among them, the well-established historical methods of source, literary and redaction criticism, and newer applications of anthropological and sociological methods. They bring these methods to historical texts, in pursuit of a set of historical questions which are conditioned by the insights of the social sciences. These questions include how a specific social structure is related to an ideology or conceptual construction of the world held by specific persons within that social structure, or, less grandly, how a given text is conditioned by and conditions its concrete social context.

Scholars sharing a social-historical approach to ancient texts also share a set of related assumptions. It is assumed that the tangible "stuff" of a time and place—who had what sort of economic resources, where one stood in a system of social relations, who held sexual rights to whom, what was eaten and when and so forth—can hold powerful explanatory value in an historical account. A second assumption distinguishing social-historical approaches more clearly from older historical investigations is that all the "players" (not only the rich and powerful, or in religious contexts those sanctioned by orthodoxy) are of value and interest.

I do not attempt to apply any specific sociological or anthropological model or method to the historical data investigated, both because this would be beyond my expertise and because of my conviction that the data available to us from the texts of earliest Christianity (and Greco-Roman society) are not sufficient to allow legitimate conclusions from such applications.

The investigation begins with the uses of sacred food and the social meanings of food in the Greco-Roman world in general and Paul's Corinth in particular (chaps. 1 to 3). The central part is an extended exegesis of 1 Corinthians 8:1-11:1 (chaps. 4 to 7). My reconstruction concludes with related events subsequent to 1 Corinthians 8-10 and with some observations about the significance of idol-food in earliest Christianity (chaps. 8 to 12).

This book would not be without the encouragement and help of many: in particular, my teacher and doctor-father, Peter Richardson; Marty Shukster; Michel Desjardins; my brother, Paul Gooch; and Margaret Gooch. I learned much from my teacher, John C. Hurd; my debt to his work is obvious.

I gratefully acknowledge that this book has been published with the help of a grant from the Canadian Federation for the Humanities, using funds provided by the Social Sciences and Humanities Research Council of Canada.

1

Table of daimonia

Introduction

Paul's response to the Corinthians concerning food offered to idols refers to specific contexts in which such food might be met: in temples, at the table of *daimonia*,[1] at the market and at meals hosted by non-Christians. This chapter will address, in part, temples and the table of *daimonia*.

Many Greco-Roman religions involved sacrificial rites at which the sacrifice or part of it was consumed by the worshippers.[2] This practice is often appealed to in commentary on 1 Corinthians 8-10, but there are few attempts to explore and apply it to Paul's discussion of idol-food in 1 Corinthians. I will set out the archaeological evidence concerning the sanctuary of Demeter and Kore on the slope of the mountain overlooking Corinth (the Acrocorinth), and the literary evidence concerning the nature of the cultus practised there. This will provide a detailed account of one cultic context that Paul would certainly recognize as a table of *daimonia*.[3]

1 The term *daimonia* is usually translated "demons." I do not use the translation because the word would have very different connotations for individuals. For Jewish-Christians, the word could carry the connotations of "demons," but for Gentiles in Corinth it would convey a more positive range of meanings similar to "Gods" (*theoi*).

2 See Ramsay MacMullen, *Paganism in the Roman Empire* (New Haven: Yale University Press, 1981, p. 34-42) for a wonderful description of the variety and extent of the connections between eating and religious expression in the Empire. H.-J. Klauck discusses the varieties of religious occasions in Greco-Roman society where food was consumed, in an attempt to trace the origin of the Christian sacramental meal (*Herrenmahl und hellenistischer Kult. Eine religionsgeschichtliche Untersuchung zum ersten Korintherbrief*, Neutestamentliche Abhandlungen, neue Folge, Band 15, Herausgegeben von J. Gnilka [Münster: Aschendorff, 1982], p. 31-233).

3 I provide an account only of the sanctuary of Demeter and Kore because of the

Demeter and Kore: Archaeological evidence

The sanctuary

Only one section of the ancient road to Acrocorinth (the fortified acropolis above Corinth) has been excavated, and only one sanctuary—that of Demeter and Kore—has been uncovered there.[4] Happily, the results of this excavation are highly significant for the investigation of eating practices in Roman Corinth. Many small dining rooms lie within and near the precinct of the sanctuary, with the clear implication that eating was connected to the cultic activities of the sanctuary.[5]

The Greek and Roman sanctuaries were laid out in the same pattern on three terraces (see Fig. 1). In the lower area (that closest to the road) were found eating facilities; further in, on the middle terrace, was

---

limits of archaeological evidence from Roman Corinth. The size and construction of other temples in Corinth and their location in the *agora* indicate that the purpose these buildings served was significant. What that purpose was, what rituals were practised there and what role these played in social, political and religious life are questions that are not addressable to the archaeological data. Even the identification of these temples is problematic: the standard procedure for identification is to situate the structure on a "map" derived from Pausanias's second-century C.E. travelogue (Pausanias, *Description of Greece*, vol. 2, trans. W. H. S. Jones and H. A. Omerod [Loeb Classical Library, 1918], p. 1-5). See *Corinth: Results of Excavations Conducted by the American School of Classical Studies at Athens* (Cambridge and Princeton: Harvard University Press and The American School of Classical Studies at Athens, 1932-1977), a many-authored series of detailed reports (cited hereafter as *Corinth*, followed by volume number). Summary descriptions of the archaeological investigations of Corinth can be found in James Wiseman, "Corinth and Rome I: 228 B.C.-A.D.267" (in *Aufstieg und Niedergang der römischen Welt*, 2.7.1. [Berlin: de Gruyter, 1979]) and Oscar Broneer, "Corinth: Centre of St. Paul's Missionary Work in Greece" (*Biblical Archaeologist*, 14 [1951]: 78-96). W. McDonald provides an earlier and less useful account in *Biblical Archaeologist*, 5 (1942): 36-48.

4 Wiseman, "Corinth and Rome I," p. 469.

5 The following description is based on a series of preliminary reports of the team excavating the sanctuary under the American School of Classical Studies at Athens: Ronald Stroud, "The Sanctuary of Demeter and Kore on Acrocorinth. Preliminary Report 1: 1961-1962," *Hesperia*, 34 (1965): 1-24; R. Stroud, "The Sanctuary of Demeter and Kore on Acrocorinth: Preliminary Report 2: 1964-1965," *Hesperia*, 37 (1968): 299-330; Nancy Bookidis, "The Sanctuary of Demeter and Kore on Acrocorinth: Preliminary Report 3: 1968," *Hesperia*, 38 (1969): 297-310; Nancy Bookidis and Joan E. Fisher, "The Sanctuary of Demeter and Kore on Acrocorinth: Preliminary Report 4: 1969-1970," *Hesperia*, 41 (1972): 283-331; N. Bookidis and J.E. Fisher, "The Sanctuary of Demeter and Kore on Acrocorinth: Preliminary Report 5: 1971-1973," *Hesperia*, 43 (1974): 267-307. I will cite these in what follows as "Preliminary Report," followed by report number.

a "theatral area"; on the highest terrace were buildings for the display of the cult images.[6]

Two features of the sanctuary stand out in the investigators' reports. First is the continuity of the sanctuary. The lowest strata of finds show the sanctuary in existence very early in the Archaic period, and the precinct gives evidence of continuous, unbroken use until the fourth century C.E. Second is the sanctuary's popularity. The sheer volume of votive objects attests to this, as does their quality. The vast majority of votives found were crudely made and inexpensive, and thus witness the use of the sanctuary by many persons of lower classes; the votives have the character of "simple, personal" offerings.[7]

While the sanctuary was not elaborate[8] it was not small. Dining rooms have been found to extend 50 metres to both sides of the central stairway "without any sign of termination" where the excavations stopped; furthermore, a cursory dig outside the boundaries of the sanctuary revealed buildings similar to the dining rooms, suggesting that they continued down the hillside. At least 40 dining rooms have been uncovered within the sanctuary.[9] These vary in layout and size within a general pattern, usually accommodating eight or nine diners (see Fig. 2). There is little direct evidence of cooking spaces.[10]

The dining rooms of the sanctuary were not restored in the Roman recolonization of the city. The monumental stairway on either side of which the dining rooms were built was covered over to form a ramp, and the dining rooms probably levelled to the slope of the hillside and filled in.[11] Early in the Roman period, however, the sanctuary's cultic buildings and theatral area on the higher terraces were restored, and the masses of pottery, coins and other artifacts from the

---

6 Bookidis and Fisher, "Preliminary Report 5," p. 267-70.

7 Stroud, "Preliminary Report 1," p. 1-2, and confirmed in later reports.

8 The cultic buildings on the upper terrace were large enough to hold only the cult images and an offering table; a mosaic floor shows no unusual skill or quality; the "theatral area" in the Roman period sat no more than 85 persons (Bookidis and Fisher, "Preliminary Report 4," p. 307, 312; "Preliminary Report 5," p. 267, 272, 278-80).

9 Bookidis and Fisher, "Preliminary Report 5," p. 267-68.

10 Often a smaller room was found directly adjacent to a dining room, whose function was not apparent from anything found within it. These rooms could have been storage areas, or rooms that held portable braziers for cooking (R. Stroud, "Preliminary Report 2," p. 316) or perhaps "sitting rooms" for diners before or after a meal (N. Bookidis and J. Fisher, "Preliminary Report 5," p. 277). In one such room at least clear traces of burning and substantial amounts of cooking and utility vessels were found (N. Bookidis and J. Fisher, "Preliminary Report 4," p. 296; "Preliminary Report 5," p. 273).

11 Bookidis and Fisher, "Preliminary Report 4," p. 315.

Roman period make it certain that the sanctuary continued to be active and popular from the beginning of the Roman colonization up to the late fourth century C.E.[12] The excavators found large quantities of Roman cooking ware, enough to justify the conclusion that despite the lack of dining halls the custom of dining continued. Bookidis suggests that dining may have gone on in less durable buildings, or "in more temporary circumstances, either out of doors or in tents."[13] We may conclude, then, that eating was as much a feature of the Roman sanctuary as the Greek.

Archaeological evidence concerning the role of eating in the cultus of Demeter and Kore

Was the eating in the sanctuary cultic? If so, how integral was it to the cultus of Demeter and Kore? The place of the dining rooms in the sanctuary suggests that eating was not a central rite: the rooms were found on the lowest level of the sanctuary closest to its entrance, and the sanctuary seems to have been structured so that the more sacred the place the higher it was set in the sanctuary. This conclusion is strongly reinforced by the discovery of dining rooms outside the sanctuary.

Other evidence suggests a different assessment of the importance of eating in the sanctuary. From the sheer number of dining rooms found and the amount of cooking ware found, it is certain that eating was an important activity at the sanctuary, and therefore part of the cultus in some way. Further, fragments of statuary show clearly the association of the Two Goddesses with food,[14] and votive offerings included many representations of cakes and fruits.[15] Finally, there is evidence of animal sacrifice: votive pits, where votive offerings were thrown[16] sometimes

---

12 Stroud, "Preliminary Report 2," p. 312-14; Bookidis and Fisher, "Preliminary Report 4," p. 307-15, and throughout all the Preliminary Reports.

13 Bookidis and Fisher, "Preliminary Report 4," p. 315. The lack of surviving eating facilities is probably consonant with the quality of Roman building in the sanctuary generally; the architectural remains (distinct from pottery or coins) of the Roman sanctuary are meagre, and Stroud claims that the Roman buildings were poorly constructed and susceptible to pillage and erosion ("Preliminary Report 2," p. 312).

14 Stroud, "Preliminary Report 1," p. 22-23. Many statues of Demeter were found showing her in a standard pose with a torch in her left hand (many lamps were found in the sanctuary) and a pig in her right, or holding stalks of wheat and a seed pod from a poppy.

15 Stroud, "Preliminary Report 1," p. 10; "Preliminary Report 2," p. 300. There were votives representing many objects. Female figures dominate in numbers, but children, horses, doves, cocks and other animals are also represented ("Preliminary Report 1," p. 17-18).

16 Depositing offerings into a pit may be connected to the myth of Kore's descent into the underworld. Compare the ritual of the Two Goddesses' festival of

contain, along with miniature votives, coarse cooking pots and much ash, and among the ashes many bones that can be clearly identified as those of young pigs.[17] Since we have clear evidence on the one hand of much eating in the sanctuary, and on the other hand of the sacrifice of pigs and the dedication of cereals and fruits, we can confidently link the two and conclude that cultic meals occurred in the sanctuary.

It is possible that the spatial organization of the sanctuary reflects not so much the "importance" of activities taking place there as the accessibility to those activities. Pausanias reports that the cult images were not on display, and the buildings holding them were not large.[18] The theatral area was screened from the rest of the sanctuary, held approximately 85 persons and was probably used to present some sacred drama or sacred objects, so it was probably used in connection with the mysteries and accessible only to initiates.[19] The dining rooms held many more persons and were more accessible, even though the meals held within them were connected to the ritual of the sanctuary. All these activities were important to the cult, and an integral part of its functioning.

Demeter and Kore: Literary evidence

An account of the uses of food in the cultus of Demeter and Kore might illuminate the question of the social and religious uses of food in Paul's Corinth. Such an account immediately runs into two important obstacles: first, there is no abundance of evidence concerning the rites of Demeter worship (even minor festivals fall under a ban of secrecy similar to that of the other Mysteries[20]); second, what is known of that worship is known chiefly of Eleusis, the cult centre, and cannot be applied uncritically to the sanctuary at Corinth.

The worship of Demeter and Kore

George Mylonas finds it no exaggeration to characterize the cultus of Demeter and Kore as the most exalted, gentle and wholesome religion of antiquity, and his disappointment at its demise under the oppro-

---

Thesmophoria, where piglets were thrown into pits and a short while later their partially decomposed carcasses retrieved and mixed with seed to ensure the seed's fertility. (See Allaire Chandor Brumfield, *The Attic Festivals of Demeter and their Relation to the Agricultural Year*, Monographs in Classical Studies, ed. W. R. Connor [New York: Arno Press, 1981], p. 77-79.)

17 Stroud, "Preliminary Report 1," p. 8-10; "Preliminary Report 2," p. 300. One terracotta pig was found in the same pit as the bones of pigs; Stroud suggests that "one worshipper seems to have been unable to afford a live pig and substituted a small terracotta one."

18 Bookidis and Fisher, "Preliminary Report 4," p. 312; Pausanias 2.4.7.

19 Stroud, "Preliminary Report 2," p. 306.

20 Brumfield, *Attic Festivals*, p. 83.

brium of Christianity is palpable.[21] The basic elements of the cultic myth are well known: the rape and abduction of Persephone (or Kore, "the maiden"); the grief and wandering of Demeter her mother; Demeter's coercion of Zeus by causing famine; the resolution of the crisis by a yearly three-month sojourn of Persephone with Plouton in the underworld and Demeter's instruction to men in the art of cultivation. The myth is intriguing, and its obvious function as an aetiological myth of the seasonal cycle makes it no less appealing, then or now.

By the time of the establishment of the Mysteries, Demeter had come into close association with Plouton, the God of the underworld, and her worship was connected with a hope for blessedness after death in that other world. This seems an important aspect of the cultus of Demeter (perhaps even the central aspect of the cultus for many individuals socially or economically distant from agricultural occupations), but even this aspect is not far removed from explicitly agricultural conceptions of death and rebirth, and agricultural elements and symbols are entwined with chthonian symbols and conceptions in all aspects of the worship of Demeter.

The myth of Demeter and the maiden is openly agricultural, and the festivals of the cultus frame the agricultural year: at the time of ploughing, *Proêrosia*; of sowing, *Thesmophoria*; of the mid-winter when the sown seed seemed dead in the earth, *Halôa*; of the first green shoots heralding the harvest, *Chloaia*; of the storing of the seed until next sowing, *Skira*.[22] Many epithets of Demeter are clearly linked to harvest, threshing, grinding and baking.[23]

The cultic myth of Demeter and Kore, the relation of her festivals to the agricultural year, and the many explicit identifications of Demeter and her gift of the art of cultivation make it plain that her cultus was intimately connected with food.[24] How food was used in her cultus, however, is the question to which I turn.

---

21 George E. Mylonas, *Eleusis and the Eleusinian Mysteries* (Princeton: Princeton University Press, 1961).

22 Brumfield, *Attic Festivals*, p. 54, 70, 104, 131, 173. Brumfield spent much time and effort studying and experiencing present subsistence farming in Attica, and this research gives her book both force and colour.

23 Ibid., p. 148-49.

24 In addition to the obvious agricultural nature of the cultus, U. Bianchi's collection of iconographic evidence concerning the Mysteries can be used as a rough index: of 52 plates concerning the Eleusinian Mysteries, 18 depict the cultus's deities in connection with food—either at a banquet, or receiving food offerings, or holding stalks of grain or cornucopiae (Ugo Bianchi, *The Greek Mysteries*, Iconography of Religions, Section 17: Greece and Rome, Fascicle 3 [Leiden: E. J. Brill, 1976], plates 1-52).

Sacrifice and food in the Mysteries of Demeter and Kore

My discussion of the Mysteries necessarily focusses on purification rituals of the *mystae* and especially the sacrifice of pigs as part of these, on Clement of Alexandria's report concerning the watchword of the Mysteries, and on other sacrifices involved in the celebration of the Mysteries.

To be initiated into the Mysteries of Demeter required elaborate preparation. One had to have been already initiated into the Lesser Mysteries at Agrai near Athens a year earlier, which served to purify the candidate. The Greater Mysteries began with a six-day period prior to the procession from Athens to Eleusis, during which various rites and sacrifices were enacted in Athens for the purification of the *mystae*.[25] At the beginning of these preparations a declaration was made concerning who could participate: "anyone of clean hands and intelligible speech [Greek, of course] who is pure of all pollution and whose soul is conscious of no evil and who has lived well and justly."[26] Candidates probably fasted during the day and ate at night, and it may also be assumed that sexual abstinence was required.[27]

A central rite in this process of purification was the sacrifice by each initiate of a piglet, after the initiate bathed in the sea with it.[28] It may be inferred with confidence from Aristophanes that these pigs were eaten: in *Frogs*, a slave whose dominant comic characteristic is an eye to the main chance responds to the sight of initiates with "O Mistress most worshipful, Daughter of Demeter—how sweet a scent of pork I get!" to which his master replies, "Hold your tongue and you might get a string of sausages."[29]

---

25 Mylonas, *Eleusis*, p. 243 and Brumfield, *Attic Festivals*, p. 142.

26 Mylonas, *Eleusis*, p. 247.

27 Lewis Richard Farnell, *The Cults of the Greek States,* 5 vols. (Oxford: Clarendon Press, 1896-1909), 3:168. Farnell cites Porphyry's list of many foods forbidden to initiates: several sorts of fish, eggs, beans, domestic birds, pomegranates, apples, and the flesh of animals improperly killed.

28 Note the regular association of pigs with Demeter. Pigs were sacrificed also in the purification of the Sacred Field, the sanctuary of Eleusis and the Priestess's house there (Mylonas, *Eleusis*, p. 249). Pigs and serpents held chthonic associations and thus were "the peculiar animals and most frequent companions" of Demeter (Farnell, *Cults*, 3:220).

29 Aristophanes, *Frogs*, 337 (Aristophanes, *Plays*, trans. Patrick Dickinson [Oxford: Oxford University Press, 1970], 2:194). Note other references in *Frogs*, whose context is the procession to Eleusis: the chorus, representing initiates, chants "Fall in like men; You've eaten enough. . . . On your way!" (Aristophanes, *Frogs*, 370-75, in Dickinson, *Plays*, 2:195). and again, "Goddess, patroness, . . . we'll do our best for you—Do yours, after the feast, and put us first!" (ibid., 384-89, in Dickinson, *Plays*, 2:196).

Another significant source for the religious use of food in the Mysteries is Clement of Alexandria's report of the "watchword" (*synthêma*) of the Eleusinian Mysteries. Delatte has investigated the uses of the term *synthêma*, and concludes that it reflects a context of questions to and answers from the initiate[30]—questions concerning the candidate's fitness for initiation. Clement reports the initiates' response as follows: "I fasted, I drank the *kykêon*, I took from a chest, I did something, I put into a basket and from a basket into a chest."[31] This aphoristic saying stands as one of our few hints of the rites of the Mysteries—the ban on speaking of the Mysteries was very well kept, but Clement of course felt no such compunction in his critique—and much effort has been expended in its interpretation. My discussion will centre on the drinking of the *kykêon* (a mixed drink).

A *kykêon* was made from hulled and crushed (not milled) grain, especially barley, stirred into a liquid (water, milk, wine, honey or oil) and sometimes seasoned with herbs. It was a simple food or drink that carried (outside the Mysteries at least) connotations of primitive rural life. Reay Tannahill suggests that such grain and liquid mixtures were among our first uses of grain as food. Such a mixture was an "epoch-making discovery in pre-historic times, enabling man (*sic*)—despite the limits of his technology—to make a quantity of solid food out of tiny, insubstantial seeds."[32] This would make the *kykêon* a most fitting element of the rites honouring Demeter's gift of cultivation.

The *Homeric Hymn to Demeter* gives both an aetiological story for the use of *kykêon* and an indication of its nature and elements in the cultus of Demeter. N. J. Richardson has concluded from a comparison of the *Hymn* and what is known of the Mysteries that the *Hymn* functioned as an "official" cult myth.[33] The passage concerning the *kykêon* refers to Demeter taking the drink "to observe the sacrament." [34] In the *Hymn*'s narrative the bereaved Demeter has refused all food and

---

30 Armand Delatte, *Le cycéon. Breuvage rituel des mystères d'Eleusis*, Collection d'études anciennes publiée sous le patronage de L'Association G. Bude (Paris: Société d'Édition Les Belles Lettres, 1955), p. 699. (This small monograph is an excerpt from the *Bulletin de l'Academie Royale de Belgique*, Classe de Lettres et Sciences morales et politique, 5 serie, tome 40, 1954.)

31 Clement, *Protrept.* 21.2 (Stählin).

32 Reay Tannahill, *Food in History* (New York: Stein and Day, 1973), p. 35-36. Compare Delatte, *Cycéon*,p. 711.

33 N. J. Richardson, ed., *The Homeric Hymn to Demeter* (Oxford: Clarendon Press, 1974), p. 12.

34 *Homeric Hymn to Demeter*, 210 (the translation cited is that of Hugh G. Evelyn-White, from *Hesiod, the Homeric Hymns and Homerica*, Loeb Classical Library, 1970, p. 303).

drink, and, finally persuaded to take something, requests that meal be mixed with water and mint. With this she breaks her fast.[35]

Drinking the *kykêon*, then, was part of the rites of the Mysteries. It was more than a casual or practical breaking of the fast before the Mysteries. It was a solemn conscious imitation of the act of Demeter in her bereavement and was done in accordance with her command; it was a commemorative act that allowed the initiate to participate in the story of Demeter, and was part of the way in which her blessing was bestowed on him or her.[36] It was part of the larger pattern of the rites of the Mysteries, which very likely were, or included, a sacred re-enactment of the story of Demeter and the maiden.[37]

The central feature of the Mysteries was something *seen*: the climax of the initiation came when in a blaze of light the sacred things were shown, and our sources speak of initiation often in the vocabulary of seeing.[38] Thus drinking the *kykêon* would be preparatory to initiation, the way in which the candidate ritually broke the fast of purification, and the rite probably occurred after the procession of initiates had arrived at the sanctuary at Eleusis and before they were admitted to the Telesterion for initiation.

Another relevant element of the cultus was the *kernophoria*, the offering of *kernoi*, that very likely was the last act of the *pannychis* (a night feast involving singing and dancing) after the arrival at Eleusis.[39] A *kernos* was an earthen dish with several smaller compartments that were filled with various foods—mostly seeds and grains, but also liquids such as honey, milk, oil or wine.[40] *Kernoi* were used also in the cults of other deities, but were found often in the rites of Demeter worship, in the Mysteries and in other festivals.

Those offering from the *kernoi* also ate from them. Athenaeus preserves a fragment of Polemon that provides evidence of this: the priest "celebrates mystic rites, takes out the objects . . . and distributes them to those who have borne the *kernos* aloft. . . . And he who has carried

35 *Homeric Hymn to Demeter*, 192-211.

36 Farnell, *Cults*, 3:194-97; Paul Foucart, *Les mystères d'Eleusis* (Paris: Libraire des Archives Nationales et de la Société de l'École des Chartes, ed. A. Picard, 1914), p. 382; Mylonas, *Eleusis*, p. 259; Klauck, *Herrenmahl*, p. 100-101. For an older view, see F. B. Jevons, *Introduction to the History of Religion* (n.p., 1896).

37 The most comprehensive and convincing discussion of the general question of what occurred in the Mysteries is that of Mylonas, *Eleusis*, p. 243-76. Regarding the sacred drama, see p. 261-72.

38 See, for example, Farnell, *Cults*, 3:197; Mylonas, *Eleusis*, p. 273; Klauck, *Herrenmahl*, p. 102.

39 Farnell, *Cults*, 3:186; Mylonas, *Eleusis*, p. 257.

40 Ibid., p. 221.

them, that means he who has borne the *kernos* aloft, tastes these articles."[41] Both Farnell and Mylonas apply this passage to the preliminary rites of the Mysteries.[42] The eating connected to the *kernophoria* was very likely carried out by all or many initiates.

Both the drinking of the *kykêon* and the eating from the *kernoi* are significant instances of the religious use of food in the Eleusinian Mysteries. Though these acts were not part of the central rites of initiation into the Mysteries, they were clearly sacred acts integral to preparation for initiation; moreover, they stood close to the religious meaning of the Mysteries that in large part celebrated the seasonal cycle of regeneration and the Goddess's gift of cultivation and the consequent abundant supply of food.

Other festivals

The Lesser Mysteries (the preliminary initiation held at Agrai in the early spring) demanded, as did the Eleusinian Mysteries, purification rites of fasting, sprinkling of water or bathing and sacrifice. A *kernophoria* also took place in a similar context of singing and dancing. Our conclusions concerning the religious use of food in the Eleusinian Mysteries are valid regarding this festival also.[43]

The Thesmophoria does not stand in such a close relationship with the Mysteries, nor was its celebration restricted to Eleusis or Agrai. This festival was held in Pyanopsion (October/November), the month of sowing, and its central rite was the throwing of piglets into underground chambers (*megara*).[44] After two or three days the rotting remains were retrieved and then mixed with seed to bestow fertility in the sowing soon to follow. This festival was everywhere restricted, at least in its central rites, to women.[45] It is likely that with the throwing of pigs into the *megaron* there were sacrifices that in turn may have been eaten: Farnell reports that it is attested of the festival that

---

41 Athenaeus, 478c. The text is given by Farnell, *Cults*, 3:357, n. 219d. I have quoted the translation offered by Mylonas, *Eleusis*, p. 271.

42 Farnell, *Cults*, 3:186; Mylonas, *Eleusis*, p. 271.

43 Regarding the Lesser Mysteries, see Mylonas, *Eleusis*, p. 239-43 and Brumfield, *Attic Festivals*, p. 139-47.

44 A *megaron* means normally a large chamber, and in religious contexts refers often to oracular shrines or sanctuaries of temples. In the context of Demeter worship, and especially the Thesmophoria, it means an underground chamber. See Brumfield, *Attic Festivals*, p. 100, n. 53.

45 For general discussions of the Thesmophoria see Farnell, *Cults*, 3:83-121; Ludwig August Deubner, *Attische feste* (Berlin: Akademie-Verlag, 1956 [first published Berlin: Verlag Heinrich Keller, 1932]), p. 50-60; Brumfield, *Attic Festivals*, p. 70-95.

worshippers ate pig's flesh and took "very probably . . . a sacramental meal."[46]

Three other aspects of this festival are of particular relevance: the *pannychis* celebrated on the first night, feasts held on the last day, and sacrificial cakes. On the first night of the festival women gathered to drink[47] and participate in rites of foul, abusive language and sexual joking (*aischrologia*).[48] This *aischrologia* was also part of the Mysteries and especially the procession to Eleusis, and its sexual themes are very likely connected to the fertility themes and purposes of Demeter worship. It is reasonable to suppose that, where women gathered to drink and rose up to play, food would be eaten.[49] There is evidence for feasts held on the last day of the festival, presided over by women elected to office in the cultus.[50] Finally, associated with the festival are sacrificial cakes made into the shape of phalli, which also were thrown into and brought out of the underground chamber.[51] These, or similar ones, would also be eaten: Brumfield cites a scholion to Lucian describing an initiation given only to women at Eleusis, where *aischrologia* was spoken and obscene joking took place, and where wine, every kind of food (except that forbidden in the Mysteries) and sexual organs made from pastry were set out on tables.[52]

The remaining festivals of the cultus of Demeter and Kore exhibit very similar features. There was a *pannychis* involving *aischrologia* also at the Haloa, and it may be concluded that this occasion included feasting.[53] All these other festivals involved sacrifices of various sorts, both animal and cereal, but apart from the Haloa, commentators report little evidence specific to feasts or the religious consumption of food.

Evidence concerning *pannycheis*, feasts and the use of sacred cakes in other festivals of Demeter show, then, that the religious role and

---

46 Farnell, *Cults*, 3:90, citing evidence set out at p. 326, n. 75a.

47 Aristophanes' *Thesmophoriazusai* is full of allusions to women drinking at this festival (for example, l. 626-35, 730-38).

48 Farnell, *Cults*, 3:104; Deubner, *Feste*, p. 52-53; Brumfield, *Attic Festivals*, p. 80-81.

49 Ibid., p. 80-81.

50 Ibid., p. 83. A sacred calendar of the Demeter cultus shows provisions made in the Thesmophoria for banquets in honour of the two deities (Sterling Dow and Robert F. Healey, *A Sacred Calendar of Eleusis*, Harvard Theological Studies 21 [Cambridge, Mass.: Harvard University Press, 1965], transcription and translation of calendar). Aristophanes in *Thesmophoriazusai* has the chorus summon Demeter and Kore to the women's feast (1145-47).

51 Deubner, *Feste*, p. 50; Brumfield, *Attic Festivals*, p. 77-78.

52 Ibid., p. 108. Aristophanes, *Thesmophoriazusai*, 280 refers to the offering of cakes. Mylonas describes a bakery, perhaps for this purpose, found within the precinct at Eleusis (*Eleusis*, p. 171).

53 Brumfield, *Attic Festivals*, p. 113-15.

significance of food in these festivals was similar to that in the Mysteries.

Conclusions

The consumption of food was an integral and important part of the cultus of Demeter and Kore. Because the cultus of Demeter centred so clearly on the Goddess's gift of the art of cultivation, it is also probable that the consumption of food played an even more prominent role than extant sources evidence. The food described above was sacred to the Goddess, and these instances of eating were sacramental acts of thanksgiving and obedience to, and commemoration of, the Two Goddesses.

Eleusis and Corinth

This conclusion begs to be applied to Paul's problem of sacred food (*hierothyton*), but a significant obstacle still stands in the way of such an application: most of the evidence surveyed derives from Eleusis and Athens, and cannot be translated uncritically to the sanctuary of Demeter on the lower slopes of the Acrocorinth.

Rites connected with both the Lesser and Greater Mysteries took place only at Agrai, Athens and Eleusis. This restriction of place is likely true of other festivals—in particular, Haloa and Chloaia, which are evidenced only at Eleusis.[54]

In contrast, other festivals were not so restricted. Harvest festivals seem to have been entirely local, and both the Proerosia and the Thesmophoria are attested elsewhere. The Thesmophoria especially is called, with good reason, a "pan-Hellenic" festival: it is attested at Thebes, Ephesus, Miletus and many other cities[55]—and among them, most happily, Corinth.[56] Further, what evidence exists concerning the festival in these diverse places suggests that it was celebrated everywhere similarly.[57] *Prima facie*, then, one may assume both that much evidence concerning the Thesmophoria at Eleusis is relevant to Corinth, and that general conclusions concerning the role of food in Demeter worship are equally valid concerning her cultus practised in Corinth.

---

54 Ibid., p. 116, 135.

55 The Thesmophoria is attested in at least 30 cities in Greece, Asia Minor and Sicily (Brumfield, *Attic Festivals*, p. 70; Farnell, *Cults*, 3:66-83). Regarding the Proerosia, see Brumfield, *Attic Festivals*, p. 61.

56 Farnell, *Cults*, 3:93. There is nothing in the source which Farnell cites that is relevant to this discussion, apart from its indication that a Thesmophoria was celebrated in Corinth.

57 Farnell, *Cults*, 3:98-99.

The excavations of the sanctuary of Demeter and Kore on Acrocorinth add the weight of evidence to this assumption. Many elements of the cultus of Demeter as seen in Eleusinian sources reappear on Acrocorinth. A "theatre" was found there, though large enough only for the presentation of a small-scale, simple sacred drama.[58] Also found were chthonic elements and symbols, torches and lamps strongly suggesting *pannycheis*,[59] evidence of sacrifices of pigs, pits perhaps serving as *megara*,[60] votive offerings depicting fruit and grain, and, most significantly, votive *kernoi*. When this evidence is added to that of the many dining rooms found in and near the sanctuary, it is certain that the significant use of food integral to Demeter worship at Eleusis occurred also in her sanctuary at Corinth.

Demeter and Kore and the table of daimonia

The rites of Demeter worship in Corinth are a clear and explicit example of what Paul would call sharing in the table of *daimoniôn* (1 Cor 10:21). To eat from the *kernos* in the sanctuary of Demeter, or to share in pork from a sacrifice offered to her, or to eat a cake representing the fertility brought by Demeter would be to eat food sacred to Demeter, and to share in the rites of her worship. Moreover, it seems very likely that any food whatever in her sanctuary would be in some sense sacred to her. How could one eat in Demeter's sanctuary and not remember, or be reminded by word or symbol or ritual act, that the fruit of the fertile ground was her gift? This conclusion is not surprising, of course, but it is happy to find so clear and well evidenced an example of *hierothyta* in Corinth, especially concerning a cultus that was active and popular[61] at the time of Paul, and very likely well used by persons of economic and social standing similar to that of Paul's community.

---

58 Regarding the Eleusinian Telesterion, see Richardson, *Homeric Hymn*, p. 24.

59 Bookidis and Fisher, "Preliminary Report 4," p. 302.

60 I offer the identification as *megara* of the shallow pits found in the sanctuary filled with votive offerings and remains of animal sacrifices. It seems an obvious solution to the function of these pits which puzzled the excavators, but they did not identify the pits as *megara* (nor, it should be noted, discussed this possibility).

61 The importance of the cult in Corinth is not sufficiently appreciated by commentators. The archaeological evidence is especially important because we have very few literary accounts of the cult in Corinth, despite the Goddesses' great popularity there.

2

In an idol's temple

Were meals at temples distinct from cultic meals?

Paul refers both to the table of *daimonia* and to eating in an idol's temple in 1 Corinthians (10:21 and 8:10), and provides distinct assessments of these: the table of demons is to be shunned, but eating in an idol's temple might cause one of the weak to fall. A common-sense reading of 1 Corinthians might suggest that these two contexts are the same. But because Paul uses different vocabulary in the two instances and assesses them differently, a question is raised whether eating in a temple may be distinct from participating at the table of *daimonia*. This chapter explores the possibility that there were meals in temples that were not necessarily connected to religious rites carried out in those temples, or, in other words, that the inextricable association of meal and cult (as in the worship of Demeter and Kore) was not necessary in all cases.

Asklepios: Archaeological evidence from Corinth

Some 500 metres north of the *agora*, against the northern wall of the city, was found the precinct sacred to Asklepios and, immediately to the west of it and to some degree integrated with it, the fountain house of Lerna. Both the Asklepieion and Lerna are important to our investigation because, under the chief cultic building of the Asklepieion, opening on to the courtyard surrounding the fountain of Lerna, are found three dining rooms.[1]

1 The excavation of the American School of Classical Studies at Athens is reported by Carl A. Roebuck in *Corinth: Results of Excavations Conducted by the American School of Classical Studies at Athens*, vol. 14, *The Asklepieion and Lerna* (Princeton: American School of Classical Studies at Athens, 1951 [cited hereafter as *Corinth* 14]). A brief summary of Roebuck's report and brief discussion of the cult of Asklepios is found in Mabel Lang, *Cure and Cult in Ancient Corinth: A Guide to the Asklepieion*, American Excavations in Old Corinth, Corinth Notes, no. 1 (Princeton: American School of Classical Studies at Athens, 1977).

The Asklepieion and Lerna were developed by the late fourth century B.C.E. into the monumental building complex that survived (with modifications) into the Roman period (see Fig. 3). Carl Angus Roebuck describes Lerna as a "resort" built around a spring, a courtyard surrounded by a continuous colonnade in whose shade persons could rest. On the north was a small staircase leading from the cultic building of the Asklepieion down to a small courtyard north of the dining rooms.[2] The Asklepieion consisted of a precinct surrounded also by colonnades, and within the precinct a large altar, a temple, an *abaton*, two pits perhaps for the holding of sacred snakes and possibly wooden structures to hold displays of votive objects.[3] The most important building within the precinct was the *abaton*, a large building that was used for the rite of incubation. The person seeking healing would spend a night in this large, communal chamber designed for the visitation of the God.[4]

The access provided by the staircase between the Asklepieion and Lerna gives rise to the following questions. Was Lerna included in the Asklepieion? How far was Lerna integrated into the functions of the Asklepieion? What was the role of the dining rooms in the Asklepieion's cultus?[5]

Persons coming to the Asklepieion would very likely make use of the facilities of Lerna for relaxation. The spaciousness of the colonnades of Lerna, the volume of water within its reservoirs and its proximity to other recreational buildings—the theatre, the gymnasium—make it likely, however, that Lerna was more a public fountain that was also used by visitors to the Asklepieion.[6] This division into "sacred" (the Asklepieion) and "secular" areas (Lerna) is paralleled in the Asklepieion in Troezen, where a courtyard and rooms, including dining rooms, are separate from the temple and sacred precinct.[7]

---

2 Roebuck, *Corinth* 14: 23-24.

3 Ibid., p. 29-40. These votive objects—terracotta representations of parts of the body healed by the God and dedicated in gratitude or in fulfilment of a vow—are abundantly preserved in the precinct. Roebuck concludes his volume with a thorough discussion of these, with fascinating photographic plates.

4 Ibid., p. 23, 46-51.

5 Before the Roman reconstruction there was a large ramp between the Asklepieion and Lerna, providing very ready access between them (Roebuck, *Corinth* 14: 23-24). In the Roman period the ramp was filled in and other structures added. This adds force to questions of the relationship of the sites.

6 Roebuck, *Corinth* 14: 25-26. See also Pausanias's description in *Description of Greece* 2.4.5.

7 Roebuck, *Corinth* 14: 1, 24-26.

If Lerna was a public resort happily proximate to the Asklepieion, it is likely that the dining rooms on the east side of the Lerna colonnade, even though directly beneath the *abaton* of the Asklepieion, were not a part of the precinct but simply convenient for the use of visitors to the Asklepieion and others. Roebuck suggests that these rooms could have been used not only for eating but also for sleeping,[8] but he is confident that these rooms would not have been used for incubation. This conclusion is reached partly on archaeological grounds. A structure built above the rooms and part of the precinct seems to have been used for this purpose, and the dining rooms were not easily accessible from the precinct for priests and cult officials. This conclusion is also supported by other evidence. "There is no indication," Roebuck claims, "that taking meals was a part of the ritual of incubation."[9] The excavation report concludes, then, that it is likely that the dining rooms of Lerna played no official or cultic role in the Asklepieion.[10]

The dining rooms of Lerna provide valuable evidence of the physical arrangements for eating in Roman Corinth. There were three dining rooms, each opening onto the east side of the courtyard of Lerna. The floors of the rooms were hard concrete, the walls covered in red stucco. In the centre of the south room (presumably the other rooms followed the same arrangement) was a square block, blackened and cracked with heat; this served as a brazier. Around the perimeter of the room were couches, each cut from a single stone block; five couches are preserved, but the arrangement of these and the dimensions of the room allow the conclusion that 11 persons could recline. There is no evidence of a kitchen near the rooms, but the braziers in the rooms were used, and possibly the open courtyard to the north of the rooms (into which the north staircase from the Asklepieion exits) could have been used for the preparation of food.[11] The decoration of the couches and rooms and their location in the "resort" of Lerna make it likely that the dining rooms were relatively expensively appointed and pleasant places to eat. (See Fig. 4.)

Archaeological evidence of other Asklepieia

The excavators concluded with confidence that the dining rooms of Lerna were probably not formally or functionally related to the cultus of the sanctuary, but were an extension of the recreational function of

8 Ibid., p. 55.

9 Ibid., p. 57.

10 This conclusion seems well warranted on the basis of the archaeological evidence of the Corinthian Asklepieion and Lerna, but my argument below will show that this conclusion must be softened.

11 Roebuck, *Corinth* 14: 51-57.

the fountain of Lerna.[12] The significance of the dining rooms in Lerna requires assessment, however, in the light of evidence from other Asklepieia and literary sources concerning the cult of Asklepios. Evidence of the association of springs and dining rooms with other sanctuaries of Asklepios and evidence from literary sources concerning the use of food in the cultus of Asklepios will lead to different conclusions regarding the association of the dining rooms of Lerna with the Asklepieion, that will in turn allow a more firmly based exploration of implications for the issue of idol-food in Paul's Corinth.

Springs and Asklepieia

Though our interest centres on the dining rooms of Lerna, it is significant none the less that Lerna was a fountain. Many Asklepieia were founded around springs or sacred wells, and water was an important element of cure. All of the major centres of the cult that have been excavated—Epidauros, Pergamon and Kos—have facilities for springs and/or baths. Smaller sanctuaries show the same feature: that in Troizen contained a monumental fountain, and in Athens the Asklepieion included a cave and its sacred spring.[13]

Vitruvius demands that Asklepieia be built in healthful locations near wholesome fountains: "There will be a natural appropriateness if, for all temples in the first place, the most healthy sites be chosen and suitable springs of water in those places in which shrines are to be set up, and for Asclepius in particular [and other Gods of healing]. . . . For when sick persons are moved from a pestilent to a healthy place and the water supply is from wholesome fountains, they will more quickly recover."[14]

Other literary sources strongly reinforce the association of springs and the cult of Asklepios. The *Sacred Tales* of Aelius Aristides are a

---

12 Ibid., p. 24-26.

13 Excavation reports of these Asklepieia are as follows: Epidauros: R. A. Tomlinson, *Epidauros*, Archaeological Sites, ed. Malcolm Todd (London: Granada, 1983); R. A. Tomlinson, "Two Buildings in Sanctuaries of Asklepios," *Journal of Hellenic Studies*, 89 (1969): 108-17; Kos: Paul Schazmann, *Asklepieion. Baubeschreibung und Baugeschichte, Kos*, Ergebnisse der deutschen Ausgrabungen und Forschungen, 1(Berlin: Heinrich Keller, 1932); Pergamon: Otfried Deubner, *Das Asklepieion von Pergamon* (Berlin: Verlag für Kunstwissenschaft, 1938); Troizen: Gabriel Welter, *Troizen und Kalaureia* (Berlin: Verlag Gebr. Mann, 1941); Athens: John Travlos, "The Asklepieion," in *Pictorial Dictionary of Ancient Athens* (New York: Praeger, 1971), p. 127-37; John Travlos, "Spring House of the Asklepieion," in *Pictorial Dictionary of Ancient Athens* (New York: Praeger, 1971), p. 138-39.

14 Vitruvius, *On Architecture*, 1.2.7, as found in Emma J. Edelstein, and Ludwig Edelstein, *Asclepius. A Collection and Interpretation of the Testimonies*, 2 vols. (Baltimore: Johns Hopkins Press, 1945), 1:370.

major source for the reconstruction of the cult—they are a disconnected diary of the orator's many salvations at the hand of Asklepios, full of both intriguing detail concerning the cult and Aristides' tedious vanity—and the *Sacred Tales* make many references to Aristides' instructions from the God to bathe or refrain from bathing. Aristides takes warm baths, cold baths, baths in lakes, rivers, springs and the ocean, in Asklepieia and outside them.[15] He provides an oration praising the water of the Asklepieion in Pergamon.[16]

It is likely, therefore, that Lerna was more strongly associated with the sanctuary of Asklepios in Corinth than the excavation report suggests. While Roebuck suggests that the visitors to the sanctuary simply made use of the facilities of Lerna for pleasure and relaxation, it is more accurate to suggest that Lerna was used by visitors as part of their cure at the suggestion of the God, and was perceived by them as part of the facilities of the Asklepieion.

Dining halls and Asklepieia

Just as most Asklepieia had facilities for the use of water similar to that of Lerna, some Asklepieia had facilities for eating similar to that of Lerna. These dining halls are not always found, and their characteristics vary, but their presence in other Asklepieia suggests also that the dining halls of Lerna were associated in some way with the sanctuary in Corinth. The Asklepieia of Troizen, Epidauros and Athens give clear evidence of facilities for eating.

A parallel to the dining rooms of Lerna may be found at Troizen (see Figs. 5 and 6). Roebuck perceives these as set apart from the sanctuary, so that he calls them "secular" space distinct from the sacred space of the sanctuary.[17] This division of space, however, is not as clear as Roebuck suggests. The building containing the dining rooms is part of the group of buildings comprising the sanctuary, and may be entered directly from, and only from, the *temenos* (the area of land dedicated to the God) of the sanctuary. It is hard to imagine a clearer instance of dining rooms strongly associated with a sanctuary, and these rooms at Troizen are as much a part of the sanctuary of Asklepios as the dining rooms in the sanctuary of Demeter and Kore on Acrocorinth. The building that housed the dining rooms was built around a central peristyle court open to the sky with a pool in its centre, and

---

15 P. Aelius Aristides, *The Complete Works*, 2 vols., trans. Charles A. Behr (Leiden: Brill, 1981). *The Sacred Tales* are *Orations* 47-50, found in vol. 2. References to bathing are too numerous to cite, but are concentrated in *Tales* 1-3.

16 Aristides, *Oration* 39. 1-18 (found in Edelstein, *Asclepius*, 1:406-13); compare *Oration* 53. 1-5 (found in Edelstein, *Asclepius*, 1:413-15).

17 Roebuck, *Corinth* 14: 24-26.

this arrangement is similar to Lerna.[18] These rooms may also have been used for incubation.

At the sanctuary of Asklepios near Epidauros another large building used specifically for dining was found (see Figs. 7 and 8). The sanctuary at Epidauros was the major centre for the cult of Asklepios, and the most complex sanctuary known. It held many structures, including a gymnasium, stadium and theatre spread over an area almost a kilometre square. One of the largest structures within the sanctuary was the banqueting hall. It was built around an open peristyle court like the building at Troizen, but it was much larger (75 × 70 metres). Like that at Troizen, it had rooms of varying dimensions. Evidence of supports for couches clearly arranged in the form of a dining room identify the structure as a banqueting hall.[19]

The banqueting hall at Epidauros bears a strong resemblance to that of Troizen. Both structures are clearly within the sanctuaries; both hold several rooms, small and large; both show dining rooms with wooden couches arranged in squares. The building at Epidauros is on a much larger scale, consistent with Epidauros's status as the major cultic centre.

The small sanctuary of Asklepios in Athens also shows a nearby building containing dining rooms (see Fig. 9). Unlike the buildings for this purpose in the sanctuaries in Troizen and Epidauros, this building is not inside the *temenos* of the sanctuary of Asklepios. Rather, it is clearly in the category of "auxiliary buildings": at the time when the sanctuary was active its boundaries were disputed, and inscriptions concerning the dispute show that this building falls outside the boundaries of the sanctuary. The building contained four square rooms whose off-centre openings and size show they each held 11 couches.

Though this building is not inside the sanctuary, it was very likely clearly associated with it. Its construction soon after the shrine of Asklepios probably prompted the dispute concerning the proper boundaries of the sanctuary. Further, the entrance to the whole complex of buildings lies between it and the buildings of the sanctuary, and the buildings form a clear architectural unit distinct from structures nearby. Finally, its close proximity to the temple and *abaton* of the sanctuary makes it likely that its dining rooms were used by visitors to the shrine.[20]

The presence of banqueting halls within or very near sanctuaries of Asklepios in Epidauros, Troizen and Athens makes it much more likely that the dining rooms of Lerna were associated with the sanctuary of

---

18 Welter, *Troizen*, p. 31-32.

19 Tomlinson, *Epidauros*, p. 78-84; Tomlinson, "Two Buildings in Sanctuaries of Asklepios," 89: 109.

20 Travlos, "Asklepieion," p. 127-28.

Asklepios in Corinth. Since springs were associated with Asklepieia, the fountain of Lerna probably strengthened the perceived association with the sanctuary.

It must be noted, however, that this association was not requisite. Not all Asklepieia had banqueting rooms. Dining rooms were not integral to the performance of the cultus of Asklepios or necessary to those persons seeking the salvation of the God. Where banqueting halls are found in sanctuaries, these halls were not of central importance. These halls were built after the main buildings of the sanctuaries, and set outside the *temenos*, on its edge, or away from the main cultic buildings among other auxiliary structures.

Sacrifice and food in the cultus of Asklepios

The central rite of an appeal to the salvation of Asklepios as witnessed by literary sources and inscriptions was incubation.[21] After rites of purification and sacrifice the suppliant would sleep in the porticos or the *abaton* of a sanctuary and hope to receive a dream or vision or visit from a sacred snake, all means by which the God healed the suppliant or proposed a course of treatment to be followed.[22]

The use of food was thus not a central feature of the cultus of Asklepios. Still, it played a part. Three aspects of this use of food are attested. First, sacred food was used in the rites of the cultus. Second, sacred food was eaten by priests and worshippers inside the sanctuary, and taken outside the sanctuary for consumption elsewhere. Finally, there is attested the use of ordinary food (that is, food not sacrificed) either prescribed or prohibited by the God to effect a cure.

Sacrifices were offered to Asklepios in several contexts: as part of the regular priestly duties for the maintenance of the cult; by priests on behalf of cities and citizens, as part of the public function of the sanctuaries; as part of the private rites preparatory to incubation; and as thank-offerings after a cure or a vision or to fulfil a vow.[23] Other sources make brief reference to tables and couches of the God.[24]

---

21 Literary sources are chiefly Aristides and Aristophanes; the main body of inscriptions is set up on steles at the sanctuary of Epidauros.

22 For a general discussion of the cult of Asklepios, see Edelstein, *Asclepius*. Volume 1 is a collection of literary testimony to the cult; volume 2 interprets this evidence. See also Alice Walton, *The Cult of Asklepios*, Cornell Studies in Classical Philology, no. 3 (Ithaca, NY: Cornell University Press, 1894; reprinted, New York: Johnson Reprint Corporation, 1965), and C. Kerényi, *Asklepios. Archetypal Image of the Physician's Existence*, Bollingen Series 65 (New York: Pantheon, 1959).

23 Walton, *Asklepios*, p. 28.

24 Cited in Edelstein, *Asclepius*, 1:278, 1:309-10, and 1:374; see also Pausanias, *Description of Greece* 10.32.12.

Private sacrifices are both better attested and of more interest for our present purposes. It is very likely that everyone seeking the aid of the God, and especially coming to sleep in an Asklepieion, brought sacrifices to the sanctuary. These were bloodless offerings—cakes sweetened with oil, wine or honey; or cheese-cakes; or figs—that were laid on an altar (and perhaps entirely consumed by fire) or sometimes fed to the sacred snakes of the Asklepieion.[25] Thank-offerings, made in fulfilment of a vow or in gratitude after a cure or vision, were more often animal offerings, but could be anything from money to pictures to songs.[26] Such a thank-offering is described by Herondas: a woman apologizes to the God for the humble cock she brings and says "For we draw no bounteous nor ready spring; else might we, perchance, with an ox or stuffed pig of much fatness and no humble cock, be paying the price of cure from diseases which thou didst wipe away, Lord, by laying on us thy gentle hands."[27]

After sacrifices had been offered to the God they were put to various uses. Portions were given to the priests, sacred food was consumed by suppliants within the sanctuary, and sacred food was carried outside the sanctuary.

Several testimonies survive concerning the portion of sacrifices given to the priests.[28] Aristophanes provides a delightful corroboration of this practice, in the mouth of a slave describing the incubation of the blind God Wealth (Ploutos) in the Asklepieion. The slave relates his own interest (while in the *abaton* with Ploutos) in an old woman's bowl of porridge (probably not sacred food in any sense but the woman's breakfast for the coming morning[29]):

> Carion [the slave]: A bowl of porridge by an old woman's head tempted me madly. I was set to wriggle towards it; then taking a quick look around I saw the priest nicking the cakes and figs from the holy table; then he made a circuit of the altars and sanctified everything—simply by putting it into a bag. So thinking this was a truly religious practice, I got up to go for that bowl of porridge.
>
> Wife: You wicked man! Weren't you afraid of the God?
>
> Carion: You bet I was—in case he got there before me,

---

25 Edelstein, *Asclepius*, 1:290-94, 2:187; Walton, *Asklepios*, p. 16. See Aristophanes, *Ploutos*, c. line 660. Such an offering may be depicted on a relief from the Asklepieion at Athens, that shows a family in front of an altar or table laden with fruit and cakes (reproduced in Travlos, "Asklepieion," pl.185, p. 137).

26 Edelstein, *Asclepius*, 1:294-301; 2:189.

27 Herondas, *Mimiambi* 4.1-95, as found in Edelstein, *Asclepius*, 1:274-77. If this language sounds like caricatured piety, it is no accident; Herondas's mimes are acid.

28 Edelstein, *Asclepius*, 1:280-81; 1:313-14.

29 Walton, *Asklepios*, p. 78.

crowned as he was, and got at the porridge. But I saw what to do from what the priest did.[30]

The second category of the use of sacred food is food consumed in the sanctuary by suppliants of the God. Several sources attest such a practice. The most direct of these is Aristides, who reports that the God instructed him in a dream to "go to the holy shrine and offer perfect sacrificial animals to Asclepius and set up holy craters and distribute holy portions to all the fellow-pilgrims."[31] Pausanias reports that at Epidauros and at Titane "the sacrifices, whether offered by one of the Epidaurians themselves or by a foreigner, are consumed within the bounds" and an inscription from Athens forbids the removal of meat from the sanctuary.[32] On the basis of such evidence, Edelstein claims that not only would the richer suppliants of the God eat their part of a sacrifice in the sanctuary, but the poor also might be offered meals in Asklepieia in honour of the philanthropy of the God.[33] The evidence of the banqueting halls found in Asklepieia corroborates the eating of sacred food in sanctuaries of Asklepios.[34]

The third category of the use of sacred food is sacrificial food consumed outside the sanctuary. Though at some Asklepieia the removal from the sanctuary of sacrificed meat was not permitted, other evidence shows that sacred food could be, and was, removed. The most explicit evidence of this is found in Herondas, where awoman who has given a priest his portion says, "The rest [of the cock and the holy bread] we will eat at home; and remember to take it away."[35]

Ordinary food was also used in the cultus of Asklepios, eaten or refrained from under the instructions of the God. Several sources collected by Edelstein briefly attest such instructions concerning diet: one inscription indicates that the God prescribed simple foods of cheese and bread, celery and lettuce, milk and honey; another instruction (for a patient with a rather different condition, one hopes) forbids cold drinks and recommends partridge stuffed with frankincense.[36]

---

30 Aristophanes, *Ploutos,* l.670-90, in Dickinson, *Plays*, 2:319.

31 Aristides, *Orations* 48.27, in Edelstein, *Asclepius*, 1:286-87.

32 Pausanias, *Description of Greece* 2.27.1; *IG.* 2.2.1364. Both are found in Edelstein, *Asclepius*, 1:290.

33 Edelstein, *Asclepius*, 2:177.

34 The banqueting hall "would be used, perhaps, by the healthy worshippers of Asklepios at his special festivals. . . . The meal, which presumably included the sacrificial meat, may well have been part of the ritual, and the *hestiatoria* [banqueting halls] were more than mere hotels or restaurants" (Tomlinson, "Two Buildings," p. 111). Compare Tomlinson, *Epidauros*, p. 84.

35 Herondas, *Mimiambi*, 4.92-93 (Edelstein, *Asclepius*, 1:275, 277).

36 Edelstein, *Asclepius*, 1:247, 249 (see also testimonies in 1:252, 259).

Our clearest indication of this sort of use of food comes from Aristides. Aristides is almost as preoccupied with whether he should eat as whether he should bathe, and the *Sacred Tales* are full of references to fasting and emetics. Aristides is also concerned with what sorts of food he ought to eat, and a notable discussion of the God's instructions concerning this matter is found in *Sacred Tale* 3 (*Oration* 49, l. 34-37), set out below as Appendix 2. Ordinary food recommended by the God is not to be offered to the God, and thus is not in any strong sense sacred food. The God's command to eat or not eat is sacred, but the food is food, and simply part of a regimen of healthful living or course of treatment that might include also exercise and bathing.[37] In no significant sense would foods prescribed by the God be considered sacred food (*hierothyta*).

It is certain, then, that sacrifice and the consumption of sacred food played a part in the cult of Asklepios, in the maintenance of the cultus by the priests, in the rites that accompanied incubation, and as thank-offerings for the God's salvation. Animals that had been offered in thanks for a dream or a cure would be eaten by priests and suppliants, often in facilities in or near Asklepieia, and sometimes taken home. Sometimes a suppliant who happened to be in the sanctuary at the right time might be given a share of a large offering made by a wealthy or particularly grateful worshipper.

Such a consumption of sacred food was not central to the cult, but incidental. The central rites of the cult concerned incubation and the visitation of the God. Sacrifices were ancillary to this rite, preparatory to it and following its completion. There is no indication that the offerings of cakes and fruits preparatory to incubation were ritually eaten by the suppliants. The sharing of the thank-offering between the God and the suppliant was not the focus of this rite of sacrifice; rather, the suppliant offered the animal in gratitude to the God and then received what was left, to enjoy and perhaps to share with his or her friends.

Implications for the problem of idol-food

This series of conclusions concerning the association of Asklepieia with springs and dining rooms and the use of food in the cult of Asklepios carries implications for the problem of idol-food. The evidence gathered here allows the reconstruction of a concrete social situation—eating a meal in the dining rooms of Lerna—whose character would potentially raise the problem of food offered to idols for Paul's associa-

37 Evidence is set out at ibid., 1:247. Most importantly, the picture provided in Aristides's *Sacred Tales* of his many-faceted participation in the cult of Asklepios strongly supports this conclusion.

tion of Christians in Corinth. Moreover, it would raise the problem in a way that is very difficult to resolve, for the question of whether eating in the dining rooms of Lerna was "reclining in an idol's temple" (1 Cor 8:10) or "sharing the table of *daimonia*" (1 Cor 10:21) has no unqualified answer. Further, it could not be determined simply from the setting whether or not what one ate in the dining rooms of Lerna had been offered to Asklepios or another God.

Whether the dining rooms of Lerna were part of the Asklepieion has no precise answer. On the one hand, in the Roman period Lerna may have been used by persons who were not visiting the sanctuary of Asklepios or using the waters as part of their treatment, and there was no necessary association between Lerna and the Asklepieion. On the other hand, this association was obvious. The presence of springs and banqueting halls in other Asklepieia, and the role that bathing and eating played in the cult of Asklepios, would have made a connection between Lerna and the Asklepieion easy to draw.

The ambiguity of the status of Lerna—a public fountain and place of relaxation, yet associated with the Asklepieion—might lead very easily to difficulties of interpretation among the group of Christians in Corinth. If there were Christians who were worried by any contact with other Gods and Lords, these might well find the dining rooms of Lerna too strongly associated with the sanctuary of Asklepios. Yet the ambiguity of the status of Lerna would provide support to any Christians who found it desirable to eat there and wished to defend the practice (even if they accepted the premises of the first group, let alone if they rejected those premises). Even if there was unanimity concerning the wrongfulness of sharing in the table of demons (as in the case of a meal in the sanctuary of Demeter and Kore), the dining rooms of Lerna would present an awkward case.[38]

Just as the question of whether the dining rooms of Lerna were tables of demons could not be answered without qualification, so it is very likely that the question of whether food offered to idols was served there cannot be answered simply. On the one hand, suppliants sometimes would have consumed in the dining rooms of Lerna their portions of animals sacrificed as thank-offerings on the altar of the sanctuary. Further, if priests were permitted to sell their portions of the offerings, it is again highly likely that some of this *hierothyton* would be prepared for consumption in the dining rooms of Lerna. Finally, it is possible that sacrificed food would be distributed to those in or near

---

38 Compare J. Murphy-O'Connor, *St. Paul's Corinth. Texts and Archaeology* (Wilmington, DE: Michael Glazier, 1983), p. 162-67. Murphy-O'Connor's discussion is addressed below, in chap. 8.

the Asklepieion and consumed in the dining rooms of Lerna. Thus some of the food some of the time could be called *eidôlothyton* ("offered to idols"). On the other hand, it is likely that not all of the food prepared for diners in the rooms of Lerna stood in such a relation to the cult of Asklepios. It seems reasonable to speculate that a group of diners could request particular foods, and, if so desired, request food without a history of sacred use.

It would be no simple matter to determine whether food served in these dining rooms was or was not idol-food. This is a situation closely analogous to, or perhaps identical with, that of 1 Corinthians 10:27-29 ("If some unbeliever invites[39] you . . ."): a Christian invited to a meal held at Lerna might be served food offered to the God (perhaps sacrificed earlier by the host, perhaps sacred food merely bought by the host).[40] Further, as 10:28 suggests (If someone says to you, "This is sacred food [*hierothyton*] . . .), the Christian might well be ignorant of the history of the food served, or choose to remain ignorant of this history, or choose simply to ignore it.

The dining rooms of Lerna and the eating that occurred there stood in an ambiguous relationship to the cultus of Asklepios, likely leading to well-supported but differing assessments by Christians of whether it was acceptable to eat there.

---

39 Often 1 Cor 10:27, *Ei tis kalei hymas tôn apistôn*, is taken to refer to an invitation to an unbeliever's home. The verb *kalein* is not followed here, however, by *eis* and a place or event (the normal construction [Bauer, Arndt, Gingrich, *s.v. Kalein*, b.]), so the place or event remains unspecified. The situation Paul sets out here could refer, then, to a meal at Lerna. This reading is supported by Hurd and others (John Coolidge Hurd, Jr., *The Origin of 1 Corinthians* [New York: Seabury Press; London: SPCK, 1965], p. 129, n. 2).

40 Murphy-O'Connor postulates several occasions on which invitations in the dining rooms of Lerna might be offered and cause problems for the "weak": invitations by family members; spontaneous invitations to join others, perhaps when the weak were using the waters and shade of Lerna for recreation; invitations by an employer or other such person whom the weak could not afford to offend (*St. Paul's Corinth*, p. 164-65).

3

"If someone invites you . . ."

Introduction

The archaeological data and literary evidence from the cults of Demeter and Kore and of Asklepios have allowed some conclusions concerning the use of idol-food in cultic centres. This chapter gathers evidence concerning the uses of sacred food in everyday settings, and the social import of eating. This evidence is found in the literature of the period. This survey is limited by time period—to literary sources conventionally dated from *c.* 200 B.C.E. to *c.* 200 C.E. This may seem a wide chronological range, but basic social patterns such as household structures and conventions of social intercourse are fairly durable, and in this survey a strikingly consistent picture of eating practices emerges from materials of diverse character and period.

This survey is also limited by genre. There is no literature that sets out to answer our questions concerning the social uses of sacred food in contexts that we would think of as secular. The categories of literature most fruitful for our purposes are those that deal with situations of daily life, often in telling detail, and thus include biography, letters, romances and drama. An exhaustive survey of these genres is included here, limited only by the chronological limits described above and the exclusion of fragmentary works. The genres that have been excluded are historiography, which generally is concerned with great events and persons, philosophical works (with some exceptions, noted below) and papyri.[1]

---

1 Many papyri (particularly papyri showing contracts and private letters) provide invaluable evidence of daily life, but that evidence does not concern the contexts in which we are interested. Much is revealed of commercial dealings, contracts for goods and services and social relations in these contexts, but this category of materials provides too little evidence concerning daily meals, the rites which attend them and the foods which are consumed to warrant a careful survey of them.

A list of the sources surveyed will be useful:[2]

Biography

Plutarch, *Lives* [Mestrius Plutarchus, *c.* 50-120 C.E.]
Lucius Apuleius, *Metamorphoses* [*c.* 123 C.E.-?]
Philostratus, *Life of Apollonius* [Flavius Philostratus, *c.* 170-245 C.E.]

Satires

Herondas [Herondas or Herodas, 3rd century B.C.E.]
Plautus [Titius Maccius Plautus, ?-*c.* 180 B.C.E.]
Terence [Publius Terentius Afer, *c.* 190-160 B.C.E.]
Horace [Horatius Flaccus, 65-8 B.C.E.]
Persius [Persius Flaccus, 34-62 C.E.]
Petronius [Petronius Arbiter, second half of 1st cent. C.E.]
Juvenal [Decimus Iunius Iuvenalis, *c.* 60 C.E.-?]
Lucian of Samosata [Loukianos, *c.* 120-after 180 C.E.]

Letters

Cicero [Marcus Tullius Cicero, 106-43 B.C.E.]
Seneca [Lucius Annaeus Seneca, *c.* 4 B.C.E.-65 C.E.]
Pliny the Younger [Gaius Plinius Caecilius Secundus, 61-*c.* 112 C.E.]

Romances

Dio Chrysostom [Dio Cocceianus, *c.* 40-after 112 C.E.]
Xenophon [Xenophon Ephesius, late 1st-mid-2nd cent. C.E.]
Achilles Tatius [2nd cent. C.E.]
Longus [name and dates uncertain; 2nd cent. C.E.]

I have included some other useful sources. Some philosophical works provide glimpses of table practices and the social significance of shared meals: ethical discourses by Epictetus and Musonius Rufus and Plutarch's accounts of philosophical table-talk. Other materials are also relevant: Seneca's tragedies (for their temporal closeness to our period), Catullus's poems (for their autobiographical nature and their rootedness in social relations) and Pausanias's travelogue of Greece in the second century C.E.

Catullus, *Poems* [Gaius Valerius Catullius, 84-54 B.C.E.]
Seneca, *Tragedies* [*c.* 55 B.C.E.-40 C.E.]
Musonius Rufus, *Discourses* [*c.* 30-101 C.E.]
Plutarch, *Convivial questions* [*c.* 50-120 C.E.]
Epictetus, *Discourses* [*c.* 55-135 C.E.]
Pausanias, *Description of Greece* [2nd cent. C.E.]

2 Full names and estimated dates are those of the *Oxford Classical Dictionary*, 2nd ed. (Oxford: Clarendon, 1970).

While these materials are diverse in language, purpose and literary character, they allow well-evidenced conclusions concerning both the social importance of shared meals and the frequent use of sacred food in contexts of shared meals. The picture of meals which emerges from these texts is surprisingly consistent, especially given the diverse nature of the sources.

It might seem dubious that a consistent picture of eating practices should emerge from such a wide range of materials; the concern, of course, is that one reads in these sources only what supports desirable conclusions. I must stress, then, that this survey is a virtually exhaustive reading of these sources, for the specific issues with which we are concerned and in no way presents merely a selected group of texts.

The conclusions that these sources allow concerning shared meals in Greco-Roman society are hardly unexpected: meals in Greco-Roman society were a central focus of social intercourse, food was a significant marker of social status, food which had been used in sacrifice was often eaten (especially on occasions of social significance) and the consumption of what Paul would call idol-food was unavoidable in normal social intercourse.

Greco-Roman meals

Literary sources from this period reveal a standard picture of a typical main meal. Whether in houses of the rich or in cottages of the poor, the main meal took place in the early evening. It included not only food but also, whenever possible, entertainment.[3] Among the rich, and especially among the ostentatious, this entertainment could be lavish, including dramatic and/or musical entertainers;[4] among the cultural elite it often included readings of literature and learned discussions. For example, Pliny (who prefers learned conversation to flute girls) chides a friend for rejecting an invitation: "You would have heard a comic play, a reader or a singer, or all three if I felt generous. . . . What a feast of fun, laughter and learning we were going to have."[5]

The most elaborate example of learned conversations at table are Plutarch's *Convivial Questions*,[6] which show the range of philosophical,

---

3 Compare Dennis E. Smith, "Meals and Morality in Paul and his World," *SBL Seminar Papers*, 20 (Chico, CA: Scholars Press, 1981): 319-21.

4 See, among numerous examples, Lucian of Samosata, *The Dream or the Cock* 11, in *Lucian*, 8 vols., trans. A. M. Harmon, Loeb Classical Library, 1919-1925, 2:193, and Pliny, *Letters* 1.15, 9.17, 9.36 in *Pliny. Letters*, 2 vols., trans. Wm. Melmoth, Loeb Classical Library, 1915.

5 Pliny, *Letter* 1.15 (*The Letters of the Younger Pliny*, trans. Betty Radice [Harmondsworth, Middlesex: Penguin, 1963], p. 48-49).

6 Plutarch, *Symposiakôn problêmatôn*, of which only Books 3 and 5 survive

literary-critical and scientific discourse among persons of Plutarch's class and education. While these may not represent actual conversations, it may be concluded that such conversations were held during and after meals, since Plutarch continually maintains the fictive context of the conversations through narrative details. Pretensions to learned table-talk are satirized in Epictetus: "But if a man . . . resorts to philosophers merely because he wants to make a display at a banquet . . . what else is he doing but trying to win the admiration of some senator sitting by his side?"[7] One of Catullus's poems provides a glimpse of the table-talk of those with literary interests: he is asked to read his host's dreadful speeches.[8] Among even the poor, the sources suggest simple musical performances, table-talk and games at table.[9]

These entertainments often had strongly religious overtones. Songs and instrumental music are often mentioned in association with meals (especially those on important occasions or special festivity among the wealthy), and typically retold ancient stories of the Gods, or offered praises to them. Horace says "the lyre inherited from the Muses the right to celebrate Gods and their sons, . . . and uninhibited drinking"[10] and he calls a lover to a feast to be completed with responsive songs to many deities.[11] In Lucius's wonderful description of his trials as an ass (*Metamorphoses*), even the bandits who have stolen him follow their feast, wine and laughter with hymns in honour of their patron, Mars.[12]

(612C-748D of the *Moralia*). The edition cited is Plutarch, *Moralia*, vols. 8 and 9, trans. P. A. Clement and H. B. Hoffleit, Loeb Classical Library, 1969.

7 Epictetus, *The Discourses as Reported by Arrian, the Manual [Encheiridion] and Fragments*, trans. W. A. Oldfather, Loeb Classical Library, 1925, 2 vols., 1.26.9 (compare 2.19.9).

8 Catullus, *Poem* 44 (*The Poems of Catullus*, trans. Peter Whigham [Harmondsworth, Middlesex: Penguin, 1966], p. 103).

9 Simple entertainment: Longus, *Daphnis and Chloe* (*Three Greek Romances*, trans. Moses Hadas, p. 17-100 [Garden City, NJ: Doubleday, 1953]), p. 61-63; Lucius Apuleius, *The Golden Ass* (*Metamorphoses*), trans. Robert Graves (Harmondsworth, Middlesex: Penguin, 1950), p. 99-109. Games at table: Plutarch, *Convivial Questions* 673B (Loeb, *Moralia* 9:373), which indicates that simple, un-literary people take up the game of Names and Numbers after dinner—a most interesting aside, which casts an unusual light on Rev 13:17-18.

10 Horace, *Epistle* 2.3., l. 84-86 (*Satires and Epistles*, trans. Niall Rudd [Harmondsworth, Middlesex: Penguin, 1979]).

11 Horace, *Ode* 3.28 (*The Odes of Horace with Five Prefacing Epodes*, trans. Margaret Ralston Gest, and ed. M. M. H. Thrall [Kutztown, PA: Kutztown Publishing Company, 1973]).

12 Lucius Apuleius, *Golden Ass*, trans. Graves, p. 109. Lucius's *Metamorphoses* is an amusing and revealing collection of stories, which sadly is not well known among current New Testament scholars—just as are many of the sources cited in this

Sacrificed food

Not only songs and stories over meals honoured the Gods but the meals themselves. On many occasions in private homes food which had been offered in sacrifice to a God was eaten by host and guests. Not every meal involved the consumption of food used in religious rites. There are many instances in the literature surveyed where meals are mentioned without any reference, either overt or implied, to sacrifice or rites. There are also many references, however, to meals which included food used in rites, and these are enough to ground conclusions of importance to the task at hand.

Some generalizations can be made from all the relevant sources concerning sacrificed food. First, it would be a mistake to think of the social contexts under discussion in categories of "sacred" and "secular."[13] Meals involving sacrifice in private homes were not occasions focussing exclusively on high religious ritual and demanding solemn religious dedication from participants, but neither were they bracketed by habitual, formal and essentially empty rites. Rather, they were often meals of some social importance. This is seen most clearly in the occasions of meals involving sacrifice: these occurred most often on celebratory occasions, such as weddings, birthdays, the visits of returning friends or important persons and religious holidays. They are meals where quantities of food are eaten, wine flows freely, and conviviality reigns—true meals and not simply ritual events. At the same time, the rites performed over the food were of significance: just as the occasions called for spirited eating they also called for authentic thanksgiving to the Gods.

Many instances can be found of this consumption of sacred food in the setting of shared meals. Examples of such eating show the range and character of these references.

Holy days or feasts explicitly dedicated to Gods

Juvenal describes a public festival: "a big feast day . . . the fun of the party, the tables that would be spread by every temple and crossway for the

---

chapter. These have high intrinsic value, and significant value as "background" in studies of early Christianity. Lucius's *Metamorphoses* stands out even among these interesting sources. Graves's introduction provides a provocative comparison to Augustine's *Confessions*, and his literate translation is itself wonderful.

13 W. L. Willis arrives at a similar conclusion regarding even cultic meals. He rejects earlier interpretations of Greek sacrificial meals as sacramental (denoting mystical participation in the God, or "acquiring the deity"), and stresses their character as joyful and boisterous communal occasions (*Idol Meat in Corinth. The Pauline Argument in 1 Corinthians 8 and 10*, SBL dissertation series, 68 [Chico, CA: Scholars Press, 1985], p. 21-61).

day and night junketing."[14] Admittedly this does not describe eating in a private context, but such feasting was not confined to temples alone.[15]

In one of Persius's satires, a wealthy patron gives oil, bread and meat to the common people "in honour of the Gods and our beloved leader [Caligula]."[16] Whether this meat had been sacrificed or whether the distribution took place on a holy day is not clear from the context, but the identification of this food as dedicated to the Gods is explicit.

Plutarch describes a traditional sacrificial rite performed in homes. His purpose is to discuss the origins of the obscure rites, but he notes that "after completing the ritual acts we returned to table . . . to drive out ravenous hunger."[17]

Lucian, in *Timon or the Misanthrope*, provides a conversation between Hermes and Zeus:[18] they speak of Timon, who "often treated us to perfect sacrifices; the one who had just come into a fortune, who gave up complete hecatombs and used to entertain us brilliantly at his house [*par ôi*] during the Diasia . . . a man who has burned so many fat thigh-bones of bulls and goats on the altar to honour us."

Lucian, in *The Double Indictment*: Pan complains that the Athenians only come up to him three times a year, sacrifice a goat and "then feast on the meat, making me a mere witness of their good cheer and paying their respects to me only with their noise."[19] Whether this feasting is at Pan's temple or at homes is not clear, but the statement is interesting for its glimpse of the motivation of at least some religious holidays.

Lucius Apuleius, *Metamorphoses*: During Lucius's adventures as an ass, he travels with itinerant eunuch priests of the Syrian Mater Magna; a wealthy man offers to house the Goddess and shows his veneration by procuring the finest victims and dining on them with his guests, the priests.[20] After Lucius's salvation from his transformation he becomes a devotee of Isis, and his initiation into the rites of both Isis and Osiris includes sacred banquets to which he invites his friends.[21]

---

14 Juvenal, *Satire* 15, l. 39-44 (*Satires*, trans. Charles Plumb [London: Panther, 1968]).

15 Ibid. *Satire* 13, line 230, alludes to cocks offered to household Gods.

16 Persius, *Satire* 6, l. 50,51 (*Satires*, trans. Niall Rudd [Harmondsworth, Middlesex: Penguin, 1979]).

17 Plutarch, *Convivial Questions* 693F (Loeb, 8:495-96).

18 Lucian, *Timon or the Misanthrope* 7.9 (Loeb, 2:333, 337).

19 Lucian, *The Double Indictment* 11 (Loeb, 3:103).

20 Lucius Apuleius, *Golden Ass*, trans. Graves, p. 204-205.

21 Ibid., p. 285-90. Other instances of meals at times of festivals, and involving rites at table, are found in Achilles Tatius, *Leucippe and Clitophon*, in *The Adventures of Leucippe and Clitophon*, trans. S. Gaselee, Loeb Calssical Library, 1917, 12.1-2 (a festival of Dionysus); Lucian of Samosata, *The Dream or the Cock* 14 (Loeb, 2:199

It is not surprising to find explicit evidence for meals clearly associated with festivals or holy days whose menus included food which had been sacrificed. What is surprising is the pervasiveness of this practice. This is seen in the range of these sources which attest it and also in the familiarity with the practice which is assumed by the authors. The pervasiveness of holy days is seen most explicitly in a reference from Lucian, which satirizes a professional hanger-on: "the parasite celebrates 30 holidays a month [which means, it is abundantly clear from context, that he has 30 banquets] for he thinks that every day belongs to the Gods."[22]

Weddings

Many sources allude to sacrifices on the occasion of weddings. Chief of these are the romances, which of course conclude with the protagonists' marriage after long adversity and many obstacles. Longus's pastoral romance *Daphnis and Chloe* concludes with a wedding, prepared for by several days of sacrifices and feasts and celebrated in the presence of the nymphs and with many offerings.[23] Xenophon's *Ephesian Tale* describes a marriage: "Sacrificial animals had been brought in from the country, and there was a great abundance of other things. All his relatives and friends had gathered together to share in the festivities and many of his fellow citizens joined in the celebration for Anthia's marriage."[24] The marriage of the protagonists in Dio Chrysostom's *Hunters of Euboea* is impeded because of a lack of sacrifice: "Now the girl's father spoke up. 'It's not that I'm putting you off, my boy,' he said. 'Your own father is waiting until he can go and buy a victim; we must sacrifice to the Gods, you know.' "[25] The families then prepare both for the sacrifice of a pig and for a great feast which also includes the best quality and greatest quantity of other food they can muster. Other sources readily confirm the central importance of sacrifice and feasting to the celebration of marriage in that culture.[26]

[a festival of Cronus]); Longus, *Daphnis and Chloe* (celebrations in honour of Dionysus, Pan and other deities).

22 Lucian, *Parasite* 15 (Loeb, 3:267).

23 Longus, *Daphnis and Chloe* (*Three Greek Romances*, trans. Hadas), p. 94, 97.

24 Xenophon, *An Ephesian Tale* (*Three Greek Romances*, trans. Moses Hadas, p. 101-72 [Garden City, NJ: Doubleday, 1953]), p. 134.

25 Dio Chrysostom, *The Hunters of Euboea* (*Three Greek Romances*, trans. Moses Hadas, p. 173-89 [Garden City, NJ: Doubleday, 1953]), p. 188.

26 Lucius Apuleius, *Golden Ass*, trans. Graves, p. 112: A bride waits for her groom who has gone "to offer the usual sacrifices in the different temples"; Lucius also refers to a bridal banquet and entertainment (ibid., p. 121). Achilles Tatius, *The Adventures of Leucippe and Clitophon*, 5.14.1-4 (Loeb, 265-69): guests share a wed-

Birthdays

Horace invites a woman to his farm for a feast in celebration of his patron's birthday, where "our altar, wreathed with fresh boughs, asks for the sacred blood from lamb as a victim." His patron's birthday, Horace explains to his addressee, is "almost more sacred [*sanctior*]" than his own birthday.[27] This is the only clear association of offered food and birthday feasts in the literature surveyed here, but several other sources associate birthdays and shared feasts clearly: in one of his satires, Horace extols the virtue of plain food ("get your sauce by sweat")[28] but also makes clear that luxury and feasting are expected at birthdays and weddings and other festive occasions.[29]

Occasions of thanksgiving

Herondas's mimes—a series of vivid, humorous, pointed vignettes—include a scene of two women at an Asklepieion. Kynno brings a rooster (they can't afford an ox or pig) in thanksgiving for a cure,[30] and, after a prayer, says to her companion, Kokkale: "Carve a drumstick for the custodian [the priest], and give the snake a morsel,[31] quietly, in sacred silence, there on the altar. We'll eat, don't forget, the rest at home. [To the priest] Stay well, my fellow. Here now, have some bread. We'll begin with you, close to the God, in passing it around on the way home."[32] This passage is remarkable for both its explicit reference to sacrificial food consumed at home, and for its indication that sacred food, in this context at least, was shared with the

ding breakfast and the couple are urged to consummate the marriage to "propitiate the Goddess who presides over marriages" (Isis). See also: Horace, *Satire* 2.2, lines 59-69; Seneca, *Octavia*, l. 700-25 (*Four Tragedies and Octavia*, trans. E. F. Watling [Harmondsworth, Middlesex: Penguin, 1966], p. 285); Plutarch, *Pericles* 7.4 (*Lives*, trans. Bernadotte Perrin, Loeb Classical Library, 1914-26, 3:19-21); Plutarch, *Alexander* 70.12 (Loeb, 7:419); Achilles Tatius, *Leucippe and Clitophon* 2.18.1; 8.19.3; Lucian, *Toxaris or Friendship* 25 (Loeb, 5:145); Plautus, *The Rope*, Act 4, Scenes 4,5 (*Roman Comedies*, ed. George E. Duckworth [New York: Random House, 1942], p. 229-30).

27 Horace, *Ode* 4.11, l. 6-8 (*Odes of Horace*, trans. Gest).

28 Horace, *Satire* 2.2, l.20 (*Satires and Epistles*, trans. Rudd).

29 See also: Juvenal, *Satire* 12, l. 1; Persius, *Satire* 2, l. 1-2, and *Satire* 6, l. 18-22; Achilles Tatius, *Leucippe and Clitophon* 5.3.2 (a host's birthday as the occasion of an invitation to dinner).

30 Herondas, *Mime* 4.19 (*Women at the Temple*) (*The Mimes of Herondas*, trans. Guy Davenport [San Francisco: Grey Fox Press, 1981]).

31 Snakes were kept in Asklepieia, used in the cultus, and sometimes seen as manifestations of the God.

32 Ibid., *Mime* 4.88-95, p. 23.

priest in the precinct and with others that the offerer might meet outside the precinct.

Many passages indicate that sacrifices were performed and shared on other occasions of thanksgiving. These other occasions were not so explicitly linked to religious contexts as in Herondas, but were occasions simply of heightened awareness of good fortune. Juvenal describes preparations for a sacrifice of a young calf in honour of the safe return of a friend, "Corrinus . . . for whose return I rear so many altars."[33] Horace provides several clear references to feasting on occasions of thanksgiving to the Gods. He calls his friend to a feast in thanks for Horace's escape from harm when hit by a falling branch, a "vowed feast, very choice, to Bacchus with a goat pure white."[34] It is clear from the context that this is a private feast, to be shared in Horace's home with an intimate friend. Horace celebrates the safe return of a friend from Spain: "Sweet lyre's music and incense and hot red blood of bulls now we will give the Gods" in a context which refers explicitly to a feast shared at home among friends.[35] Again, over the safe return of a friend, Horace urges him to "give to Jove now feasts that you pledged him" and anticipates a drinking party with him.[36] Horace calls for a celebration of Cleopatra's downfall and Caesar's victory: "Now we must drink deep! Now with dancing foot must beat the hard earth; now . . . we'll set the Gods' sacred tables. Comrades, we're already late for the feasting!"[37]

Lucian also provides a glimpse of what might be called a proleptic thanksgiving meal: a ship captain sacrifices for a safe journey, and the Gods are "asked to the meal."[38] A thanksgiving sacrifice and subsequent meal soon after a sea voyage are portrayed also by Plautus.[39]

Funerals

Lucian provides two references concerning sacrifice and banquets in connection with funerals: *On Funerals* 24 (Loeb, 4:129) refers to funeral feasts after three days of fasting,[40] and *Pathological Liar* gibes that doctors expect sacrifices at their funerals instead of "a little honey

33 Juvenal, *Satire* 12, l. 1-12, 94 (*Satires*, trans. Plumb).

34 Horace, *Ode* 3.8, l. 5-8 (*Odes of Horace*, trans. Gest).

35 Ibid., *Ode* 1.36, l. 1-6, 16.

36 Ibid., *Ode* 2.7, l. 17-18.

37 Ibid., *Ode* 1.37, l. 1-4.

38 Lucian, *Zeus Rants* 15 (Loeb, 2:113).

39 Plautus, *Amphitryon*, l. 964-68 (Act 3, Scene 3) (*Roman Comedies*, trans. Duckworth).

40 Lucian, *On Funerals* 24 (Loeb, 4:129).

and water" like those poorer than they.[41] Lucius Apuleius also refers to "required sacrifices" eight days after death.[42]

More explicit links between funeral sacrifices and meals are found. Lucius Apuleius's bandits at a feast in celebration of their exploits also pour libations for comrades killed in their recent adventures and sing hymns in honour of their patron, Mars.[43] A scurrilous poem of Catullus portrays a woman "seen . . . often in the public cemeteries scrounging for the food-offerings placed by the half-burnt bodies, chasing the small loaves as they roll out of the fire."[44]

Seneca describes an aristocrat who was either neurotic or graphically expressive of a distinctive approach to mortality:

> [He] was in the habit of conducting a memorial ceremony for himself with wine and funeral feasting of the kind we are familiar with, and then being carried on a bier from the dinner table to his bed, while a chanting of music went on of the words "He has lived, he has lived" in Greek, amid the applause of the young libertines present. Never a day passed but he celebrated his own funeral.[45]

These references do not provide an explicit identification of sacrificed food consumed at table as part of funeral rites, but the indications both of sacrifices at funerals and feasts as part of funeral rites permit a strong inference that the two were often linked.

Sacrifices at common meals

The last group of references to be presented show sacrifices held at shared meals without any special occasion.

Plutarch indicates the sorts of meals at which the table-talk he records took place: "Most of the dinners were portion-banquets, and each man at the sacrifices was allotted his share of the meal."[46] Plutarch also remarks on a particularly appreciated entrée: "the cock, that [the

---

41 Lucian, *Satirical Sketches*, trans. Paul Turner (Harmondsworth, Middlesex: Penguin, 1961) p. 208.

42 Lucius Apuleius, *Golden Ass*, trans. Graves, p. 227.

43 Ibid., p. 109.

44 Catullus, *Poem* 59 (*Poems of Catullus*, trans. Whigham, p. 119).

45 Seneca, *Letter* 12.8 (*Letters from a Stoic*, selected and trans. Robin Campbell [Harmondsworth, Middlesex: Penguin, 1969], p. 58). See also Seneca, *Letter* 122.3, which describes persons wasting their lives over dinner tables: "what in fact they are doing is not banqueting but celebrating their own last rites" (ibid., p. 221). The context only reinforces the implication that funeral rites included formal meals.

46 Plutarch, *Convivial Questions* 642F (Loeb, 8:183).

cook] had set before the diners though it has just been[47] slaughtered as a sacrifice to Heracles, was as tender as if it had been a day old."[48]

Horace depicts a meal when friends arrived or "neighbours dropped in for a friendly visit on a wet day." Host and guests would share a chicken or kid and play drinking games, "and Ceres, receiving our prayer that she would rise high on the stalk, allowed the wine to smooth away our worried wrinkles."[49] It is likely that such a prayer would be accompanied by a libation or offering, and that this rite would hallow the food and drink. Horace also makes explicit reference to sacrifice at a meal whose chief characteristic is its simplicity and lack of social pretension: "Ah, those evenings and dinners. What heaven! My friends and I have our own meal at my fireside. Then, after making an offering, I hand the rest to the cheeky servants."[50]

Sacrifices were made at meals marking social occasions that were not as significant as birthdays, weddings or funerals. On whatever occasions friends met to eat, some sacrifice could readily occur to honour the meal and the event.

Conclusions

Many meals in Greco-Roman society included food that had been sacrificed to Gods before the meal or as one of the events of the meal. This is obviously the case for meals that are part of the celebrations of religious festivals. It is more noteworthy, however, that sacrifice was probably very often paired with meals of a heightened social significance. Whenever meals marked important social transitions (weddings or funerals) sacrifices were likely to occur. Similarly, whenever meals marked celebratory occasions (birthdays, the reunion of friends, the success of adventures or simply an elaborate meal for the pleasure of guests) then, too, sacrifice and the eating of sacrificed food were likely. This pairing of rite and meal in contexts of social importance is found in texts throughout the period, in descriptions of meals among both elite and common classes. It is remarkable that this conclusion is so clearly supported by the sources, especially given the incidental glimpses of such meals the sources afford.

This is important for the assessment of the social effects of abstinence from idol-food. If Corinthian Christians following Paul's advice were to attempt to avoid any situation where they would be asked to eat food explicitly identified as idol-food, then it is very likely that they could not accept invitations to frequent and important occasions. They could not attend weddings, funerals, celebrations in honour of

---

47 *kai tôn arti*

48 Ibid., 696E (Loeb, 8:511).

49 Horace, *Satire* 2.2, l. 115-25 (*Satires and Epistles*, trans. Rudd, p. 93).

50 Ibid., *Satire* 2.6, l. 65-66, p. 116.

birthdays, or even formal or relatively elaborate banquets—special meals of whatever occasion—since rites performed at the meals or referred to by the participants would mark the fare as idol-food.

The social impact of this cannot legitimately be down-played by an uncritical appeal to 1 Corinthians 10:27-28 claiming that Paul is saying that believers can accept such invitations as long as no one explicitly identifies the fare as idol-food. Even if Paul's caveat in 10:28 is interpreted this narrowly, it would still very likely apply to the contexts described by the references above. These citations make overt connections between shared meals and sacrificed food. Since the sources incidentally reveal these connections, the participants in the meals would have perceived those connections at least as acutely. These rites were connected in important ways to the occasions and purposes of the meals.

Some shared meals in that culture may not have included idol-food (the sources include many references to shared meals which are not connected by the sources with religious rites) and thus were akin to 1 Corinthians 10:27 (a simple invitation to eat). But the sources suggest strongly that socially significant occasions would more likely be akin to 1 Corinthians 10:28 (where a participant makes explicit the sacred character of the food): the ubiquitous use of hallowed food to celebrate socially significant events makes it certain that often the food (and fellowship) would be explicitly set apart as special by religious rite, and therefore—according to Paul—dangerous to eat.

The social importance of meals

The social impact of a refusal to consume idol-food is strengthened by another important conclusion that emerges from the literary sources: shared meals were a central feature of social intercourse in Greco-Roman culture. This conclusion is again not surprising, but it is useful to set out the evidence: food as a marker of social distinctions, meals as social requirements and shared meals as expressions of friendship.

Meals and food are markers of social status. In Greco-Roman society, you were what you ate, and—more important—you were whom you ate with. Elaborate feasts and rare, expensive food were the signs par excellence of wealth. In Petronius's nasty satire, Trimalchio is the worst sort of pretentious social climber from the lowest classes, ridiculous in his caricatured cultural aspirations—except that no one will laugh, since Trimalchio's wealth is staggering. The central expression both of Trimalchio's wealth and his ostentation, and the focus of Petronius's satire, is a feast at Trimalchio's house.[51] A small sample of Petronius's description shows the character of the menu:

---

51 Petronius, *Satyricon*, l. 31-41, trans. Michael Heseltine (Loeb Classical Library, 1930), p. 53.

> There was a round plate with the twelve signs of the Zodiac set in order, and on each one the artist had laid some food fit and proper to the symbol; over the Ram ram's-head pease [chick-peas, drawing a pun on the Latin], a piece of beef on the Bull, kidneys over the Twins, over the Crab a crown, an African fig over the Lion, a barren sow's paunch over Virgo . . . over Capricornus a lobster, over Aquarius a goose, over Pisces two mullets.[52]

One of Juvenal's satires is entirely a description of a hapless client at his wealthy patron's dinner, and the satirical drive throughout is provided by the contrast between the elaborate and costly fare served the patron and the miserable fare served the client.[53] Pliny makes a similar point more directly in a letter of advice to a young man. He complains of his treatment while guest at another man's table: "The best dishes were set in front of [the host] and a select few, and cheap scraps of food before the rest of the company. He had even put the wine into tiny flasks, divided into three categories. . . . One lot was intended for himself and for us, another for his lesser friends (his friends are all graded) and the third for his and our freedmen." Pliny's advice to his addressee: don't make class distinctions at table; serve all the guests the same food.[54]

Persius provides a telling aphorism showing the strong association of luxurious eating and wealth: "Twins born under the same star vary in temperament. One, for a birthday treat, will dip his dry greens in brine. . . . He personally shakes the precious pepper on his plate. The other, a stylish lad, chews through a huge inheritance."[55]

Seneca's letters also provide important glimpses of wealth spent on meals. One of the most interesting of these describes at length a dining room which is for Seneca the pinnacle of useless folly: this room was a wonder of technology and luxury, even to the extent that its ceiling could change pattern for every course.[56] Another letter describes the employment of useless wealth: it turns first to the embellishment of the person (clothes and ornament), then houses, then tables—"where novelty is all."[57] Another refers to snow melting in wine, and to "a whole boar lying somewhere where people can see it, conveying the impression that it has been banished from the table as being too cheap and ordinary a piece of meat to be on it."[58]

---

52 Ibid., 35 (Loeb, p. 53).

53 Juvenal, *Satire* 5.

54 Pliny, *Letter* 2.6 (*Letters*, trans. Radice, p. 63).

55 Persius, *Satire* 6. 18-22 (*Satires*, trans. Rudd, p. 230-31).

56 Seneca, *Letter* 90 (*Letters*, trans. Campbell, p. 165-66).

57 Ibid., *Letter* 114, p. 215.

58 Ibid., *Letter* 78.22-28, p. 138.

Social practice over meals was a strong marker of status in the Greco-Roman world. The rich ate very well. Moreover, a prime means of displaying wealth, and the social status dependent on it, was time, effort and money spent on lavish meals and novel foods.[59]

Sources also show participation at meals to be an essential element of ordinary social intercourse. Indications of the importance of meals are diverse, but support a consistent picture of meals as the main means of establishing and maintaining social relations.

Participation in sacrifice (and sharing the meals which ensued) was a requirement of holding public office. It is of course a commonplace of discussion of Greco-Roman religion that it was tied intimately to the social and political structure of the *polis*. Pausanias, in his *Description of Greece*, describes a round structure near the Council Chamber in Athens, and adds that "here the Presidents sacrifice."[60] Pliny relates how he was given the office of augur, and it is clear that Pliny sees this primarily not as a religious office but as a public honour and a reward for public service.[61] A papyrus fragment provides a list of public duties to be performed by a high public official that include participation in many sacrifices to various Gods.[62] Achilles Tatius describes a sacrifice to Artemis, at which the members of the council assist.[63] Active participation in political life in Greco-Roman cities would require participation in sacrifice, and—in every likelihood, though our sources do not show this—participation in the formal banquets likely to follow such sacrifice.

The sources also show a more pervasive social requirement of shared meals—more pervasive in number and context of occasions, and throughout the social classes. The importance of shared meals to social intercourse was likely to have been of much significance to the earliest Christian groups such as those in Corinth.

---

59 Other references include: Juvenal, *Satire* 3, *c.* l. 140 (a man's wealth can be measured by the number of courses he serves); Lucian, *The Dream or the Cock* 11 (a comic description of a poor man at a rich man's dinner, who is overwhelmed by the "learned" conversation, the entertainments, and the many courses [Loeb, 2:193]); Lucius Apuleius, *Metamorphoses* (*Golden Ass*, trans. Graves, p. 249, 252); Plutarch, *Lycurgus* 10 (*Lives of the Noble Greeks*, ed. Edmund Fuller [New York: Dell, 1968], p. 50-51); Seneca, *Letters* 89 and 95 (*Ad Lucilium Epistulae Morales*, 3 vols., trans. Richard M. Grummere, Loeb Classical Library, 1925, 2:393; 3:67,70-71,73-77); Horace, *Satires* 2.4 and 2.8.

60 Pausanias, *Description of Greece* 1.5.1, in vol. 1, trans. W. H. S. Jones and H. A. Omerod, Loeb Classical Library, 1918.

61 Pliny, *Letter* 4.8.

62 A. S. Hunt, and C. C. Edgar, *Select Papyri*, vol. 2, *Non-literary Papyri*. Public documents, Loeb Classical Library, 1954, p. 161.

63 Achilles Tatius, *Leucippe and Clitophon* 8.7.6.

Musonius Rufus provides an unconscious witness to the social importance of shared eating by providing a catalogue of table vices:[64]

> At each meal there is not one hazard for going wrong, but many. First of all, the man who eats more than he ought does wrong, and the man who eats in undue haste no less, and also the man who wallows in the pickles and sauces, and the man who prefers the sweeter foods to the more healthful ones, and the man who does not serve food of the same kind or amount to his guests as to himself.

Musonius is drawing common examples from his readers' experiences to make a serious point concerning Stoic moderation and control of all appetites. My point, of course, is different: that Musonius draws on these examples is good evidence of the social importance of meals, both to hosts and guests.

Pliny's letters offer more telling evidence for the central social role of meals. In two letters, Pliny offers extensive descriptions of his home near Rome, referring to only three kinds of public space: outdoors (including ball courts), baths and dining rooms. These dining rooms were carefully thought out—varied in size, and oriented for view and ventilation. Even on the grounds of his estate there was what must have been a thoroughly delightful dining area—a curved bench with hidden pipes so that "water gushed out as if pressed out by the weight of people sitting there," filling a pool on which floated serving dishes "shaped like birds or little boats."[65] The inference to be drawn from the space given to social use in Pliny's house is that the major social activity was dining. This was true also of classes less wealthy than Pliny. Though Pliny's house was unusual in its size and luxury, there is no reason to think it unusual in its culturally determined functional division of space.[66]

The sources also show that social advancement required attendance at meals. Many references can be found to the *parasitus*. "Parasite"

---

64 Musonius Rufus, *Discourse* 18B, l. 29-34 (*Discourses*, trans. Lutz, p. 117).

65 Pliny, *Letters* 2.17; 5:6 (*Letters*, trans. Radice, p. 75-79; 139-44).

66 Houses of the less wealthy, of course, less often survive and, until recently, were not often excavated. One excavation report supporting these general conclusions, however, comes from the American excavation at Corinth, which describes a Roman villa west of the city (Theodore Leslie Shear, *Corinth: Results of Excavations Conducted by the American School of Classical Studies at Athens*, vol. 5, *The Roman Villa* [Cambridge, MA: Harvard University Press, 1930]). The report focusses almost exclusively on three well-preserved mosaic floors, and nothing is said whatever of the possible functions of the rooms of the structure. Only two rooms are large enough to be public space, and one of these is an atrium with a concrete pool filled from an opening above it. The other room is shown on a diagram (*Roman Villa*, p. 14) to contain what seems to be couches along the perimeter, though the text—most frustratingly—does not refer to them.

means a guest in its primary sense, but in its common use, a social inferior servile to his host in order to win a meal in the short run and in the long run social advancement. Parasites are stock characters in satire of the period and are seen as thoroughly unpleasant characters, but it is clear that attendance at meals given by social superiors was the primary means for winning favours and benefits for many persons in that society.

Epictetus disapproves of social climbing through grasping for invitations: "You have not been invited to somebody's dinner party? Of course not; for you did not give the host the price at which he sells his dinner. He sells it for praise; he sells it for personal attention."[67]

Lucian's satirical vignettes often refer to parasites. The evil extravagances and snares of Rome include "informers, haughty greetings, flatterers, legacy hunters, feigned friendships, and dinners"; for all the toadying of those who pay court to the rich, they receive a "much-talked-of dinner," itself "the source of many evils."[68] He consistently portrays false philosophers chasing free meals more than virtue. For example: "They make laughing stocks of themselves by elbowing each other out of the way to get to a rich man's door, or going to big dinner-parties and crudely flattering their hosts, eating more than is good for them, grumbling, and preaching off-key sermons on morality in their cups, and finally passing out from a surfeit of neat alcohol."[69]

Lucian also shows the importance of meals to other professions: a young girl about to begin her career as courtesan is instructed on appropriate behaviour at table by her mother.[70]

Catullus sympathizes with a friend "forced to hang about the street corners angling for invitations."[71]

Seneca provides warning advice concerning parasites: avoid friends met in one's reception hall and at one's table, since "the more they owe the more they hate."[72] Plautus's parasite in the *Twin Menaechmi*, named Brush because he sweeps the table clean, holds the opposite point of view. If one wishes to retain control over another, then feed him well: "Give him all he wants to eat and drink every day, and he'll never try to run away. . . . The bonds of food and drink are very elastic, you know: the more you stretch them, the tighter they hold you."[73]

---

67 Epictetus, *Manual [Encheiridion]* 25.4-5 (Loeb).

68 Lucian, *The Wisdom of Nigrinus* 1:117, 121 (Loeb).

69 Lucian, *Fishing for Phonies* (*Satirical sketches*, trans. Turner), p. 184.

70 Lucian, *Mother Knows Best* (*Satirical Sketches*, trans. Turner), p. 40.

71 Catullus, *Poem* 47 (*The Poems of Catullus*, trans. Whigham, p. 106).

72 Seneca, *Letter* 19 (Loeb, 1:131).

73 Plautus, *Twin Menaechmi*, Act 1, Scene 1, l. 90-95 (*Roman Comedies*, trans. Duckworth, p. 61).

The social importance of meals is also shown in that to refuse a meal or part of a meal was to give offence. A fragment of Epictetus shows this: "Now when we have been invited to a banquet, we take what is set before us; and if a person should bid his host to set before him fish or cakes, he would be regarded as eccentric [*atopos*]."[74] *Atopos* conveys not only "unusual" but also "out of place, strange, unnatural, disgusting."

Philostratus gives an account of Apollonius's defence before the Emperor Domitian on a charge of conspiracy—really a literary opportunity for Philostratus to answer all manner of charges against the philosopher.[75] Part of Apollonius's "defence" concerns his refusal to sacrifice.[76] His reasons for this are an abhorrence of slaughter and a reverence for life. What is noteworthy, however, is that a refusal to participate in sacrifice and the intimately connected refusal to eat meat is perceived first as odd and then as requiring justification.

Seneca, too, reveals a similar concern, but much more explicitly. He argues that philosophers who lead ascetic lives—shabby clothes, long hair, unkept beards, avoidance of property—only encourage contempt from others rather than a love of philosophy or virtue. This applies also to asceticism in diet: to refuse not only extravagance and luxury, but even plain and common food, will "earn only hostility and ridicule." Seneca's generalization of this view is striking: "The first thing philosophy promises us is the feeling of fellowship, of belonging to mankind and being members of a community; being different will mean the abandoning of that manifesto."[77]

The negative social consequences attendant on unusual diet, and more particularly on the refusal of common foods, went well beyond curiosity and disapproval: it seems not to stretch Philostratus's literary plausibility to require someone to defend abstinence from sacrifice in a court, and it seems a real possibility to Epictetus and Seneca that unusual diets would breed contempt and rejection from common persons.

The positive aspect of the same social reality is that, just as abstinence from food bred hostility, shared food bred friendship. In the introductory section of Lucius Apuleis's *Metamorphoses*, while Lucius still is in human form, he is a guest at the house of a miserable and miserly man. The central vignette showing his host's meanness is a scant meal offered to Lucius but in the end cleverly not provided.[78] In another context, one of the characters in Lucius's story implores her

---

74 Epictetus, *Fragment* 17 (Loeb).

75 Philostratus, *Life of Apollonius*, 7.32-8.8, trans. C. P. Jones (Harmondsworth, Middlesex: Penguin, 1970).

76 Ibid., 8.7.10.

77 Seneca, *Letter* 5.3,4 (*Letters from a Stoic*, trans. Campbell, p. 37).

78 Lucius Apuleius, *Golden Ass*, trans. Graves, p. 41-44.

hearers to have nothing to do with a certain man: "do not eat at the same table with him, don't even talk to him."[79] Lucius also celebrates his initiation into the rites of Isis and Osiris with meals shared with friends.[80] Horace lists qualities necessary for success "in the daily business of life": one must be, first, a good neighbour, and second, a charming host; then one must be kind to one's wife, forgiving of the servants, and so forth.[81] The association of neighbourliness and hospitality, and the relative position of being a host in Horace's list, are both noteworthy. Many other references linking friendship and the table are found. Achilles Tatius makes "hearth and table" synonyms for close social relations and mutual approval.[82] Seneca quotes a proverb of Epicurus: "You must reflect carefully beforehand with whom you are to eat and drink rather than what you are to eat and drink. For a dinner of meats [*visceratio*] without the company of a friend is like the life of a lion or a wolf."[83] Epictetus:

> The man who consorts frequently with one person or another for conversation, or for banquets [*eis symposia*], or for social purposes in general [*eis symbiôsin*] is compelled either to become like the man himself, or else to bring them over to his style of living. . . . Since the risk is so great, then, we ought to enter cautiously into such social intercourse with the laymen,[84] remembering that it is impossible for the man who brushes up against the person who is covered with soot to keep from getting soot on himself.[85]

Lucian:

> Nobody invites an enemy or unknown person to dinner; not even a slight acquaintance. A man must first, I take it, become a friend in order to share another's bowl and board [*trapezês*, "table"]. . . . I have often heard people say: "How much of a friend is he, when he has neither eaten or drunk with us?"[86]

Cicero's letter to Papirus Paetus, in which Cicero playfully defends his attendance at a dinner with a famous courtesan:

---

79 Ibid., p. 188. This equation between shared meals and social acceptance is of course exactly parallel to 1 Cor 5:11: "I wrote to you not to associate with anyone . . . —not even to eat with such a one."

80 Ibid., p. 285-90.

81 Horace, *Letter* 2.2 (*Satires and Epistles*, trans. Rudd).

82 Achilles Tatius, *Leucippe and Clitophon* 8.8.11 (Loeb).

83 Seneca, *Letter* 19 (Loeb, 1.131).

84 For Epictetus, those not won over to philosophy—but note the Greek: *tais idiôtais*. Compare 1 Cor 14:23.

85 Epictetus, *Discourse* 3.16.1,3 (Loeb).

86 Lucian, *Parasite* 22 (Loeb, 3:269-71).

> "And this is the sort of dinner party Cicero goes to," you will ask. . . . I like a dinner party. I talk about any topic . . . and my griefs and my sighs are turned into shouts and laughter. . . . So this is the way I spend my time. I read or write something every day. Then lest I be denying friendship its due, I dine with my friends.[87]

In the prologue to the *Convivial Questions* Plutarch refers to the "friend-making character of the dining table."[88] Plutarch's characters claim that "the drinking party is a passing of time over wine which, guided by gracious behaviour, ends in friendship."[89] Finally, in one of Plutarch's discussions of etymologies one of his characters notes a claim which—despite its dubious etymological validity—stands well as the conclusion of this entire chapter: "they say that *cena* [Latin: dinner] has its name from *koinônia* [Greek: fellowship]."[90]

Conclusions

Earlier chapters on the sanctuaries of Demeter and Kore and Asklepios discussed Paul's instructions not to share the table of *daimonia* and not to be seen in an idol's temple, and explored the possible range of social effects of avoidance of such contexts. This survey of literary sources shows that Paul's instruction concerning invitations from non-believers was even more problematic. "Go if you wish, eat what's put in front of you," says Paul, but adds a troubling condition: "But if some one says to you, 'This has been offered in sacrifice,' then out of consideration for the man who informed you, and for conscience's sake—I mean his conscience, not yours—do not eat it."

We can now answer the following questions. In what contexts might consumption of sacred food occur? How frequently might a Corinthian Christian encounter such contexts? What social effects would follow a refusal to eat?

First, the contexts in which sacred food was consumed at homes or temples among guests were many.[91] Guests would be invited to share

87 This translation of Cicero's *Epistulae ad familiares* 9.36.2-4 is cited in *Private Letters Pagan and Christian*, ed. Dorothy Brook (London: Ernest Benn, 1929), p. 51-52. The extant correspondence of Cicero to Papirus Paetus provides an extensive example in general of the social importance of meals. The letters are full of references to banquets and playful warnings of how much Cicero expects to consume on his visits, and convey a strong impression of the frequency and importance of shared meals among those of Cicero's class (see Cicero, *The Letters to his Friends*, trans. Glynn Williams, Loeb Classical Library, 1927-1929, letters 9.15-26).

88 Plutarch, *Convivial Questions* 612D (Loeb, 8:7).

89 Ibid., 621C (Loeb, 8:57).

90 Ibid., 726E (Loeb, 9:163).

91 Compare the conclusion of Willis, *Idol Meat*, p. 15 (based on a survey of second-

meals at religious festivals. Food offered to Gods would be served at political functions, weddings, birthdays, funerals, and diverse occasions of celebration for good fortune. There was a strong possibility that food offered to Gods would be served at any meal considered special, even if its special character derived simply from its occasion of good cheer among friends.

Second, these occasions would have been encountered frequently by Corinthian Christians. It might have been possible to avoid religious festivals, but not the many other social events where sacred food would be served. This is supported by two independent features of the evidence: on the one hand "idol-food" is associated with occasions of major social significance, and on the other hand shared meals were the major means of the maintenance of social relationships in that culture.[92] Corinthian Christians could expect to receive many invitations to occasions where just the sort of exception Paul notes—the explicit identification of some of the food as offered to the Gods—would likely be met. The problem Paul describes could not be avoided.

Third, the social consequences of refusing to eat food offered to idols would be extreme. Events of central significance to family and friends would have to be avoided. A major means of social advancement, and the major means of the maintenance of friendship, would at the very least be awkward and difficult for Christians. To refuse to accept food presented at a meal, to raise questions beforehand, and to refuse food commonly eaten by virtually all other persons in that society would mark Christians as odd and repugnant. It would not be possible to maintain social relationships with those outside the Christian circle without major adjustment and the serious possibility of misunderstanding and hostility.

---

ary sources concerning Greco-Roman religion): "there would have been ample opportunity for most people . . . to have some occasion to participate" in meals involving sacrificed food. Ramsay MacMullen's extensive description of the dining facilities of temples and the role of meals in those temples also supports my conclusions strongly. He argues that the social and religious character of many meals in temples were of a piece; he also notes that temples would have been used for many meals of special significance, since even large houses usually had dining rooms which could accommodate only nine diners (*Paganism*, p. 34-42).

92 The sources surveyed show that this holds true at all socio-economic levels. Occasions where idol-food was served may have been encountered more frequently among the wealthier. Some analyses, notably that of Theissen, suggest that some members of the Corinthian group were of higher social status than is often assumed.

4

Introduction to the discussion of 1 Corinthians 8-10

The examination of the social use of sacred food in chapters 1 to 3 allows an informed approach to the passages in 1 Corinthians where Paul addresses the issue of food offered to idols. An understanding of the broad context of 1 Corinthians, however, will not of itself allow a clear understanding of the text. The letter responds to a specific set of events shared by Paul and his addressees.

Its character as a letter—as one part of an extended dialogue between Paul and his converts in Corinth—presents significant challenges to a reader who wishes to gain a valid understanding.

Most scholars approach 1 Corinthians 8:1-11:1 to discover the principles that underlie Paul's position concerning food offered to idols. Food offered to idols is not a current religious or moral issue in the contexts from which most scholars write (Christian scholars at least), so they find it difficult to enter imaginatively the problem Paul addresses. Also, the work of many scholars is controlled by a religious agenda. As a result the text is explored not at the level of the concrete social problem of idol-food but the level of principles that might be applied to other religious, social or moral conflicts.[1]

1 Cf. J. Murphy-O'Connor, "Freedom or the Ghetto (1 Cor 8:1-13; 10:23-11:1)" (*Revue biblique*, 85 [1978]): 543: "The problem of the legitimacy of the eating of meat which had formed pagan sacrifices is, in itself, of very limited interest. Paul's treatment is of perennial value because he saw that fundamental principles were involved." An explicit focus not on food but on principle informs a major part of the literature on 1 Cor 8-10: see Hans Freiherr von Soden, "Sakrament und Ethik bei Paulus," in *Urchristentum und Geschichte* (Tübingen: J. C. B. Mohr [Paul Siebeck], 1951, p. 239-51) (an abridged translation of "Sakrament" is found in *The Writings of St. Paul*, ed. Wayne Meeks [New York: W. W. Norton, 1972, p. 257-68]). Even scholars who are aware of the importance of the concrete social

If the point of the text is Paul's principles, then the centre of concern is Paul—Paul as authority, Paul as founder of a religious system or exponent of a religious/ethical approach to conflict—and not the situation or the persons he addresses. Further, if one is concerned to discover the principles Paul applies to the problem of idol-food, one has assumed that Paul approaches the problem in a principled way. If one expects to apply the principles so discovered one assumes not only that the principles exist but also that they are principles meriting approval and emulation. It is also assumed (perhaps less consciously) that Paul's approach was and is effective—that Paul's principles (if understood properly) work, and that they could have worked (if followed properly) to solve the problem of idol-food in Corinth.

The agenda of this study is social-historical, and it attempts to recover the concrete social situation originally addressed by 1 Corinthians 8:1-11:1. These chapters offer extensive and important evidence concerning the relations of Pauline Christians with Greek-speaking non-Christians, and the possible social implications of joining the Corinthian Christian club.[2] These chapters also offer a clear view of Paul's attempts to resolve concrete and specific conflicts that intertwine social and religious aspects and involve Christians and non-Christians. Our evidence concerning Paul is best, but all participants matter equally in a historical reconstruction. It will not be assumed that Paul's approach to the problem of idol-food was principled or that his approach was effective.

Paul addresses problems of food and eating in three letters—1 Corinthians, Romans and Galatians. Because Paul's letters are written

---

issues underlying the text fall under this characterization. Willis, for example, shows his central concern with Paul's ethics (*Idol Meat*, p. 116-17), and his conclusions are taken up entirely with theological themes provided by the history of scholarly Christian debate.

2 "Club" or "voluntary association" are the most accurate terms for the group of Christians in Corinth. The group was not a community: we have no evidence that they lived together or organized themselves on a model analogous to the community at Qumran, for example. The group was also not a school, analogous to the group of scholars attached to Peripatetic or Stoic teachers. The closest parallel social organization in Greco-Roman society is the social club that met for shared meals and common interests. For discussions of these clubs see Franz Poland, *Geschichte des griechischen Vereinswesens* (Leipzig: Teubner, 1909); Paul Stengel, *Die griechischen Kultusaltertümer* (*Handbuch der klassischen Altertumswissenschaft*, 5, 3 [Münich: Beck, 1920]); Marcus Tod, "Clubs and Societies in the Greek World," in *Sidelights on Greek History* (Oxford: Basil Blackwell, 1932), p. 71-96; Ramsay MacMullen, *Roman Social Relations, 50 B.C. to A.D. 284* (New Haven: Yale University Press, 1984), p. 72-87; Dennis E. Smith, "Meals and Morality," p. 323-24; and Willis (*Idol Meat*, p. 47-61).

to concrete circumstances and different audiences his treatment of food issues in these letters must not be conflated or confused. First Corinthians will be the focus of a reconstruction of Paul's views on idol-food, since it contains the most extensive discussion of the questions of permitted food. Since 1 Corinthians is probably the earliest of these three letters,[3] Galatians and Romans will be explored for evidence relevant to the problem of food offered to idols in chapters 10 and 11, below, where evidence concerning further developments in the issue of idol-food is explored.

The passages found in 1 Corinthians 8:1-13 and 10:14-11:1 address the problem of idol-food directly and at length, and are thus the passages most relevant to the issue.[4] What, however, is the relationship between these passages? Though the passages both concern food offered to idols, they are separated by Paul's defence of his practices as an apostle (9:1-26), an extended discussion of the exodus of Israel and her experiences in the wilderness, and Paul's exhortation based on those experiences (10:1-13). Some have argued that chapter 8 and 10:14-11:1 show sufficiently strong differences in content that they are not to be treated as two parts of one answer to a problem. Instead, they

---

3 Romans 15:26 shows Paul planning to leave for Jerusalem after having completed the collection in Achaia, so Romans is later than 1 Cor where the collection has just begun (1 Cor 16:1-4). The place of Galatians in the sequence of Paul's letters is much more problematic. Concerning the sequence of Paul's letters, see J. C. Hurd, *Origin*, p. 12-42.

4 Paul writes of food and eating in several other places in 1 Cor. In 3:2 he complains that the Corinthian Christians are ready only for milk and not food; in 5:6-8 he refers to celebrating a festival with unleavened bread; in 6:13 he quotes disapprovingly a chiastic proverb, "Food for the stomach, and the stomach for food"; in 11:20-34 he criticizes the Corinthians for the divisive manner in which they eat the Lord's meal and commands them to do otherwise; in 15:32 he quotes (disapprovingly again) the proverb, "Let's eat, let's drink; tomorrow we'll die." Though these passages are not directly relevant to the issue of idol-food, there may be associations with it (Paul often thinks and writes associatively): 3:2 may be a pointed allusion to idol-food ("You think yourselves spiritual, able to treat all food as lawful, but you are ready only for milk"); 5:8 (celebrating the festival) is followed by Paul's demand that his readers not eat with a brother guilty of (among other things) idolatry; the proverb in 6:13 is linked to the issue of idol-food ("All things are lawful for me," in 6:12 is repeated at 10:23); the proverb in 15:32 echoes Paul's citation of Exodus in 10:7, where eating and drinking are expressive of idolatry, and this link might explain the following proverb in 15:33, "Bad company corrupts good habits," that reads oddly in its context. Chapter 11:20-34 addresses a situation apparently quite distinct from the eating of idol-food, yet here too are links between the issues. As 10:21-22 shows, Paul thinks of (at least some) idolatrous eating as directly parallel to the Christian cultic meal in meaning and function.

are seen as two answers to one problem (in particular, that the passages belong to different letters), or as two answers to different aspects of one problem.

Before these passages can be used in a social-historical reconstruction their literary relationship must be determined. I am convinced that 1 Corinthians 8:1-11:1 must be read as Paul's integral response to the Corinthians' question concerning idol-food. The entire section bracketed by the two explicit discussions of the issue must be understood as one unit, and everything in the unit is directly relevant to Paul's response. The clear associative links among the unit's sections warrant this conclusion. Paul's defence of his apostolic rights in 9:1-27 seems to break in at 9:1 out of nowhere, but by 9:12 the connection to the issue of idol-food is implicit and by 9:22 explicit: just as in 8:9 Paul warns that the liberty or right (*exousia*) of the Corinthians to eat idol-food might become an obstacle to the weak, so in 9:12 Paul forgoes his liberty or right (*exousia*) in order to cause no hindrance to the gospel of Christ. If Paul demands concessions to the weak in 8:9 he can point to his own practice toward the weak in 9:22.[5] The example from Scripture and Paul's application of it in 10:1-13 has explicit links also to the issue of idol-food. Though the "fathers"—the Israelites in the wilderness—ate spiritual food and drink just as the Corinthians have, they became idolaters who "sat down to eat and drink." Paul's strong conclusion (*dioper*, "for this very reason") is that the Corinthians must also avoid idolatry expressed in meals sacred to other Gods (10:14-22). The entire section from 8:1 to 11:1 must be considered a unitary response.

Even if Paul's defence of his practices and his exposition of the Exodus narrative belong to his response concerning idol-food, still there remains one obstacle to treating 8:1-11:1 as a unit. A strong tension has long been noted between Paul's depiction of idol-food in 8:1-13 and 10:23-11:1 on the one hand and in 10:1-22 on the other. In the former passages Paul seems to think idol-food itself harmless and the harm to lie in the attitudes of others toward it; eat, he says, unless it makes a problem for another. In contrast, 10:1-22 depicts the consumption of idol-food as participation in the worship of demons, and thus an act that violates partnership with the Christians' Lord.

---

5 The relevance of chapter 9 as Paul's extended example of his renunciation of his own *exousia* is widely acknowledged in the commentary on 1 Cor 8-10: see, for example, Heinrich August Wilhelm Meyer, *Critical and Exegetical Handbook to the Epistles to the Corinthians*, vol. 1, *First Epistle, Chapters 1-13* (Edinburgh: T. & T. Clark, 1877), p. 251; Johannes Weiss, *Der erste Korinthbrief* (Göttingen: Vandenhoeck & Ruprecht, 1910), p. 242-44; Hans Lietzmann, *An die Korinther I.II* (Tübingen: J. C. B. Mohr [Paul Siebeck], 1931 [first ed., 1907]), p. 39; von Soden, "Sakrament," p. 244; Hurd, *Origin*, p. 110-12, 127-28.

The tensions between these passages must not be ignored or obscured in an exegesis of these chapters.[6] If the tensions exist because the two passages belong to distinct letters later redactionally conflated into the canonical form of 1 Corinthians, a very different account of Paul's response to the problem of idol-food, and also a different reconstruction of the dialogue between Paul and the Corinthians, would be required.

Arguments for the partition of 1 Cor 8-10 on these grounds are set out most cogently by Weiss, and developed by von Soden.[7] Hurd has provided an extensive and persuasive analysis of the question of the integrity of 8:1-11:1,[8] responding to von Soden's claims[9] that the two sections show different premises regarding the reality of demons, different conclusions concerning the permissibility of eating idol-food, and different world views. Hurd's counter-arguments are cogent: the unreality of demons in 8:4 is not Paul's view but a Corinthian slogan; Paul's conclusions that abstinence for the sake of the weak and abstinence to avoid idolatry are complementary rather than conflicting; and the "sacramental" world view of 10:1-22 is not inconsistent with Paul's views concerning the magical effects of the Lord's table and of baptism shown elsewhere in 1 Corinthians.[10]

In addition to the arguments set out by Hurd, a consideration of Paul's aside in 10:19 makes this proposed partition theory untenable. This aside—"What do I imply, then? That food offered to idols is anything, or that an idol is anything?" (Revised Standard Version)—runs across the grain of Paul's argument in 10:14-22, whose point is that idols *are* demons and that eating idol-food *is* partnership with demons. Further, the aside recalls 8:4—"we know that there is no idol in the world and that there is no God but one"—and seems more consonant with his views in 8:1-13 and 10:23-11:1. The aside indicates that Paul

---

6 C. K. Barrett—to provide one example out of many possible—claims that the question of Paul's consistency in 1 Cor 8-10 is at the heart of the matter ("Things Sacrificed to Idols," in *Essays on Paul* [London: SPCK, 1982] [First published in *New Testament Studies*, 11 (1964-65): 138-53], p. 40).

7 Von Soden's arguments are addressed directly by Hurd; see my account immediately below. I address Weiss's views at length, below, in Appendix 1. Other partition theories are set out by Jean Héring, *Le première épître de Saint Paul aux Corinthiens*, deuxième ed. (Neuchatel: Delachaux et Niestle, 1959), p. 11-12, and Walter Schmithals, *Gnosticism in Corinth. An Investigation of the Letters to the Corinthians* (Nashville: Abingdon Press, 1971), p. 90-96.

8 Hurd, *Origin*, p. 131-37.

9 Von Soden, "Sakrament," p. 254-57.

10 See also Hurd's discussion of the literary integrity of the letter as a whole: *Origin*, p. 43-47.

himself is aware of the tensions in his response (and perhaps not entirely at ease with them), and is thus a clear indication that 10:1-22 belongs to the same response as chapter 8 and 10:23-11:1.[11]

The discrete passages in 8:1-11:1 are all integral to Paul's response to the problem of idol-food raised by the Corinthians, and as a consequence the entire section must be investigated as a complex whole.[12]

Because this investigation is a social-historical reconstruction of the events and arguments over the issue of idol-food, my exegesis of 1 Corinthians 8-10 will not proceed verse by verse, but will address to the text a series of questions necessary to this reconstruction: (1) What is idol-food? (2) For whom is idol-food a problem, and why? (3) What is Paul's proposed solution to the problem of idol-food? My answers to these questions form chapters 5, 6 and 7 respectively.

In Appendix 1 I set out my response to significant different views concerning 1 Corinthians 8-10 that have been argued by other commentators. I restrict my discussion to six scholars: Johannes Weiss, John Hurd, C. K. Barrett, Gerd Theissen, Jerome Murphy-O'Connor and Wendell Lee Willis. These commentators have provided distinct and extensively argued positions that present significant challenges to the conclusions I present below. The appendix summarizes their arguments, acknowledges my debts to their work, and sets out reasons for rejecting their views.

---

11 Compare a similar argument in Hurd, *Origin*, p. 134. Weiss is aware of the difficulty 10:19 poses for his partition theory and explains it thus: the verse did belong in the earlier letter as an aside, and gave occasion to the criticisms of the Corinthian strong, who developed it into the slogans to which Paul responds with chapter 8 (Weiss, *1 Kor*, p. 261). This solution may be ingenious, but only underlines the unpersuasiveness of Weiss's partition theory, which cannot account for the intertwining in both chapter 8 and chapter 10 of the supposedly distinct Pauline views.

12 Most recent scholarship also affirms the literary integrity of 1 Cor 8-10: Gordon Fee, "2 Cor 6:14-7:1 and Food Offered to Idols," *New Testament Studies*, 23 (1977): 148; Murphy-O'Connor, "Freedom," p. 543; Willis, *Idol Meat*, p. 112-13. A significant exception to this consensus is Hans-Joseph Klauck (*Herrenmahl*, p. 272, 282-84), who resurrects a partition theory with affinities to those of Weiss and Schmithals.

5

What is idol-food?

Idol-food and sacrifices

Though it is very often assumed that all idol-food is meat,[1] there is nothing in the text to make this a certainty. "If food puts an obstacle in the way of my brother I will never again eat meat (*krea*)" (8:13) shows clearly that the idol-food Paul has in mind most readily is meat. It cannot be inferred from this, however, that only meat could be idol-food: Paul's reference to refusing to eat meat is rhetorical,[2] and in 8:13 what might cause a brother to fall is *brôma*—a general term for "food."

Other terms used for idol-food in 1 Corinthians are not specific to one sort of food. Arndt and Gingrich translate *eidôlothyta* (8:1,4,7,10; 10:19) as "meat offered to an idol."[3] This is a judgment made from an unwarranted understanding of the passages here in question and from a

---

1 Some scholars claim explicitly that idol-food was meat: Morton Scott Enslin, *Christian Beginnings* (New York: Harper, 1938), p. 251; Archibald Robertson and Alfred Plummer, *A Critical and Exegetical Commentary on the First Epistle of St. Paul to the Corinthians* (Edinburgh: T. & T. Clark, 1911), p. 163; Margaret E. Thrall, *The First and Second Letters of Paul to the Corinthians* (Cambridge: Cambridge University Press, 1965), p. 61. Most scholars do not address this question directly, but only imply the identification of *eidôlothyta* and meat: Hans Conzelmann, *A Commentary on the First Epistle to the Corinthians* (Philadelphia: Fortress Press, 1975 [translated from *Der erste Brief an die Korinther*, Göttingen: Vandenhoeck und Ruprecht, 1969]), p. 142; Kirsopp Lake, *The Earlier Epistles of St. Paul: Their Motive and Origin* (London: Rivingtons, 1911), p. 198; Willis, *Idol Meat*, p. 1. The only scholar who makes much of the explicit identification of meat and *eidôlothyta* is Gerd Theissen, in "The Strong and the Weak in Corinth: A Sociological Analysis of a Theological Quarrel," in *The Social Setting of Pauline Christianity. Essays on Corinth by Gerd Theissen* (Philadelphia: Fortress, 1982), p. 121-44.

2 Compare 1 Cor 9:19-23.

3 William F. Arndt and F. Wilbur Gingrich, *A Greek-English Lexicon of the New Testament and Other Early Christian Literature*, 4th ed. (Chicago: University of Chicago Press, 1952).

set of assumptions concerning the practices of sacrifice. The strongest evidence for the identification of *eidôlothyta* with meat is a common meaning of *thyô* as "to kill in sacrifice," something possible only of animals. Arndt and Gingrich claim in the entry concerning *thyô*, however, that its proper and most common meaning is simply "to sacrifice." Because many sorts of food were offered to Gods—grain, wine, honey, as well as many sorts of animals—it is likely that "things sacrificed to idols" might include foods other than meat. *Thyô* (and *thysia*, compare 10:18) has a range of connotations, from "sacrifice" to the wider concept "to offer." This wider connotation is certainly possible: Liddell and Scott suggest that it is sometimes used in explicit contrast to *sphazô*, "to slaughter, especially for sacrifice."

Another indication of the sort of food Paul spoke of has been sought in 10:25: "Eat everything sold in the market [*en makellôi*]." Arndt and Gingrich include a set of assumptions in the translation of this word also, which they give as "meat market." The RSV echoes this judgment. *Makellon*, however, has a more general sense of "food market."[4]

The hypothesis that *eidôlothyta* may refer to more sorts of food than meat is strengthened by 8:4, where Paul uses the expression *brôsis tôn eidôlothytôn*. *Brôsis* here means "eating," but it is also a general term for food, with no necessary connotation of meat (compare Cor 2 9:10, where it clearly refers to bread). Similarly, less direct indications of what was eaten or avoided are non-specific: 8:10, "If someone sees you . . . reclining (*katakeimenôn*) in an idol's temple" (*katakeimenôn* here means simply "to recline to eat"); 10:21,22, "you cannot drink . . . the cup of demons . . . you cannot have a share in the table of demons"; 10:27, "eat everything set before you"; 10:30 "If I partake"; 10:31, "whether you eat or drink."

Though the most ready meaning of *eidôlothyta* is meat from sacrificed animals, there is nothing in the text of 1 Corinthians to limit Paul's use of the term exclusively to meat. Many other sorts of food were used in the rites of various cults, and there is no evidence from non-Christian sources to support such a restriction of the term. Idol-

4 The term is a borrowing from Latin, in which it carries no particular association with meat and means simply "provision market" (*Oxford Latin Dictionary* [Oxford: Clarendon, 1968], p. 1057). Liddell and Scott translate *makellon* as a direct equivalent to *macellum* and render it simply "market" (*A Greek-English lexicon*, rev. H. L. Jones [Oxford: Clarendon Press, 1940], 2:1074). Cadbury notes that all sorts of food were sold in *macella* ("The Macellum of Corinth," *Journal of Biblical Literature*, 53 [1934]: 141).

food ought to be understood as any food associated with the rites of or participation in other cults.[5]

Idol-food and idols

Idol-food in 1 Corinthians may include many foods: meat or grain, oil and honey. Is there any evidence to limit the specific nature of these foods' associations with idols?

One instance of this association is set out in 8:10: the problematic food is eaten *en eidôleiôi* ("in a temple of an idol"). Because it is eaten in a temple, it is likely that the food, or the act of eating, was part of the rites of the cult.[6] Other references in 1 Corinthians 8-10 support this conclusion: 10:14-22 explicitly makes idolatrous eating analogous to the supper rite of the Christian group, a rite laden with religious meaning for Paul and very likely for the Corinthian Christians, and in 10:7 the very act of eating makes the Israelites idolaters.

Yet there are other indications in these chapters of a more tenuous connection between idol-food and cult. Paul speaks of problematic food bought at the market (10:25) or served by a host (10:27). This too is idol-food, even if Paul does not label it explicitly as such. It raises problems because it has once been used in a non-Christian rite, and some portion either taken to market to be sold, or served by a host (who in turn had either used the food in a sacred rite or bought such food at market). Here the connection between idolatry and idol-food lies in the food's history and not in the present use of the food; in the present the food is put to secular use (if such an anachronistic distinction is legitimate) but its sacred past remains religiously significant.

Since in some instances Paul clearly refers to idol-food as part of idolatrous rites, and in others to food that was once but is not now so used, is idol-food problematic because the food itself carries the contagion of idolatry, or because the idolatrous practices associated with the food are harmful, and not the food itself? Paul's advice can be made to support either possibility. Sometimes Paul seems to indicate very clearly that food and idolatry are quite distinct: if one possesses the

---

5 Celsus argues against Christian avoidance of idol-food on exactly these grounds: "But when they eat food, and drink wine, and take fruits, and drink even the water itself, and breathe even the very air, are they not receiving [*lambanousin*] each of these from certain daemons, among whom the administration of each of these has been divided?" (cited by Origen in *Contra Celsum* 8.28 [*Origène. Contra Celse*, t. 4 (livres 7 et 8) (Introduction, texte critique, traduction et notes par Marcel Borret, Sources chrétiennes, no. 150 [Paris: Les éditions du Cerf, 1969]); translation by Henry Chadwick, *Contra Celsum* [Cambridge: Cambridge University Press, 1953 (reprinted with corrections, 1965)], p. 471-72).

6 Likely, but not certain, as shown by chapter 2, above.

knowledge that idols have no existence (8:4), and recognizes that food cannot present believers to God (8:8), and denies that food offered to idols is itself anything (10:19), then one can conclude that idol-food as food is of no harm. This conclusion can be strengthened by the argument that Paul condemns not idol-food but certain effects of eating it; the food can be bought at market or eaten at another's invitation, but if the eating of it causes difficulty for others the right to consume it should be renounced.[7]

On the other hand, sometimes Paul seems to indicate clearly that the food itself has religious effect. To eat idol-food can make one a partner (*koinônos*) with demons (10:20). Just as consumption of the Christian ritual meal effects *koinônia* with Christ, so consumption of the drink and food of demons destroys that *koinônia* and provokes the jealousy of the Lord (10:20-22). Paul believed the Christian rite carried something akin to infection: he believes improper eating causes illness and even death (11:30). It can be asserted, then, that Paul believed idol-food to carry the contagion of demons in the same way that the meal of the Lord infects with the Lord's blessing.[8]

---

7 The standard view is that Paul found food itself harmless and urged avoidance of idolatry and/or harm to others. Early on, Meyer claimed that food was for Paul *adiaphoron* (the Stoic technical term for matters of no moral consequence, over which the enlightened person would invest no care) and that Paul's objection was over idolatry (*1 Cor*, p. 245, 294, 297). Von Soden assumes that food per se for Paul is of no concern: "Eating as such constitutes no case of conscience, but rather eating as a demonstrated and confessed act towards others. . . . Conscience is spoken not of things but of persons" (von Soden, "Sakrament," p. 245 [my translation]). See also John C. Brunt, "Rejected, Ignored or Misunderstood? The Fate of Paul's Approach to the Problem of Food Offered to Idols in Early Christianity," *New Testament Studies*, 31 (1985): 114-15; Conzelmann, *1 Cor*, p. 147-48; Paul Gooch, "The Burden of the Weak: 1 Corinthians 8-10," chap. 5 of *Partial Knowledge. Philosophical Studies in Paul* (Notre Dame, IN: University of Notre Dame Press, 1987), p. 111; Wayne A. Meeks, " 'And Rose up to Play': Midrash and Paraenesis in 1 Corinthians 10:1-22," *Journal for the Study of the New Testament*, 16 (1982): 73; C. A. Pierce, *Conscience in the New Testament* (London: SCM Press, 1955), p. 77; Robertson and Plummer ("The 'weakness' [of the weak] consists in giving moral value to things that are morally indifferent"), *1 Cor*, p. 179-80; Schmithals, *Gnosticism*, p. 227-28; Weiss, *1 Kor*, p. 264.

8 Kirsopp Lake stresses this view, and argues that many persons would hold no clear idea in cultic settings of the relationship between the food and the God it honoured (*Epistles*, p. 195-97). Lake makes explicit reference to the notion of infection: "It is noteworthy how very nearly demonic possession played the same part in ancient pathology as bacterial infection does in modern" (ibid., p. 196, n.1).

Attempts to reconcile the tensions between 1 Cor 8 and 1 Cor 10

This apparent contradiction—that sometimes food as food is not harmful, and at other times is the vector of contagion—has caused discomfort to commentators who have perceived it, who have then attempted several interpretive reconciliations.[9]

The most extended example of an attempted reconciliation is the work of Willis. He rejects the view that Paul believed eating at the table of the Lord or of *daimonia* is a consumption of the God and has either magical or quasi-magical powers of salvation (a "sacramental" view). Willis argues that Paul's concern in chapter 10 is not *daimonia* but rather the table and cup—the fellowship with others in idolatry. Willis concludes that Paul's warning against *koinônia* in the table of demons in chapter 10 does not reflect a fear of contagion, but rather a desire to have the Corinthians avoid fellowship with idolaters. This reading in turn makes chapter 10 more consistent with Paul's warnings against idol-food in chapter 8 on the basis of its effect on the weak rather than its nature as food.[10]

Despite the thoroughness of Willis's arguments and their careful structure, his position remains an elaborate interpretative reconciliation of the unreconcilable. The chief weaknesses of Willis's view are that (1) it pays insufficient attention to Paul's understanding of *koinônia* and (2) it runs counter to Paul's belief in the reality of *daimonia.*

Koinônia at the Lord's meal is effected in and through the elements of the meal. Willis's attempt to distinguish between *koinônia* in the Lord through the meal (which, he believes, Paul doesn't mean) and on the other hand *koinônia* with other believers at the meal (which, he believes, Paul does mean) simply violates the evidence here and elsewhere of Paul's understanding of the Lord's meal and the nature of the believers' relationship in Christ. *Koinônia* in the Lord and *koinônia* with other believers are for Paul one and the same: 10:16-17 intertwines

---

9 See discussion of partition theories, above. Not many commentators address the tensions in Paul's views of idol-food in terms of whether the food itself carries contagion. Those who do usually argue that Paul sees no danger in food itself. Gordon Fee attempts an extended argument that idol-food in chapter 8 and 10:23-11:1 has only to do with food per se and that 10:1-22 deals only with idolatry ("*Eidôlothyta* Once Again: an Interpretation of I Corinthians 8-10," *Biblica*, 16 [1980]: 176-79)—a view that might work in theory, but would not work, even as 1 Cor shows, in concrete social practice. Hurd admits to the unreconciled tension in Paul's views: Paul "carefully did not specify whether the danger from demons attaches itself to the intention of the one who eats or to the actual meat wherever it is eaten" (*Origin*, p. 143).

10 Willis, *Idol Meat*, p. 184-88; 191; 215-19.

associations among the body of the Lord in the bread and the body of believers in the Lord. Chapter 11:29-30 shows that the Lord's meal itself carries direct physical effect.[11] Finally, Paul's faith is shot through with a religious understanding that can be described as participatory or mystical—an understanding calling on the interconnectedness of the experience of believers and the experience of Christ, and the saving action of God through or in Christ that is mediated not only in works of belief but also in bread, wine and water. While Willis's root point seems correct—that Paul did not see the table of the Lord as some crude theophagy—his conclusion that Paul held no sacramental view of the Lord's meal is overstated. Paul saw the Lord's meal as a powerful medium of salvation, just as he saw baptism as such (Rom 6:3-11).[12]

Second, Paul believes that *daimonia* are real. Willis's view that *koinônia* in the table of the Lord is only a community of believers, and that *koiônnia* in the table of demons is wrong because believers find themselves associated with idolatry, is incomplete without an answer to the question of why such association with idolatry would be harmful. In Willis's exegesis of chapter 8 the question of the reality of other Gods is passed over very quickly. He argues, correctly, that 8:5—"there are many Gods and many Lords"—is Paul's correction of the Corinthians' confident assertion of the unreality of idols,[13] yet he is not entirely comfortable with Paul's view here, as revealed in his conclusion concerning the issue: "Paul himself is seeking to establish the reality of the pagan gods and especially their influence on Christians, *however he may regard them*" (emphasis added).[14] Despite Willis's discomfort, he knows and says how Paul regards *daimonia*: they are real and dangerous.

Conclusions

The problem with the table of demons is that for Paul demons are real, and *koinônia* at their table will destroy *koinônia* effected through the

---

11 Hurd, *Origin*, p. 135-36.

12 Compare Hurd, who notes not only 11:29 as a clear indication of Paul's understanding of the "magical" nature of the Lord's meal, but adds that baptism on behalf of the dead (1 Cor 15:29) and the solemn judgment of the incestuous man (1 Cor 5:1-5) also indicate Paul's belief in the sacramental power inherent in these rites (*Origin*, p. 135-37). See also Lake (*Epistles*, p. 213) and Weiss (*1 Kor*, p. 257-60 [excursus on *koinônia*]). Klauck's conclusions are the same: for Paul *koinônia* intertwines conceptions of *Gemeinschaft* and participation, person and object (*Herrenmahl*, p. 260-61).

13 Willis, *Idol Meat*, p. 86.

14 Ibid., p. 87.

Lord's table.[15] In chapter 10 the meal of *daimonia* infects those who share it, just as the Lord's meal immunizes the believer against death. This view of the nature of idol-food remains in tension with that of chapter 8, where idol-food is a problem not in itself but because its associations might draw a believer again into idolatry.

It should be recognized, however, that Paul or the Corinthian Christians very likely did not perceive or admit the distinction between problems with food per se (chapter 10:16-22) and its associations (chapter 8). Certainly Paul was aware of the apparent inconsistency of his discussion (10:19), but despite his awareness—and the attempts of commentators to find an underlying consistency—his discussion retains a strong tension between a view of idol-food as infectious and idol-food as itself harmless. This tension will be explored more fully below.

---

15 Compare Conzelmann's arguments concerning Paul's intended and explicit parallels between the Lord's table and the table of demons (*1 Cor*, p. 170-74). Similar arguments stressing Paul's treatment of the meals as parallel are made by Robertson and Plummer (*1 Cor*, p. 210), and Schmithals (*Gnosticism*, p. 225).

6

For whom is idol-food a problem, and why?

Introduction

Idol-food is a problem both for Paul and the Corinthians. The Corinthians have addressed a question or set of questions to Paul concerning idol-food,[1] and Paul sets out an extensive response. It might be thought, then, that the situation is straightforward: the young and inexperienced group looks for guidance.

There is, however, a more complex interaction between Paul and the group in Corinth. The Corinthians have done more than ask Paul questions concerning idol-food. They have made claims concerning the issue to which Paul responds, and the Corinthians' letter to Paul is not the first stage of their interchange concerning the issue. Further, Paul's response to the Corinthians' letter implies that the group of Christians in Corinth cannot be thought of as holding one undifferentiated position concerning the issue of idol-food. Finally, Paul refers to situations involving non-Christian Corinthians, so the persons involved in the matter are not simply Paul and the Corinthian group. These complicating factors disallow simple assumptions concerning the matters or events that gave rise to the Corinthians' questions to Paul concerning idol-food, and require a careful examination of the origin of the issue in Corinth.

For whom was idol-food was a problem? For the Corinthians or some of the Corinthians? For persons outside the Corinthian Christians' circle? For Paul? Or for some combination of these players?

---

1 *Peri de* in 8:1 echoes 7:1 and 7:25, where Paul clearly responds to a letter from the Corinthians. The structural formula recurs at 12:1, 16:1 and 16:12.

The Corinthian Christians

It has long been recognized that 1 Corinthians includes quotations from (or at the very least allusions to) the Corinthian letter to Paul.[2] These are indicated by a repeated feature of Paul's letter that is hard to explain otherwise: occasionally Paul will make a bold aphoristic statement which immediately he retracts or strongly qualifies. For example, in 6:13 he says "Food for the belly, and the belly for food, *but* God will make nothing both one and the other." Four times Paul says "All things are permitted" (6:12; 10:23) and each time immediately suggests otherwise: "*but not* all things are helpful or constructive" and "*but* I won't be mastered by anything."[3]

These bold statements which Paul qualifies are consistent with a specific position concerning idol-food (among other things), which in turn Paul attributes to (some of) the Corinthians. The putative quotations centre on the possession of knowledge and authority, and Paul portrays such knowledge and authority as grounding the practice of Corinthian Christians (8:9-10).

These three features of the texts—that Paul sets out bold statements but then qualifies them, that the bold statements represent a consistent point of view, and that central elements of that point of view are attributed by Paul to Corinthian Christians—support the claim that these statements represent quotations from or allusions to a letter from Corinth.

The quotations may be recognized by both their aphoristic quality and Paul's hasty subversion of them.[4] The four instances of "All things are permitted," the chiastic proverb concerning the belly and food, "We all have knowledge" (8:1), and "There is no idol in the universe" (8:4) are all commonly seen as quotations, and the RSV puts each of them in quotation marks.[5] "There is no God but one" (8:4) also echoes the Corin-

---

2 For a full discussion, see Hurd, *Origin*, p. 120-23, and all of chap. 3 of *Origin*. See also Jerome Murphy-O'Connor's discussion of 1 Cor 6:12-20: here Paul also refers to Corinthian quotations and contradicts them ("Corinthian Slogans in 1 Cor. 6:12-20," *Catholic Biblical Quarterly*, 40 [1978]: 394-95).

3 I have not added the emphasis. It is found in Paul's syntax (*ho de theos* [6:13]; *all'ou*; *all'ouk* [6:12; 10:23]).

4 Willis also argues that Paul rejects the Corinthian quotations (*Idol Meat*, p. 116, 120). Others have argued vigorously that Paul does not subvert the Corinthian position but only qualifies or re-directs it. This scholarly stance will be addressed at length below.

5 Paul does not immediately counter the claim of 8:4 concerning the reality of idols, but his introduction of "so-called" Gods and Lords in 8:5, and his claims concerning *daimonia* in 10:20-22, show clearly that he does not agree with the aphorism. The monotheistic slogans of 8:4 meet the criterion, then, of Paul's subversion, and thus seem Corinthian quotations.

thian letter (despite the desire of many commentators to have Paul agree unconditionally with this monotheistic claim) because of its close association with the saying concerning idols in 8:4 and because Paul qualifies it in 8:5-6. "Food will not bring us before God; if we don't eat we are not lacking, and if we do we don't excel" (8:8) is also a quotation of the Corinthian letter,[6] since 8:9—"But beware lest this liberty of yours become an obstacle"—is best read as a qualification of the saying in 8:8.[7]

Paul's quotations from the Corinthians' letter to him show that 1 Corinthians 8:1-11:1 does not respond to a simple request on the part of the Corinthians for wisdom in the matter of idol-food. The quotations indicate not confusion over what is to be done concerning idol-food but a straightforward position on the part of the Corinthian writers that any limitation of their diet is foolish. They know that idols are nothing, and deduce from this that idols cannot contaminate food. The Corinthians writing to Paul had no problem with idol-food.[8]

Yet it is the Corinthians who have raised the issue in their letter, so some attempt must be made to determine why the issue was a problem for them. There are two possibilities. The first is that the Corinthians were divided in their assessment of the hazards of idol-food. It may be that the letter was written by those on only one side of a divisive issue, or that Paul quotes only the arguments of one side. The second possibility is that the Corinthian group was troubled by someone outside the group who has suggested a view of idol-food contrary to their normal practice. In either case the Corinthians would have written to Paul both to express their own views and to seek his.

An overwhelming majority of scholars find the first explanation the most likely.[9] On their reconstruction the Corinthian group is not uni-

---

6 See Murphy-O'Connor, "Food and Spiritual Gifts in 1 Cor 8:8," *Catholic Biblical Quarterly*, 41 (1979): 292-98. Murphy-O'Connor argues that 8:8 is a quotation of the Corinthians, and that it is to be understood as a claim of the Corinthian strong in response to criticism of the weak that the strong are not harmed by eating and the weak do not please God by abstention.

7 It is also possible, but less likely, that 8:10 contains an echo of a Corinthian argument: the Corinthians might have claimed that the consciousness of the weak might be "built up" to eat without harm, to which Paul ironically replies, "built up? to destruction" (8:11). Compare Murphy-O'Connor, "Freedom," p. 547; Robert Jewett, *Paul's Anthropological Terms: A Study of Their Use in Conflict Settings* (Leiden: Brill, 1971), p. 423-24; Theissen, "Strong and weak," p. 140; Willis, *Idol Meat*, p. 97-98.

8 Hurd justifiably goes further: the Corinthians not only had no problem with idol-food but their approach to the issue was sufficiently blunt and critical that it was probably taken by Paul to be "veiled hostility" (*Origin*, p. 113).

9 This standard view is effectively challenged only by Hurd. Weiss presents the classic arguments for the presence of weak Christians in Corinth (*1 Kor*, p. 211-12),

fied, and Paul in 1 Corinthians 8:1-11:1 seeks to mediate between competing views of idol-food. There is evidence to support this reconstruction. In 8:7-13 Paul warns those who hold the views expressed in the Corinthian quotations that their *gnôsis* and their *exousia* might cause other brothers to fall into sin. There is not knowledge in these others; rather, because of the intimacy (or habit) of idols which they have still, they eat idol-food as idol-food (8:7).

That these others are still intimate with idols might lead to the suspicion that Paul is referring to non-Christians whose sensibilities must be accommodated in order to win them (compare 9:19-23), but Paul identifies these others as Christians: the consciousness of these who eat idol-food as idol-food is weak and is polluted by the act of eating (8:7); this weak one is a brother[10] for whom Christ died (8:11).

In this view, then, there are two groups of Christians in Corinth, or at least two differing views concerning the hazards of idol-food. These two sorts of Christians are labelled "the weak" on the basis of 8:7-13, and on the basis of obvious contrast (and the possible allusion of 10:22), "the strong." There is support elsewhere in 1 Corinthians for this postulated division of the group. Paul refers explicitly to reported divisions (*schismata*) of the Corinthian group (11:18) and complains of quarrels that apparently take the form of divided allegiances (1:11-12). He refers to the weak explicitly as a group in 9:22, and the "someone" (*tis*) raising questions concerning the origin of food at a dinner party (10:28) has been taken to be a weak Christian.[11]

---

as does Lietzmann, *1 Kor*, p. 43. See also: C. K. Barrett, *The First Epistle to the Corinthians* (London: Adam and Charles Black, 1968), p. 194-95, 215; Conzelmann, *1 Cor*, p. 14, 147; Arnold Ehrhardt, "Social Problems in the Early Church. I. The Sunday Joint of the Christian Housewife," chap. 12 of *The Framework of the New Testament Stories* (Manchester: Manchester University Press, 1964), p. 277; Lietzmann, *1 Kor*, p. 42-43; Murphy-O'Connor, "1 Cor 8:8," p. 297, and "Freedom," p. 547-48; Theissen, "Strong and Weak," p. 121; Willis, *Idol Meat*, p. 76-78, 118. Many scholars simply assume the presence of the weak from the face of the text: Enslin, *Beginnings*, p. 251; Héring, *1 Cor*, p. 63, 67-68; Klauck, *Herrenmahl*, p. 246; Lake, *Epistles*, p. 199-200; Meyer, *1 Cor*, p. 243; Robertson and Plummer, *1 Cor*, p. 169; Thrall, *First and Second Letters*, p. 63-64; von Soden, "Sakrament," p. 242 (and Meeks's translation, p. 261).

10 *Adelphos* is Paul's standard term of address to those to whom he writes and his preferred designation for members of the Christian group. Only in Rom 9:3 is it used otherwise—there to refer to Jews, Paul's *suggeneis kata sarka*—and everywhere else it denotes a member of the Christian group. Perhaps the clearest example of this is found in 1 Cor 5:9-11 where *adelphos* is clearly contrasted to someone *tou kosmou toutou*—outside the group. The identification of "weak one" and brother in 8:11 shows clearly that the weak with whom Paul is concerned are members of the Christian group.

11 Barrett, *1 Cor*, p. 239; Meyer, *1 Cor*, p. 309-10; Murphy-O'Connor, "Freedom," p. 570, n.79; Weiss, *1 Kor*, p. 265.

This evidence from outside 8:7-13, however, cannot be made to support easily a division between "strong" and "weak" Christians. The *schismata* of 11:18-22, 33-34 also have to do with food, but in a different context and in a different way: the two groups are here not weak and strong, with or without *gônsis*, but rather surfeited or lacking.[12] There is no obvious link between having *gnôsis* or *exousia* and being drunk (11:21), or between recent intimacy with other Gods and being hungry (11:21). Such a link might be traced,[13] but it would depend much more on a series of inferences than a simple observation of the texts of 8:7-13 and 11:18-34. Even more obvious is the lack of correspondence between those "of Paul . . . of Apollos . . . of Cephas . . . of Christ" in 1:12-13 and the strong and weak of 8:7-13.[14] Evidence from outside 1 Corinthians 8:1-11:1 does not help, then, to support a reconstruction of two groups within the Corinthian Christians with opposing views of idol-food.

The passages found at 9:22 and 10:28 are stronger corroborative evidence for the existence of a group of weak Christians but, even so, difficulties arise. The "weak" of 9:22 cannot be read directly into the context described in 8:7-13 since the weak of 9:22, like the Jews and

---

12 See Theissen, "Social Integration and Sacramental Activity: An Analysis of 1 Cor 11:17-34," in *The Social Setting of Pauline Christianity. Essays on Corinth by Gerd Theissen* (Philadelphia: Fortress Press, 1982). See especially his summary at p. 160-62.

13 It is sometimes argued that the strong Corinthians' *exousia* led them into deliberate libertinism, including sexual immorality and drunkenness (Barrett, "Things sacrificed," p. 54-55; Murphy-O'Connor, "Freedom," p. 549; Schmithals, *Gnosticism*, p. 221-26).

14 Some have attempted to link the weak with Jewish-Christian scruples held by a party of Peter in Corinth. Barrett: "the problem of *eidôlothyta* would never have arisen in a Gentile Church like that of Corinth if the Jewish Christians (the Cephas group perhaps) had not raised it" ("Things Sacrificed," p. 49); Klauck, *Herrenmahl*, p. 230; Ehrhardt, *Framework*, p. 277; Manson, "The Corinthian Correspondence (1) (1941)," in *Studies in the Gospels and Epistles*, ed. Matthew Black (Manchester: Manchester University Press, 1962), p. 193-96). Peter Richardson develops an extended argument concerning Jewish-Gentile conflicts among Christians in Corinth (*Israel in the Apostolic Church* [Cambridge: Cambridge University Press, 1969], p. 199). This view has had a long history: F. C. Baur argued it (*Paul the Apostle of Jesus Christ. His Life and Work. His Epistles and his Doctrine*, 2 vols. [London and Edinburgh: Williams and Norgate, 1876], 1:260-66). I do not accept these arguments. Concerning a Jewish-Christian group in Corinth, I take the view forcefully put by Enslin, who finds "no scintilla of evidence" linking the parties of chapter 1 with gnostics or Jewish Christians (*Beginnings*, p. 249). Compare Lake (*Epistles*, p. 114-16, 125-30, 239), Conzelmann (*1 Cor*, p. 14), and Hurd (*Origin*, p. 117-25). See also my critique of Barrett in Appendix 1.

those "under the law" and "those outside the law" of 9:20-21, are not Christians: they are not brothers but those Paul has sought to win.[15] If we accept the presence of weak Christians on the basis of 8:7-13, then the weak of 9:22 might be linked to these more readily, but apart from 8:7-13 neither the weak of 9:22 nor the passage in which they are found (9:19-23) would be considered evidence of two groups of Christians in Corinth.

Only 8:7-13 stands as clear evidence for the existence of two groups of Corinthian Christians, the strong and the weak, each with opposing views concerning idol-food. The standard reading of 8:7-13 makes a very basic assumption: since Paul refers to weak Christians who may be harmed by the practice of the strong, such weak Christians must have existed. This assumption, however, is hardly ever noticed, let alone questioned, and there is good reason to suspect its validity. Nothing in 8:7-13 indicates that Paul knows of specific weak Christians or of specific objections they might have raised concerning idol-food. While 8:1-4 echoes the views of the strong, there are no similar echoes of the views of the weak; while in 8:1 and 8:4 we hear the *Corinthians*, in 8:7-13 we hear not weak Corinthians but Paul.[16]

This conclusion is supported not only by a lack of any quotations of the weak (admittedly an argument from silence) but by the tentative and conditional nature of Paul's objections and the hypothetical situations to which he alludes. Paul's objections to the strong are conditional (8:9, "lest in some way"; 8:13, "*if* food is an obstacle"), and he sets out a clearly hypothetical situation (8:10, "if[17] someone sees you . . . in an idol's temple"; compare 10:28, "But if someone says 'This is sacred food' ").

It can be objected, of course, that Paul's advice is conditional because that is its essence (there is nothing wrong with eating *unless* it is harmful). While this explanation is plausible, two considerations make me hesitant to accept it. First, Paul is very well informed about the group in Corinth at the time of writing 1 Corinthians (better informed concerning his addressees in this case probably than in the case of any of his other extant letters). He holds in hand a letter from the Corinthians and he has received at least one if not two oral reports (1:11; 5:1; 11:18; 16:17). He refers not only to topics raised in the

15 Contra Lietzmann, *1 Kor*, p. 43.

16 See Hurd, *Origin*, p. 117-25. Much of what follows concerning the weak in Corinth is derived from Hurd's arguments.

17 *Ean* can sometimes "approach" the meaning of *hotan*, "whenever, when" (Bauer, Arndt, Gingrich, *Ean* 1.d), but here it must be taken to set out a simple hypothetical condition, both because that is the primary meaning of the word and because Paul uses it in this way in 8:8.

letter from Corinth but also to specific situations in the Corinthian group (1:12; 5:1; 6:6,7; 11:20,21). If there are weak Christians seriously threatened by specific practices of strong Christians Paul would very likely refer more to these in less hypothetical terms.

The second consideration concerns the practice of the strong to which Paul alludes—eating in an idol's temple (*en eidôleiôi*). If Paul knew of Corinthian Christians eating in temples or sanctuaries, his lack of urgency is very surprising. It is rather more likely that he would demand a delivery of these to Satan, as in the case of the sexually immoral person of 5:1-5: after all, to become table partners with demons is for Paul idolatry (10:14-22), and the Corinthians are not to associate or eat with someone who is supposedly a brother but is an idolater (5:11-13).[18]

There could be some persons recently attached to the Christian group in Corinth who would meet Paul's description of the weak. Paul is apostle to Gentiles, and (at the very least) there is no reason to deny the presence of Gentiles in the Corinthian Christian group. Some of these Gentiles would have been intimate with or be used to idols very recently (8:7).[19] Paul felt that this appeal to the weak would make some sense to the Corinthians.

On the other hand, it is also very likely that joining the Christian group involved some sort of acceptance of the unreality or illegitimacy of other Gods. The affirmation in 8:4, "There is no God but one," was a central feature of proselytism to Judaism of all sorts (including Christianity), and thus it seems equally likely that "weakness" of the sort Paul appeals to would indicate an uncertain or uncommitted adherence to the Christian group.[20]

---

18 Some scholars argue that the strong did eat in temples. Some assert this because they see temples as *loci* for normal social intercourse and argue that the Corinthian strong did not wish to forgo such social contacts (Weiss, *1 Kor*, p. 211; von Soden, "Sakrament," p. 264 [Meeks's translation]; Ehrhardt, *Framework*, p. 279, and Willis, *Idol Meat*, p. 21-61). Other scholars argue that the strong's blatant exercise of their *exousia* led them to flaunt their freedom in specifically religious contexts (Fee, "*Eidôlothyta,*" p. 149-50 [arguing specifically contra Hurd]; Meyer, *1 Cor*, p. 246; Murphy-O'Connor, "Freedom," p. 549; Schmithals, *Gnosticism*, p. 221, 226).

19 Most scholars take this verse to be an indication that the weak were Gentiles: Barrett, *1 Cor*, p. 194-95; Paul Gooch, "Burden," p. 115; Héring, *1 Cor*, p. 67; Lietzmann, *1 Kor*, p. 38; Robertson and Plummer, *1 Cor*, p. 169, 221; Thrall, *1 and 2 Cor*, p. 64; Weiss, *1 Kor*, p. 227; Murphy-O'Connor, "Freedom," p. 552-54; Willis, *Idol Meat*, p. 91-95. A small minority of scholars reject the identification of the weak with Gentiles, and see the weak as Jews. See my discussion of Barrett in Appendix 1.

20 J. Murphy-O'Connor has argued that the phrase *he syneidêsis autou . . . oiko-*

It is difficult to know how to balance these probabilities without more specific evidence. It is very likely that many Corinthian Christians had worshipped other Gods until very recently, but it is also very likely that they had adopted a very different understanding of that past worship in order to join the group of Christians at Corinth. It is much more certain, however, that *if* there were weak Christians at Corinth they had no voice either in the letter to Paul or among the messengers that brought Paul reports of the community. Paul's guess at their presence might be better than ours—but he had a point to make that depends on their presence, and we do not.

The question is for whom idol-food was a problem. It was certainly not a problem for the strong—for the Corinthians who wrote to Paul concerning the issue. There is less evidence that idol-food was a problem for the weak. Most likely there was no *party* of weak Christians in Corinth, and perhaps not even weak individuals troubled by the practices Paul describes. If these weak existed we know of no complaint made to Paul on their behalf. All the harm of which Paul speaks is potential and hypothetical. Even if weak individuals existed in Corinth this would not account for why the issue is raised in the Corinthian letter to Paul. If idol-food might be a problem to such persons we have no evidence that any event(s) occurred involving them to account for the argumentative nature of the Corinthian query and Paul's extended response.

Outsiders

The second possibility is that the problem developed not out of the Corinthian group itself but from external pressure upon it concerning the eating of idol-food. Once again the logical possibilities may be set out and argument harnessed to evidence. Since the Corinthian Christians seem to have no problem with idol-food yet raise the issue with Paul, it is clear that some objection has been brought to Corinthian Christian practice concerning idol-food or that some advice had been offered contrary to that practice. This could come from non-Christian Corinthians or from Christians outside the Corinthian group—Paul, his co-workers or Christians not associated with him.

---

domêthêsetai in 8:10 is Paul's ironic echo of another Corinthian claim, that "weak" Christians should have their consciousness raised (to add to Paul's ancient irony a modern pun on the Greek) to allow an unfettered and fearless eating of idol-food. ("Freedom," p. 547). See also Theissen, "Strong and Weak," p. 140; Willis, *Idol Meat*, p. 97-98; and Paul Gooch, "Burden," p. 105.

Non-Christians

One of these possibilities may be rejected immediately. There is no evidence whatever that non-Christians were objecting to Christians eating idol-food. The one reference to a non-Christian explicitly connected to the issue is found in Paul's hypothetical dinner invitation, where the non-Christian host serves idol-food rather than objects to it (10:27). This accords with the obvious certainty that persons other than Jews or Christians would find nothing dangerous or offensive about food offered to their Gods.[21]

Christian outsiders

It is similarly certain that other Christians not associated with Paul in his mission are not responsible for the problem. They have not put pressure on the Corinthian group to abstain from idol-food. There is abundant evidence in other letters that Paul does not hesitate to attack apostolic poachers on his groups, but in 1 Corinthians there is no persuasive evidence of such an attack.[22] Even if other apostles came up with a view of idol-food that Paul agreed with, still Paul would view such as an incursion on his rights over the Corinthian group: while the attacks in Galatians and Philippians are motivated by disagreement over circumcision, no similar difference animates the attacks on the "false apostles" of 2 Corinthians 10-13 but rather a bitter resentment at their usurpation of Paul's authority over the Corinthian group. There Paul makes clear that he views the Corinthians as his own territory appointed to him by his God.[23] If the Corinthians were troubled or

---

21 A minority of commentators suggest that the "someone" (*tis*) of 10:28 is a non-Christian guest at the meal (the "someone" calls idol-food by its proper, non-Christian term, *hierothyton*). See Lietzmann, *1 Kor,* p. 51; von Soden, "Sakrament," p. 250-51. Willis provides a history of the discussion of the identity of the *tis* (*Idol Meat,* p. 240-42). Even if this "someone" is not a Christian this would not mean that non-Christian pressure was the root of the idol-food problem. Even if "someone" did in actuality raise the issue of *hierothyton* with a Christian, the "someone" would do so on the basis not of his or her own scruples but on the basis of the scruples the "someone" expected to find in his or her Christian guest/friend/table companion.

22 Richardson argues that there is a Jew-Gentile conflict in Corinth, and that Paul's attempted resolution of it betrays none of the standard themes of this conflict since he is trying to enter the fray as irenically as possible ("On the Absence of 'Anti-Judaism' in 1 Corinthians, in *Anti-Judaism in Early Christianity*, vol. 1 *Paul and the Gospels*, Studies in Christianity and Judaism, no. 2 [Waterloo, ON: Wilfrid Laurier University Press, 1986], p. 72).

23 2 Cor 10:13-18; 11:2; compare 1 Cor 9:1-2 and Paul's understanding of the extent and limit of his mission in Gal 2:1-10.

confused by other apostles Paul could be depended upon to attack these interlopers openly.[24]

Paul's associates

Some apostles associated with Paul, however, have been in Corinth since Paul's first visit there. Apollos has visited the group (1:12; 3:1-10) and likely spent considerable time there (the parallelism of 3:6—"I planted, Apollos watered"—suggests this); the Corinthians would like him to return (16:12). Some of Paul's associates may have carried the letter to which Paul refers in 5:9, and it is to be expected that Paul regularly sent associates to the cities where his groups were found (see, for example, 16:10-11). It is possible that someone associated with Paul demanded or advised a different practice concerning idol-food, which in turn prompted the Corinthians to defend their practice and perhaps to seek Paul's view in their letter to him.

Once again there is no persuasive evidence to support this suggested origin of the problem of idol-food. Paul's own associates seem—as far as the letters allow us to see them—colourless and docile, faithful bearers of Paul's messages (and one suspects that the Paul one comes to know in the letters would hardly demand less). If they brought advice or demands concerning idol-food, it would be Paul's.

The one associate in 1 Corinthians with any independence of Paul is Apollos (they have worked separately and Apollos is free to reject Paul's urgent requests of him [16:12]), but Paul nowhere indicates disagreement or tension between himself and Apollos (3:5-9; 16:12). It is possible that Apollos urged a different practice concerning idol-food, and the Corinthians turned to Paul in their letter for advice, but this remains speculation.[25] The evidence we do have, I will argue, points in a different direction.

Paul

The eating of idol-food is not a problem for the strong Corinthians, and Paul appears to know of no harm to weak Corinthians. Non-Christian Corinthians would not have objected to the eating of food offered to their Gods. Christian apostles from outside the Pauline circle

---

24 For this reason attempts by Barrett and others to link the weak and Peter, or Peter's associates, may be rejected (see also Appendix 1).

25 Richardson takes a different view of the relations between Paul and Apollos: Paul is skeptical and suspicious of Apollos, whom Paul links to wisdom and to those who put too much store in wisdom (citing 1 Cor 3:5-8), and who refuses to do what Paul wishes (1 Cor 16:1) ("Anti-Judaism," p. 65). Even if Richardson's view is correct, there is still no direct evidentiary link between Apollos and idol-food.

have not imposed the issue on the group, nor have associates of Paul. This of course leaves only one party to the issue on which to rest responsibility for raising the problem: Paul himself.

The claim that Paul himself is responsible for the problem of idol-food in Corinth does not depend only on this process of elimination but on positive evidence from 1 Corinthians. This evidence is of two sorts: first, Paul's view of idol-food and, second, the communication between Paul and the Corinthians before the writing of 1 Corinthians.

A full discussion of Paul's views concerning idol-food will be left to chapter 7, but some obvious points can be acknowledged immediately. The Corinthian Christians object to restrictions concerning idol-food and defend their position. In contrast Paul does have problems with idol-food. If eating such food puts an obstacle in the way of his brother, Paul will not eat it (8:13; 10:28-29). Paul argues that participation in meals sacred to other Gods violates *koinônia* with Christ and provokes God to jealousy (10:14-22). Even if eating idol-food is permissible it may not be the best thing to do (8:1; 10:23-24). The only player (actual and not hypothetical!) to admit any problem with idol-food, then, is Paul.

There is yet more direct evidence. Paul's letter shows explicitly some recent problems in communication between Paul and the group in Corinth (5:9-13). Paul has written a letter to them that was misunderstood by the Corinthians or said what Paul did not intend. It is more likely that Paul's previous letter said more than he intended than that the Corinthians misunderstood. Paul's reminder in 5:9, "I wrote you in my letter not to be associated with sexually immoral persons (*pornoi*)" is directly parallel to 5:11, "But now I write not to be associated *if someone called a brother* is *pornos*" (emphasis added by the parallel structure). Verse 9 seems a quotation of Paul's earlier letter because of the parallel structure of 5:9 and 5:11 (emphasized because the structure is ungrammatical in 5:11) and because of the break in Paul's syntax at 5:10. If all that Paul did say in the earlier letter was not to mingle with *pornoi* and other problematic persons, then Paul probably did say more than he intended, and the Corinthians had reason to question his meaning, as Paul himself recognizes (5:10).

Paul's attempt in 5:9-13 to clarify his meaning gives us a glimpse of the contents of his previous letter, and that glimpse shows that Paul has himself provoked the Corinthian concern over food offered to other Gods. Since 5:9 is a quotation from Paul's earlier letter, it follows that Paul had demanded separation from persons with unacceptable sexual mores. The repetition of *pornois* in 5:10, however, at the head of a list of unacceptable persons, together with the appearance of the same list (again extended to include more persons) in 5:11 make it very likely that in the previous letter Paul had also forbidden association with defrauders, drunkards, and—note well—idolaters. Presented with this the Corinthians would have asked how one could associate with these proscribed persons, and apparently came up with a disturbing range of ways that such an exhortation could be understood—disturbing enough that in response to the Corinthians' letter Paul is obliged to clarify his own earlier letter (5:10,11).

Paul himself has provoked the problem over idol-food in Corinth. Prominent in both lists of proscribed persons in 5:10-11 are "sexually immoral person" (*pornos*) and "idolater" (*eidôlatrês*).[26] The Corinthians have written to Paul concerning what more precisely he means by the evils represented by these persons, and Paul's response in both cases[27] works to the same effect: to set out more specifically what behaviour in what contexts he finds acceptable.[28]

Conclusions

The answer to the question that began this chapter—for whom is idol-food a problem?—is now provided. Food offered to other Gods is root and branch Paul's problem. It has become a problem to the Corinthians at the time of writing of 1 Corinthians only because Paul's earlier demand to avoid any contact with idolaters has raised questions and objections concerning the eating of idol-food.

---

26 If 2 Cor 6:14-7:1 is a fragment of Paul's previous letter, it is significant to note that the exhortation against idolatry is found here also: 6:16 "what agreement has the temple of God with idols?," and even more interesting, 6:17 "and touch nothing unclean." *Porneia* is not explicitly mentioned in the fragment, but could well be implicit in 7:1: "let us cleanse ourselves from every defilement of body." There is scholarly discussion over the origin and meaning of these verses: see Gordon Fee, "2 Cor 6:14-7:1 and Food Offered to Idols," *New Testament Studies*, 23 (1977): 140-61; and Margaret E. Thrall, "The Problem of 2 Cor 6:14-7:1 in Some Recent Discussion," *New Testament Studies*, 24 (1977): 132-48.

27 Paul's explanations concerning sexual morality are in 1 Cor 7.

28 My debt to Hurd's analysis of the relationship between 1 Cor and Paul's Previous Letter is obvious and my arguments are similar to his (see especially *Origin*, p. 225-26). Though contrary to the standard view, these conclusions are not unique. Long ago Weiss argued that Paul's earlier letter, which on Weiss's reconstruction included 10:1-22, provoked the arguing slogans of the Corinthians (Weiss, *1 Kor*, p. 213). Schmithals makes a similar claim, also on the basis of a partition theory (*Gnosticism*, p. 224-25). Fee also accepts Hurd's conclusions ("*Eidôlothyta*," p. 172).

7

What is Paul's proposed solution to the problem of idol-food?

The occasion of Paul's instructions

The Corinthian solution to idol-food was to eat it without worry: "We all have knowledge" that "there is no idol in the world, and no God but one; food won't affect our status with God, and whether we eat idol-food or not makes no difference. All things are permissible" (8:1,4,8). The Corinthian appeal to knowledge (*gnôsis*) makes it likely that the Corinthians would expect to educate any of their group who thought such food harmful.[1]

Given this Corinthian position it is curious that they would raise the issue of food explicitly (*peri de tôn eidôlothytôn*, 8:1), and this curiousness is heightened when it is recalled that the reconstructed occasion of the Corinthian letter to Paul—and, as will be argued, Paul's response—focusses not on food but on the dangers of idolatry.

The explicit focus on food might have arisen either because Paul's previous letter itself raised the issue of food,[2] or because Paul's forbidding of any association with idolatry made the Corinthians see some food as problematic and led them to raise the matter with Paul. In either case, food has been focussed on because food offered to idols and the social consumption of it might be seen to be specific instances of idolatry.

---

1 The possible ironic allusion to *hê syneidêsis autou . . . oikodomêthésetai* (8:10) also supports this conclusion.

2 Some argue that the previous letter raised the issues of idolatry in general and idol-food in particular (Weiss, Schmithals, and especially Hurd in *Origin*, p. 225-26), or criticized the Corinthians' practice (see, for example, Willis, *Idol Meat*, p. 97-99, 258). Alternatively, it is possible that the previous letter might have raised the issue of food indirectly with allusions akin to 1 Cor 10:7 ("The people sat down to eat and drink").

It is useful in this connection to compare 1 Corinthians 8-10 with 1 Corinthians 7.[3] The discussion of sexual immorality (*porneia*) there covers several specific contexts and persons, and the structure of the chapter suggests that Paul is responding to specific issues raised by the Corinthians. The clearest evidence of this is 7:25-26, where the discussion of unmarried women is introduced by "Now concerning (*peri de*) unmarried women I have no command of the Lord." The *peri de* formula is understood elsewhere in 1 Corinthians to refer to topics raised in the Corinthian letter, and its presence here is reason to suspect that the Corinthians have asked a specific question concerning unmarried women. If this is the case, then it seems more likely that other abrupt introductions of different classes of persons (7:8,10,12) may also reflect the content of the Corinthian letter. The Corinthians may have pressed Paul concerning just what was sexual immorality: Were they to have no sexual intercourse? What of those married? Should they separate? Is sleeping with a non-believing spouse associating with a sexually immoral person? Should young persons not marry at all? These may have been the Corinthian concerns, and it is likely that Paul's response addresses these concerns in turn.[4]

Because chapters 8 and 10 address a series of concerns in a similar way, probably the Corinthians raised in their letter not only the issue of idol-food in general but also asked specifically about food sold in the market and invitations to table from non-believers. Paul's transition to these topics is abrupt, and follows immediately on another quotation from the Corinthian letter (10:23), making it likely that these specific concerns were found in the Corinthian letter.[5]

Because the Corinthians seem not to object to eating idol-food, the "questions" in chapter 10 concerning food sold in the market or served

3 A similar sequence lies behind all the *peri de* sections (1 Cor 7:1-40; 8:1-11:1; 12:1-14:40; 16:1-4, and 16:12). Paul has given an exhortation in his previous letter that in turn raises potential consequences that the Corinthians find unacceptable, provoking a letter from the Corinthians expressing those concerns, to which much of 1 Cor is a response.

4 See Richardson's differing position in "'I Say, Not the Lord': Personal Opinion, Apostolic Authority and the Development of Early Christian Halakah," *Tyndale Bulletin*, 31 (1980): 65-86.

5 Hurd argues that the Corinthians almost certainly raised these specific concerns since (1) it is unlikely that Paul, urging abstinence from idol-food, would have himself raised the potential difficulties over markets and invitations, and (2) these difficulties reflect the daily life of the Gentile Christian (*Origin*, p. 145). Weiss agrees for different reasons (*1 Kor*, p. 211). Barrett claims the opposite—that Paul raised these specific issues (*1 Cor*, p. 239). Willis provides a thorough account of the possibilities, but doesn't decide (*Idol Meat*, p. 258).

by a host have rather the character of objections.[6] "If we are to avoid the contaminations of idolatry," they might have said, "what of food sold in the market, or served at our friends' banquets? This might be idol-food. Are we to avoid this as well? How separated must we be?"

What eating does Paul reject or allow?

At first reading, Paul's response is vacillating and confused.[7] On the one hand Paul does not deny the claims made by the Corinthians. Even if he modifies or limits the Corinthian claims he does not seem to reject them. He seems to agree that there are no other Gods (8:6), that idol-food is nothing (10:19,26), and that one's freedom to eat should not be condemned by someone else's sense that such eating is wrong (10:29,30). On the other hand, Paul insists that there are many so-called Gods and Lords (8:5) or *daimonia* (10:20-21), that idol-food makes one a partner with *daimonia*, and that one's freedom to eat is limited by the harm it may cause to others. This tension is at the centre of scholarly concern over 1 Corinthians 8-10 and cannot be avoided. It must be concluded either that Paul's views are more nuanced than this outline suggests[8] or that he does vacillate.[9]

There are two kinds of eating Paul finds unacceptable: eating that breaks partnership[10] with the one true God and one true Lord, and eating that harms a brother. Eating in an idol's temple is unacceptable if it causes a brother to perish from his weak consciousness, as is eating at the invitation of a non-believer if it has a similar effect. Other eating is permissible: if the sacred history of food served at a non-believer's is not

---

6 In agreement with Hurd, *Origin*, p. 126, 147.

7 See, for an example of an intuitive and undeveloped assessment of Paul's position, Cadbury's article concerning the *macellum* in Corinth: Paul is "of two minds on the question of food offered to idols" ("Macellum," p. 134).

8 Some scholars see Paul's response as very effective; in particular, see my discussion of Barrett, Murphy-O'Connor and Tomson, below, in Appendix 1. E. P. Sanders cites 1 Cor 8-10 as a self-evident demonstration of Paul's ability to engage in complex and coherent thought (*Paul and Palestinian Judaism. A Comparison of Patterns of Religion* [Philadelphia: Fortress Press, 1977], p. 549).

9 Lake finds Paul's arguments "not wholly logical" and excuses Paul's inconsistency as a human trait (*Epistles*, p. 201); Conzelmann concludes that Paul vacillates between adoption of the standpoint of the strong in chapter 8 and warnings to all in 10:1-22 (*1 Cor*, p. 137).

10 "Partnership" is the translation I offer throughout this chapter for *koinônia*. *Koinônia* carries many nuances, derived from its root sense of "held in common [*koinos*]": association, fellowship, communion. Its sense in Greek is warmer than "partnership," stronger than "association" or "fellowship," and without the religious overtones of "communion."

pointed out it is permissible to eat it. All food at market may be bought and eaten, and no questions of consciousness are to be raised over it.

Though this brief statement is accurate it is not an adequate description of Paul's position. The nuances of Paul's positions, and the interrelationships of Paul's claims and the contexts themselves must be explored.

Partnership with daimonia

Even if Paul quotes the monotheistic slogans of 8:4 and affirms that there is one God the father and one Lord Jesus Christ (8:6), this affirmation is deeply qualified. There is one God and one Lord to us (8:6), he stresses, but to others many Gods and many Lords (8:5). Even if Paul does not wish to seem to say that idol-food or idols themselves are "anything" (10:19) he believes that the things that are offered (*ha thyousin*) are offered to *daimoniois* (10:20).[11]

I resist a translation of *daimonia*, since it is ambiguous in the text. *Daimonion* could mean "God" or "a God" similar to *daimôn* (Herodotus, Euripides), or "inferior divine being" (Xenophon, Plato), or "evil spirit, demon" (LXX).[12] While Paul would certainly understand *daimonia* to be demons, the Corinthians might not hear that nuance but understand the term as a general reference to deities. Whatever the term *daimonia* connoted to Paul or the Corinthians, however, Paul understood *daimonia* to be real. There might be no idols in the world but there are Gods in heaven and on earth (8:4,5); the Corinthians could become partners (*koinônoi*) with *daimonia* and in doing so make their Lord jealous (10:20-22).[13]

---

11 *Daimoniois kai ou theôi thyousin*, 10:20, is an allusion to Deut 32:17. Paul alludes to other features of the Deuteronomy passage: the rock of Deut 32:4,13,18 becomes the rock of 1 Cor 10:4; the provoking of God to jealousy through idolatry, 1 Cor 10:22, is found in Deut 32:16,21.

12 Liddell and Scott, "*daimonion*," *daimôn*."

13 There is divergence over the interpretation of 8:5-6. Some admit that Paul's qualification of the Corinthian monotheistic slogan is substantive—that Paul did affirm the reality of demons or (as some are happier to describe them) demonic powers—but often this is admitted equivocally, since it makes Paul primitive and interferes with the common claim that Paul agreed with the content of the strongs' *gnôsis* but urged the primacy of love. See Barrett, "Things Sacrificed," p. 55, *1 Cor*, p. 191-92; Baur, *Paul*, 2:255-57; Conzelmann, *1 Cor*, p. 148; Murphy-O'Connor, "Freedom," p. 557-60; W. F. Orr and J. A. Walther, *1 Corinthians*, Anchor Bible, vol. 32 (Garden City, NY: Doubleday, 1976), p. 233, 252; Robertson and Plummer, *1 Cor*, p. 167, 215; Schmithals, *Gnosticism*, p. 226; and Willis, *Idol Meat*, p. 84. My favourite instance of equivocation in scholarly commentary is provided by Giblin: "It appears as though Paul [in 8:5] is highlighting polytheistic acclamations and diverse confessions that entail acknowledgment of multiple, relatively unconnected subjects of divine activity in the world, and not

Paul asserts that eating in some contexts effected this partnership with *daimonia*. The section 10:14-22 rests on an extended comparison between the Lord's meal, the sacrifices of Israel and the eating of food sacred to *daimonia*. The explicit analogy between the cup of *daimonia* and the cup of the Lord, and the table of *daimonia* and the table of the Lord (10:21), together with the other clear allusion to the Lord's meal (10:16), make it clear that Paul is thinking of eating that is consciously sacred to the *daimonia* or Lord it honours. He insists in 1 Corinthians 11 that the Lord's meal be eaten in the correct way (11:27)—that Christ's body be recognized and his death proclaimed by those acts of conscious commemoration (11:24-26,29). A careless and hasty consumption of food and drink is *not* (for Paul at least) the Lord's meal (11:20), and Paul makes a clear distinction between eating to satisfy hunger and the Lord's meal (11:34).

Paul might recognize, then, a distinction between eating idol-food as food to satisfy hunger and eating idol-food as partnership with *daimonia*. Whatever meal was like the Lord's meal, which had a similar religious effect, was in Paul's view entirely wrong; just as eating the Lord's meal in an unworthy way brought judgment on the Corinthians (11:27,29) so, Paul warns, eating the meals of *daimonia* would provoke God's jealousy and break partnership with Christ.

Obstacles to brothers

The second sort of eating that Paul rejects is that which harms other brothers. Paul provides a justification for rejecting this eating that is distinct from the justification he presents in 10:14-22. In that passage Paul argues that eating from the table of *daimonia* is wrong because of its effect on partnership with Christ of the one who eats, but in 8:7-13 and 10:28-29 he argues that the eating of idol-food can be wrong because of its effect on others' partnership with Christ.

Paul suggests that there might be some Corinthians without knowledge (*gnôsis*), who have a weak conciousness (*syneidêsis*) because of their very recent intimacy with idols. It is difficult to know exactly what Paul means by *syneidêsis*; probably it is an equivalent to *gnôsis*.

---

as though he is pursuing the non-existence of false gods" ("Three Monotheistic Texts in Paul [1 Cor 8:1-13; Gal 3; Rom 3]," *Catholic Biblical Quarterly*, 37 [1975]: 533-34). Some say unequivocally that Paul affirms the reality of demons: Conzelmann, *1 Cor*, p. 143, 173; Héring, *1 Cor*, p. 65; Richard A. Horsley, "Gnosis in Corinth: 1 Corinthians 8:1-6," *New Testament Studies* 27 (1981): 49-50; Hurd, *Origin*, p. 134; Klauck, *Herrenmahl*, p. 245, 265-66; and Lietzmann, *1 Cor*, p. 37. Some hold that Paul denied the reality of other Gods, demons, powers or the like altogether: R. M. Grant, *Gods and the One God* (Philadelphia: Westminster, 1986), p. 48 (Grant does not address at all 1 Cor 10).

The Corinthians' consciousness is characterized by knowledge and power (*exousia*) (8:1,9,11), but the consciousness of others may be characterized as without knowledge and weak (8:7).[14]

It is significant that Paul does not say that the consciousness of these others is false (whether ignorant or in error or deceived) but rather that it is weak. Paul would agree with such a weak person's assessment of idol-food: if such a one thought it harmful Paul would urge him not to eat. If there is someone with such a weak consciousness, and if this person would be influenced to eat idol-food wrongly by the Corinthians' freedom, then it would be wrong for the Corinthians to eat idol-food. If someone, led by the example of the Corinthians, ate idol-food as idol-food (*hôs eidôlothyton*, 8:7,10), then his consciousness would be polluted (8:7), he would have an obstacle put in his path (8:9; 8:13), and he would perish (8:10). To cause a brother to perish thus would be to sin against both the brother and Christ (8:12).

Three contexts

Paul's two justifications for the prohibition of idol-food are distinct: to avoid idolatry, and to avoid harming the weak. Are the kinds of eating prohibited by these two justifications also distinct? Is there any eating of idol-food permissible because it does not make the eater a partner of *daimonia*, yet impermissible because it might pollute the consciousness of the weak? Paul refers to three hypothetical instances where he imagines problems of conciousness being raised: when a weak brother sees a brother with knowledge at an idol's table (*en eidôleiôi*, 8:10); when food

---

14 In agreement with Horsley, "Consciousness and Freedom among the Corinthians: 1 Corinthians 8-10" (*Catholic Biblical Quarterly* 40 [1978]: 581-86), and Willis, *Idol Meat*, p. 89-92. Much discussion has concerned what Paul understood by *syneidêsis*. An older view saw *syneidêsis* as conscience, as self-awareness in the sense of a "confidant" from which nothing could be concealed (for example, Meyer, *1 Cor*, p. 243; von Soden, "Sakrament," p. 242, n. 3). C. A. Pierce's monograph, *Conscience in the New Testament* (London: SCM Press, 1955), provides an extensive analysis of the Greco-Roman background to the term and its possible meanings in the New Testament, including 1 Cor 8 and 10; Pierce's conclusion is that for Paul *syneidêsis* means a sort of pain felt when moral bounds were exceeded. M. E. Thrall holds another view: Paul understood *syneidêsis* to "perform . . . in the Gentile world roughly the same function as was performed by the Law amongst the Jews" ("Pauline Use of *Syneidêsis*," *New Testament Studies* 14 [1967]: 124). See also Paul Gooch, "'Conscience' in 1 Corinthians 8 and 10" (*New Testament Studies* 33 [1987]: 251-52); R. Jewett, *Paul's Anthropological Terms*, chap. 10; and Horsley, "Consciousness," p. 581. Tomson explores the meaning of this term extensively, comparing Greek and Jewish sources, and concludes that *syneidêsis* means consciousness, associated with intention in human action (*Paul and the Jewish Law: Halakha in the Letters of the Apostle to the Gentiles* [Minneapolis: Fortress Press, 1990], p. 208-15).

is bought in the market (*en makellôi*, 10:23); and when someone tells a brother at table with unbelievers that the food served has been offered to a God (*hierothyton*, 10:27-29).

Eating in an idol's temple

The problem

The situation set out in 8:10 and Paul's immediate treatment of it are perplexing. In the context of 8:7-13, the only complaint Paul raises against reclining at table in an idol's temple (*en eidôleiôi*) is that it might lead to the downfall of one with weak consciousness concerning idol-food. The hypothetical Corinthian doing so has knowledge—presumably the conviction that this food cannot harm him—but the weak Christian does not have this conviction, and will be set up for a fall by this example. On the face of it, however, one would expect that Paul would consider reclining at table in an idol's temple to be sharing in the table of *daimonia* and thus impermissible (10:14-22). Yet Paul in chapter 8 does not attack the knowledge of the Corinthian eating at temple[15] nor condemn the act per se, but only its potential consequences. If we possessed only chapter 8 we would suspect that Paul would condone such eating if the eater's consciousness were strong and there were no weak Christians to witness it.[16]

This apparent tension between 8:7-13 and 10:20-22 leaves us with four possibilities: first, Paul was unaware of the tension between these two passages; second, he does not condemn this eating in 8:10 because such eating was entirely hypothetical and unlikely to occur; third, eating in an idol's temple was not always sharing the table of *daimonia*; and fourth, 8:10 does not provide Paul's complete estimate of eating in an idol's temple—that for some reason Paul waits until 10:14-22 to complete his judgment concerning such eating.

The first and second explanations of this tension may be rejected. Paul is not simply unaware of the tensions between these two passages, since 10:19 shows clearly that he is thinking of chapter 8 when he writes 10:14-22. Paul does not condemn the eating of 8:10 as partner-

---

15 It is accurate to say that Paul does not attack the *gnôsis* of the Corinthians; it would also be accurate to say that Paul does not lend it unequivocal support.

16 Few scholars have addressed explicitly the question of whether Paul would condone a specific occasion of eating in a temple if no weak Christian would be harmed by it. Those who do ask the question answer it in the affirmative: Conzelmann, *1 Cor*, p. 177; Hurd, *Origin*, p. 129, n.2; and von Soden, "Sakrament" [Meeks], p. 264. Note, however, von Soden's limitation of this claim: "It is of course self-evident that Christian participation was forbidden in any meal whose circumstances or form stamped its essential meaning as that of idolatry. . . . No 'informer' needed to point out the sacrificial meat" (ibid., p. 264).

ship with demons simply because such hypothetical eating is not happening or unlikely to happen among the Corinthians, since the similarly hypothetical condition of whether or not some Corinthians did share the table of *daimonia* does not prevent him from attacking partnership with *daimonia* in 10:14-22.[17]

Temples and the tables of demons

The third possible explanation—that Paul thought eating in an idol's temple was not always sharing the table of *daimonia*—has been argued by some. Willis provides the most extended discussion, arguing that the Corinthians participated in such meals for social reasons without perceiving this as a betrayal of their Christian faith. Others have made similar claims that some Corinthians participated in meals in temples without any sense of this as wrong or dangerous,[18] or that the strong Corinthians' inflated sense of their power led them to do this as some sort of demonstration of their immunity, without any consciousness of participating in idolatry.[19]

A careful distinction must be made here between whether Paul or the Corinthians—if they did eat in temples—perceived eating in temples as distinct from participation at the table of demons, or whether Paul's distinction derives from the objective fact that there were some meals held in temples that did not involve food hallowed by religious rite. Both questions are relevant to determining whether Paul could have maintained a distinction between eating in an idol's temple and at the table of demons.

First, whether meals could be held in an idol's temple without sacred food: my survey of the use of sacred food in the Greco-Roman world allows a more thorough answer to this than others have devel-

---

17 Whether the Corinthians *did* eat in temples will be discussed in chapter 8 concerning the effect on the Corinthians of Paul's position.

18 Weiss, *1 Kor*, p. 211 (most Corinthian Christians ate in temples because they did not wish to sever social ties with family and friends); Ehrhardt, *Framework*, p. 279 (temples were the "restaurants" of the ancient world); Murphy-O'Connor, "Freedom," p. 549 (the strong originally ate idol-food in temples "without suspecting there might be a problem"); and Fee, "2 Cor 6:14-7:1," p. 151; "*Eidôlothyta*," p. 180 (the Corinthians wanted to continue to join pagan friends in feasts at temples).

19 Von Soden presents an often-cited view that the Corinthian strong had adopted a magical view of the Christian sacraments—that these protected them from any harm from hostile spiritual powers—but von Soden does not make any claim concerning whether the Corinthians ate in temples ("Sakrament," p. 259 [Meeks's translation]). Fee extends this argument to claim that the Corinthian strong justified their eating in temples by this immunity from harm (*Eidôlothyta*, p. 180). Barrett presents a similar view: the *gnôsis* of the strong was "essentially practical," giving them freedom to eat and to fornicate ("Things Sacrificed," p. 54-55).

oped.[20] There were indeed "temples"—or, more accurately, sacred enclosures—in Corinth where food was regularly consumed by small groups, most likely in a context where religious rites were mixed with conviviality (the sanctuary of Demeter and Kore). There were also eating facilities that stood in ambiguous relation to a temple (the dining rooms beneath the Asklepieion). Most meals of any social consequence involved religious rites. Many socially significant meals took place in homes. The constant theme of the literary sources with regard to meals is the theme of host and guest, of shared meals at private homes as marks of social intimacy[21]—so constant a theme that were it not for the archaeological evidence of the extensive use of dining rooms associated with cultic centres it might be concluded that no significant degree of social eating occurred there.[22] This allows an assessment of whether there might have been meals "in an idol's temple" that did not include religious rites.

The finding that the dining rooms of Lerna stood in an ambiguous relation with the Asklepieion lends support to this possibility. A situation can easily be envisaged where a strong Christian's eating at the dining rooms of Lerna could raise questions among other Christians worried over idolatrous rites. The evidence collected by Willis, which shows the essentially social purpose of many meals where religious rites were performed,[23] would also support the argument—whether made by the strong themselves or by commentators—that some meals in temples were only nominally connected to idolatry, and not in any significant way.

The other findings of my survey of archaeological and literary evidence, however, make it very clear that the dissociation of temples and

---

20 Ehrhardt's claim, for example, that temples were the restaurants of the ancient world is made without reference to sources (*Framework*, p. 279). Willis develops an extensive argument that the rites over most meals were of no religious significance, but on the basis of unrepresentative evidence (see Appendix 1).

21 The evidence collected in chaps. 1-3 should be compared with the only evidence for meals in temples commonly cited in commentary on 1 Cor 8: the papyrus inscriptions noted by Adolph Deissmann (*New Light on the New Testament from Records of the Graeco-Roman Period*, Edinburgh: T. & T. Clark, 1908, p. 351) that extend invitations to dine at the table of the Lord Serapis. The bulk of evidence, not explored by New Testament scholars, leaves a different impression of the social context of shared meals.

22 This evidence concerns not only the cults practised in temples, but the lack of facilities for dining in private homes. MacMullen notes that even the homes of the wealthy rarely included dining rooms that would hold more than nine diners, and thus the communal facilities of temples were necessary for social occasions where a larger number were to be entertained (*Paganism*, p. 34-42).

23 Willis, *Idol Meat*, p. 47-56.

meals involving religious rites was not likely. The presence of a great number of dining rooms at the sanctuary of Demeter and Kore was not coincidental: the cult and its rites centred on the provision of food. The literary evidence shows time and again that socially significant meals involved explicit religious rites.[24] If such meals involved rites even when held in private homes, it seems most unlikely that there would not be some cultic acts in meals celebrated in cultic settings. Finally, social events and religious events could not be separated in the Greco-Roman world to the same extent as they can be in ours.

An objective separation between meals eaten "in an idol's temple" and meals involving idolatrous rites was highly improbable in Paul's Corinth. It can safely be presumed that meals in temples involved food hallowed (or, depending on one's point of view, infected) by sacred rite. This presumption is all that is required: Paul argues that if those without the knowledge of the strong see the strong at table in an idol's temple they might eat idol-food to their destruction—that is, they will presume the strongs' participation in idolatry.

It is not possible, then, to maintain validly that Paul's different treatment of eating in an idol's temple in chapter 8 and the table of demons in chapter 10 rests on any *objective* difference between these.

The second possible reason for Paul's different treatment of eating in an idol's temple and the table of demons is a *subjective* distinction on the part of Paul or the Corinthians, or both, that allowed the strong, on the basis of their monotheistic knowledge and spiritual power, to participate in meals in temples without perceiving this as participation in idolatry or worship of demons. This seems a more promising approach to resolve the tension between chapter 8 and chapter 10. If Paul or the Corinthians could see a difference between eating at a cultic meal and participating in idolatry, then chapter 8 might be addressed simply to the strong to warn them that their freedom puts others (but not the strong) at risk from the idolatry forbidden in chapter 10.

This reconstruction is not persuasive because it simply does not account for the warnings of chapter 10. If Paul finds this supposed distinction on the part of the strong valid (and thus only warns them on behalf of the weak), why does he bring in the warnings of chapter 10? The warnings from the example of the Israelites in 10:1-13 are directed at the strong—the point of the Israelite story is that those who thought they stood ended up falling (so the warning in 10:12)—and thus the strong, not the weak, are warned against idolatry.[25] Even if the Corin-

---

24 This conclusion is supported even by the selective evidence Willis uses. The rites occurred, whatever the participants' or Willis's assessment of the depth of their religious meaning.

25 Robertson and Plummer, *1 Cor*, p. 198, 202, 208; Willis, *Idol Meat*, p. 123-64

thians did make the subjective distinction between cultic meals and idolatry[26] it is problematic to assume that Paul approved this distinction.

Paul the persuader

The final possible explanation of the tension between Paul's forbidding of eating in temples only on grounds that it might harm the weak (chapter 8) and his forbidding of participation at the table of demons (chapter 10) is that 8:10 does not provide Paul's complete estimate of eating in an idol's temple.

This explanation is the most plausible, and not only because other possible explanations have failed. Paul is concerned in chapter 8 to agree with the Corinthians as far as he can. He accepts their claims to knowledge (8:1,4,7,10,11)—at least almost accepts them (8:1b,2)—and goes as far as he can to appear to agree with their estimate of the reality of other Gods (8:5-6, noting especially "so-called Gods," *legomenoi theoi*). Yet Paul's significant qualifications of the Corinthian claims have already been noted, and I have argued that 10:14-22 represents Paul's true estimation of the reality of other Gods and Lords.

Paul's condemnation of the eating of 8:10 only on grounds of its effect on the weak is part of Paul's strategy of persuasion—put charitably, that Paul in 8:7-13 simply focusses on one problem with such eating, offers one argument against it, and will go on to offer another;[27]

(providing an extended discussion and history of research of 10:1-13); Wayne A. Meeks, *The Moral World of the First Christians* (Philadelphia: Westminster Press, 1986), p. 135. See also Meeks, "'And Rose up to Play,'" p. 64-78.

26 Though I am admitting here for the sake of argument that the Corinthians might have eaten in temples, it should be remembered that this claim does not rest on firm evidence. The Corinthians' claims that there is only one God and that idols are not real do not in themselves support the inference that they participated in cultic meals. To support this inference, some appeal to evidence outside chapter 8 must be made—usually 1 Cor 6:12/10:23 (the Corinthian claim that all things are lawful), or 1 Cor 6:12-20's warnings against sexual immorality, or the hypothesized Corinthian belief in the magical protection offered by the sacraments reconstructed on the basis of 1 Cor 10:1-13, or the lawless practice of later Christian Gnostics complained about in the Fathers. Chapter 6's warnings about *porneia*, however, may be a hypothetical "worst case" adduced by Paul (contra Hurd, *Origin*, p. 86-89) and so may be the eating in temples of chapter 8. Very much detail has been filled in by commentators on the basis of the aphorism "all things are lawful." What later Gnostics did (or the Fathers thought they did) is of limited application here, in my view.

27 Kirsopp Lake finds that, because Paul agrees with the strong in chapter 8 and the weak in chapter 10, his position is not "wholly logical" (*Epistles*, p. 201). Compare Conzelmann: chapters 8 and 10 deal with different topics (eating and idolatry) with resulting different conclusions (in the first case, freedom, in the second,

or, put less charitably, that Paul wishes not to lose his credibility with the Corinthians at the outset so offers a less offensive (that is, more flattering to the Corinthians) reason for not eating in an idol's temple.

If the Corinthians were eating in settings associated with cultic locations or rites, then Paul's first approach to their practice is not to condemn it outright. If the Corinthians were not eating in such contexts, still Paul's appeal to the consciousness of the weak avoids a direct challenge to the knowledge of the Corinthians. Such an oblique attack is also made on the question of the reality of other Gods.

Other letters of Paul show a similar persuasive technique: a series of unrelated arguments, developed to varying degrees, sometimes in tension with one another, linked only by their common conclusion in support of Paul's central point.[28] Paul makes the point, and if that doesn't work (or even if it does) he makes it over again in another way. Where passion and persistence count Paul is effective; where our own standards of consistency and logical development are applied Paul's arguments are less effective.

Chapters 8-10 of 1 Corinthians show this technique of Pauline persuasion, though by this claim I do not wish to minimize the strong structural links between the sections[29] or to suggest that Paul's approach is crude or unpersuasive. Paul is willing elsewhere to attempt different and not deeply related arguments to make a single point. The tension between chapter 8's lack of condemnation of eating in an idol's temple *per se* and chapter 10's forbidding of participation in cultic meals is caused because Paul does not give his complete estimation of eating in an idol's temple in the first instance.

Conclusions

Paul found eating in an idol's temple impermissible both because it might cause the weak to fall and because it broke partnership with the Lord. If Paul seems to disapprove of such eating only for its effect on the weak in 8:10, it is because of his strategy of persuasion and not because he would find such eating acceptable if the weak were not harmed by it.

---

avoidance) (*1 Cor*, p. 170-71). Thrall proposes that the letter shows us Paul's thought in progress: in chapter 8, Paul is content to argue on the terms of the strong, but "when he comes to write chapter 10 he realizes that they [the strong] could be wrong in principle as well" (*1 and 2 Cor*, p. 4).

28 The long argument concerning the inefficacy of the law in Gal 2-5, the long argument concerning the place of the Jewish people in salvation history in Rom 9-11, and the short letter to Philemon all show this distinctly Pauline structure.

29 These structural links are shown in particular by the connections between chapter 9 and the rest of the sections, and the mutual informing of 8:4-6 and 10:14-22.

Food bought at market

The problem

The second concrete circumstance that Paul addresses where questions of consciousness (*syneidêsis*) might be raised is the purchase of food at the market (10:25). Here Paul's judgment is not hedged with conditionals: "Eat," he says, "everything sold in the market, not questioning at all because of consciousness."[30] Though this pronouncement is straightforward it too leads to another tension in Paul's position: in 8:10 concern for the consciousness of the weak was to prevent eating, but here qualms of consciousness are not to be considered. It is not clear on the face of the text why consciousness is deeply relevant in one context and entirely inconsequential in another.

Paul's instructions to the weak?

Again, a number of possible explanations may be presented. The circumstances addressed in 10:25 and in 10:27 were raised in the Corinthians' letter, possibly as Corinthian objections to the extent of the consequences of avoiding idol-food. Paul's unqualified response suggests that perhaps he believes that no one would raise serious questions of consciousness concerning food sold at market or be harmed over such questions.

This first suggestion, however, does not resolve the inconsistency.[31] Paul may not know what problems of consciousness would be held by the weak Christians in Corinth, or even whether such Christians existed. More significantly, the direct point of 8:7-13 and (as will be seen) 10:27-29 is that if problems of consciousness are raised then eating is impermissible. To be consistent, then, with both his uncertainty concerning the weak and his position elsewhere, Paul would have to say in 10:25, "Eat whatever is sold at market, unless someone objects that this food is offered to a God (*hierothyton*)."[32]

---

30 The lack of hypothetical conditions is notable because of their presence in both 8:7-13 and 10:27-29.

31 It does not *resolve* the inconsistency, but it may explain it; see my conclusion below.

32 Unlike other commentators, Fee, Tomson and Willis address this inconsistency (Pierce sets out the contradiction blatantly, but does not seem to perceive it as such [*Conscience*, p. 75-76]). Fee attempts to make the inconsistency disappear in a postulated specific circumstance: the one calling attention to the sacred food at the dinner of 10:27 was not a weak Christian, and therefore the issue of *syneidêsis* here is not the same as in chapter 8 ("*Eidôlothyta*," p. 177). This is unpersuasive. Whether a weak Christian (Fee's chap. 8) or a Gentile table companion (Fee's 10:28), Paul's conclusion is the same—Don't eat on account of consciousness—*except* in 10:25-26. Tomson notes the inconsistency then argues that 10:23-11:1 are Paul's practical

Instead Paul implies the opposite: the Corinthians are to eat "in no way (*mêden*[33]) conducting an examination for the sake of consciousness." Some see this demand not to raise scruples as Paul's demand of the weak, in balance to his demands of the strong in chapter 8 and 10:28: the weak should overcome in this instance their problems of consciousness.[34] This interpretation, however, rather than reconciling the conflict only underlines it by raising further difficulties: if Paul could demand the disregard of consciousness in this context, why not—as the Corinthians may have argued[35]—urge its disregard well? in the other contexts as well?

Food, not idolatry?

Another possible explanation of Paul's disregard of consciousness in 10:25 is that Paul makes an underlying distinction between simple food and the demonic harm that can come through it. It is idolatry that harms (Paul is understood to argue), not food; since the connection to idolatry of food bought in the market is so remote, no problem of consciousness need be raised.[36]

This explanation, like the former one, does not fare well under closer examination. Some aspects of Paul's response to the Corinthians seem to show that Paul sees idol-food simply as food: 10:26 ("The earth . . . belongs to the Lord") treats idol-food sold in the market as simple food; 8:8 ("Food will not bring us before God; if we don't eat we are not lacking, and if we do we don't excel") is affirmed by Paul (whether a Corinthian slogan or not) and the limitation which Paul urges to this claim concerns not food per se but the power (*exousia*) to eat it (8:9); Paul suggests that he does not think that idol-food is "anything" (10:19). On the other hand, aspects of Paul's response show that he understands food to hold deadly contagion. Paul's warnings in 10:14-22, read together with 11:17-34, show that Paul sees the part-

---

instructions (*halakha*) to help the Corinthians determine what is or is not idol food (*Paul and the Jewish Law*, p. 202). See also Willis (*Idol Meat*, p. 240-43).

33 Baur, Arndt, Gingrich, "*mêdeis,mêdemia, mêden*," 2.b.*beta*.

34 Weiss, *1 Kor*, p. 264; Barrett, "Things Sacrificed," p. 47, 50. See also Willis, *Idol Meat*, p. 230-34.

35 *Oikodomêthêsetai* (8:10) may be an ironic reference to the vocabulary of the strong.

36 That Paul makes a distinction between food and idolatry is often argued. See, for example, Lietzmann, *1 Cor*, p. 38; Barrett, *1 Cor*, p. 236-37 ("Nothing happens to [the food] in the moment of sacrifice: it is the same as before. . . . The effect of the sacrifice lies not in the eating but in personal relations [with demons], and the consequences that flow from them"). Barrett argues the point more fully in "Things Sacrificed," p. 51-52. Peter Tomson develops this view through comparison with early rabbinic *halakha* (*Paul and the Jewish Law*, p. 219).

nership (which can lead either to God's blessing or God's rejection) inherent in food. The cup and the bread *are* partnership in the blood and body of Christ (10:16). It is the table of demons—not the allegiance to demons expressed by this rite or some such more abstract concept, but the concrete cup and table of *daimonia*—that breaks partnership with the Lord.

Paul's language in chapter 8 also reveals his concern that food itself is a vector of contagion. He makes no distinction between idolatry and food. He does not claim that the weak will come under the sway of other Gods again if they resume old patterns of behaviour. Rather he says that "they will eat [food] as idol-food" (*hôs eidôlothyton esthiousin*, 8:7) and will be encouraged to eat idol-food and perish (8:10-11). The food when it is offered to *daimonia* or when it is consumed as idol-food itself effects the destruction of partnership with the Lord and destroys the brother who consumes it.

The claim that Paul makes a distinction between food as food and the idolatry that food sometimes expresses cannot be supported from the text of 1 Corinthians 8:1-11:1. Paul instead says both things—that food can be just food and that idol-food as food can kill. If commentators shy at admitting that Paul says the latter it may be that they are embarrassed for him; if commentators argue an underlying consistency to Paul's views in this regard they go further than the text allows.

Conclusions

Both the attempts that have been made to reconcile Paul's disregard of consciousness in 10:25 with his demands for its consideration in chapter 8 and 10:28 are unpersuasive: Paul's inconsistent instructions cannot be explained away as his different instructions to the strong and the weak, and Paul does not make a distinction between food and idolatry that would reconcile his conflicting instructions. We are left with a basic conflict: concerning eating in an idol's temple, the consciousness of the weak determines the impermissibility of the act; concerning food sold in the market, consciousness is to be set aside.[37]

---

37 Willis presents an original argument that would salvage Paul's consistency: other commentators take the qualification of 10:28 ("But if someone says to you, 'This is sacred food' ") to apply only to the situation set out in 10:27 (a dinner party at which idol-food is served); Willis argues that the qualification applies to *both* the situation of 10:27 and to purchases in the market (*Idol Meat*, p. 242-43). Paul's instruction to defer to the consciousness of others would then apply to food in all the contexts Paul addresses. I do not find Willis's reading persuasive, on structural grounds. Verse 28's qualification on the freedom to eat at meals in the homes of others stands parallel to verse 26 ("For the earth is the Lord's"). Willis correctly notes that 10:26 is intended to justify, not limit, the purchase of food, while 10:28

The inconsistency between 10:25 and chapter 8 and 10:27-28 remains unaccounted for,[38] except as an instance of Paul's lack of perception of inconsistency or lack of concern over it. Whether Paul is following the Corinthians or anticipating them, he genuinely sees no danger or harm in food from the marketplace whatever its history, and hence is not concerned either to sway the Corinthians' views of it or to integrate the issues over it into his real concerns.

Eating with non-believers

The final concrete instance addressed by Paul is set out in 10:27: "If one of the unbelievers offers you an invitation[39] and you wish to go, eat *everything*[40] set before you, not questioning at all because of consciousness." Paul finds nothing wrong or dangerous with food in this context, whatever its religious history. "If, however, someone says to you, 'This is sacred food' [*hierothyton*, literally "offered to a God"], do not eat because of that one who informed you and [because of] consciousness—not your own consciousness I mean, but that of the other" (10:28-29a). This is a clear instance where in Paul's view eating is permissible by one criterion (it does not threaten partnership with the Lord[41]) but impermissible by the other (it does threaten the consciousness of another).[42]

---

limits it (*Idol Meat*, p. 243), but he does not address the structural implications of this. The justification of 10:26 is not intended to apply to other eating (at temples and at homes), and in the same way the qualification of 10:28 is meant to apply only to 10:27.

38 Another explanation is possible: *syneidêsis* really does not matter to Paul. The argument from the consciousness of the weak in chapter 8 could be only an opening manoeuvre (recall my assessment of Paul's techniques of persuasion); Paul's true position is found in his warnings against idolatry developed in 10:14-22. If this were the case the tensions in Paul's position would be slackened, but this cannot be supported from the text. I will argue below that Paul's third concrete instance of eating (10:27-29) shows that he takes problems of *syneidêsis* seriously.

39 Usually commentators take this to be an invitation to a private home (see, for example, Thrall, "Pauline Use of *Syneidêsis*," p. 122). Hurd supports a different view: the verse refers to invitations to temples (*Origin*, p. 129, n.2, noting others in support of this view). Either context or both could be addressed by Paul's description.

40 Stressed by word order: *pan to paratithemenon hymin esthiete* (10:27b).

41 The claim that in Paul's view such eating of idol-food does not threaten *koinônia tou kyriou* must be qualified. At root, Paul's concern over the consciousness of the other is a concern over the other's *koinônia* with the Lord, so to this extent Paul's arguments concerning consciousness and *koinônia* amount to the same thing.

42 See Robertson and Plummer (*1 Cor*, p. 219) who suggest that, though Paul allows such eating, it is a concession to the Corinthians. Paul's diction betrays his ill ease:

Much perplexity has been felt over the hypothetical one (*tis*) who tells the Corinthian believers that the food served at the hypothetical meal is sacred food.[43] This "one" has been taken to be a non-Christian host or invited guest, or protesting Christian not accepting the invitation, or weak Christian learning of the history of the food as it is served. This "one" has also been taken not only to be hypothetical but exceedingly unlikely.[44]

Much corresponding perplexity has also been raised over the nature of this one's consciousness. In my view, since the term "consciousness" is introduced abruptly in 10:25 and not explained further in 10:25,27,28, or 29, Paul means by it in chapter 10 what he means by it in chapter 8. Whether or not Paul's hypothetical "one" is a Christian, "consciousness" must mean here what it does in chapter 8: consciousness that this food is religiously potent, because of very recent or ongoing intimacy with "idols."[45]

"the emphasis is on *kalei*; he [Paul] suggests that without an express invitation they surely would not go. . . . [*Kai thelete poreuesthai*] is an intimation that he does not advise their going, though he does not forbid it" (*1 Cor*, p. 221).

43 I do not enter into the discussion concerning the identity of the *tis* of 10:28, for two reasons. First, my concern is to show that Paul makes a serious appeal to the consciousness of others in his instructions over idol-food, and it is not deeply relevant to this claim whose consciousness Paul has in mind. Second, I will argue below (chaps. 8 and 9) that the very indeterminateness of Paul's scenario is the most notable and significant feature of it, and may have caused serious problems to those wishing to follow Paul's instructions.

44 Proponents of the view that the *tis* is a non-Christian focus on the term *hierothyton*, arguing that a Christian would call the food *eidôlothyton* (Lietzmann, *1 Kor*, p. 51; von Soden, "Sakrament," p. 250). Lietzmann adds that the elaborate construction of 10:29a would be unnecessary if Paul were referring to a weak Christian (*1 Kor*, p. 51). More often scholars argue that the *tis* was a weak Christian: the consciousness of this one is parallel to that of the weak of chapter 8 (Klauck, *Herrenmahl*, p. 277; Meyer, *1 Cor*, p. 309; Robertson and Plummer, *1 Cor*, p. 221; Weiss, *1 Kor*, p. 265); the *tis* can't be the host or a non-Christian guest because Paul says that accepting invitations is acceptable (Meyer, *1 Cor*, p. 309-10); a non-Christian would not be concerned (Barrett, *1 Cor*, p. 239; Murphy-O'Connor, "Freedom," p. 570, n.79; and Weiss, *1 Kor*, p. 265). Hurd argues that the *tis* of 10:28 is another unreal person, like the weaker brother of chapter 8, introduced hypothetically by Paul (*Origin*, p. 125). Compare Robertson and Plummer: the situation of 10:28-29 is pure hypothesis and not very likely (*1 Cor*, p. 221). Willis provides an extensive survey of the literature on this question, and on the issue of the locale of the invitation (*Idol Meat*, p. 238-42), but draws no conclusion concerning the identity of the *tis*.

45 Thrall argues a different conception of the consciousness of the *tis* of 10:27: citing Rom 1:29 and the gospel traditions concerning judging, Thrall argues that the problem exercising Paul in 10:27-29 is not that the weaker brother will be led

Consciousness and knowledge

In 10:28-29 Paul gives a clear instance where food permissible on his criterion of partnership is not permissible on his other criterion of consciousnesss.[46] This is good evidence that Paul takes consciousness seriously, but other features of 1 Corinthians 8:1-11:1 also strongly support this conclusion. In 8:13 Paul appeals to the Corinthians to restrict their power (*exousia*) to eat in the interest of preventing harm to others by claiming that he will not eat meat if it causes his brother to fall. This claim is clearly conditional, but Paul expands and defends it with chapter 9. The point of chapter 9 is that Paul *has* restricted his own *exousia* in order to benefit the Corinthians (9:1-18, noting especially vv.5,6,12,18), and that he *has* renounced his legitimate freedom in order to win salvation for some (9:19-23).[47]

Paul thus counters anticipated Corinthian objections to the restriction of their liberty: if they do not wish to guard the interests of the weak let them look at what Paul has done: "To the weak I became weak that I might win the weak." In the same way, Paul's last word on the topic of idol-food to the Corinthians is that they should follow his example; whether they eat or drink they should put no obstacle in the way of others, not seeking their own advantage but that of others (10:31-11:1).

The conclusion that consciousness is significant to Paul means again, however, that his inconsistency over consciousness is only underlined. Every attempt to reconcile Paul's disregard of consciousness in 10:25 and his demand that it be respected elsewhere fails to be supported by the text. For Paul the consciousness of others makes eating idol-food wrong (8:7-13; 10:28-29) except that sometimes it doesn't (10:25).

---

astray but that he will condemn, "with dire consequences to himself" ("Paul's Use of *Syneidêsis* ," p. 122).

46 Paul's reason for urging care for the other's consciousness should not be forgotten: if the other is a Christian, the eating of idol-food might provoke the other into an eating that would break the other's partnership with Christ; or if the other is a non-Christian, it might legitimize his perception that the Christian he addresses is a *koinônos* at the table of *daimonia*.

47 This view of the function of chapter 9 is held with virtual unanimity, even among scholars proposing a partition of 1 Cor: see, for representative arguments, Barrett, "Things Sacrificed," p. 53; Baur, *Paul*, 1:268; Fee, "2 Cor 6:14-7:1," p. 152; Klauck, *Herrenmahl*, p. 249; Lietzmann, *1 Kor*, p. 39; Meyer, *1 Cor*, p. 251; Robertson and Plummer, *1 Cor*, p. 176-77; Schmithals, *Gnosticism*, p. 228; von Soden, "Sakrament," p. 244; Weiss, *1 Kor*, p. 242-44; and Willis, *Idol Meat*, p. 160-62. Hurd, however, finds an additional point to chapter 9: Paul is defending himself against a charge of inconsistency in his own use of idol-food (*Origin*, p. 127-28).

There is also an uncomfortable unresolved tension between Paul's response and the Corinthians' earlier claims over knowledge. Some eating is clearly permissible in Paul's view, but for the consciousness of others. Paul's response, however, in the end does not answer why the Corinthians cannot "build up" the consciousness of these others (8:10) to convince them of the harmlessness of eating idol-food. This tension resonates with Paul's inconsistency: even Paul implies that some problems of consciousness should be ignored (10:25), so why should other problems of consciousness not be ignored or addressed with knowledge? Paul himself recognizes the potential frustration of the Corinthians with his response—"For what reason is my freedom judged by another's consciousness? If *I* share a table[48] with thanks, why am I defamed because of that for which *I* give thanks?" (10:29-30).[49]

Because Paul's protest in 10:29b-30 seems from one perspective so clearly at odds with his conclusions in 10:28-29a, it might be thought that the protest of 10:29b-30 is another quotation from the Corinthian letter to Paul.[50] This possibility is reinforced since the protest is clearly consistent with the views of the Corinthians.

Two observations make this unlikely, however. First, these verses are not immediately qualified or denied by Paul. Second, both the content of the verses and the stress on the pronoun "I" clearly reflect Paul's demand for consideration of the consciousness of *others*, and since this demand seems to be introduced in 8:7-13 it is unlikely that the Corinthian letter would reflect it.[51]

---

48 The text says only *metechô*, but the expanded translation I propose is justified since the same verb is used in 10:21 in connection with the tables of the Lord and *daimonia*.

49 The emphasized "I" is conveyed in both instances by the repeated first person: *ei egô chariti metechô . . . egô eucharistô*.

50 One possibility, as noted, is that the verses are a quotation from the Corinthians. A variant of this claim is provided by Lietzmann, who suggests that Paul himself introduced 10:29-30 in the style of diatribe as an interjection of the strong (*1 Cor*, p. 51). Héring suggests that Paul directs these objections to the weak (*1 Cor*, p. 99). Yet another variant is defended at length by Weiss: the verses are a textual gloss, introduced by someone with the viewpoint of the Corinthian strong (*1 Kor*, p. 265-67). Willis provides an extensive discussion of commentary on these verses (*Idol Meat*, p. 246-50); see also Hurd's catalogue of views (*Origin*, p. 130, n. 2).

51 Paul's earlier letter might have made some reference to the objections of others concerning idol-food. If this were the case, 10:29b-30 could be seen as a quotation and the whole of 8:7-13 an answer to the *hinati* of 10:29b, and the Corinthian claim that *pantes gnôsin echomen* (8:1) given a significant new colouring: "What others? *We* all have knowledge." It must be stressed, however, that there is no evidence in 1 Cor of this earlier allusion to "others," and if the Corinthians were asking concerning who these others might be, Paul's treatment of them in 8:7-13 and 10:28-29 would hardly be adequate.

It is more likely that Paul anticipates a Corinthian objection with his protest in 10:29b-30, or protests against an anticipated misinterpretation of his demand. The verses should be seen as an expansion of the phrase "not *your* consciousness I mean" in 10:29a: "of course," Paul affirms, "it is no problem to you or me," but the consciousness of the other must still over-ride that of the Corinthians who find themselves in this context.[52]

To return, however, to the main point: Paul recognizes the potential frustration of the Corinthians with his position concerning the consciousness of others, but does not change his conclusion. Even if he does protest that his or the Corinthians' liberty is not condemned because of another's consciousness, still his protest does not alter the behaviour he demands: renounce your liberty in order that others may be saved or other brothers might not fall. To the protest that the obstacle of idol-food might be removed by knowledge, however, Paul says, in the end, nothing.

Did Paul reject the Corinthian position concerning idol-food?

Has Paul rejected the Corinthian position? Paul has qualified every Corinthian claim, but does this qualification indicate basic disagreement with the Corinthian position concerning idol-food?

One point of unqualified agreement may be found—but an agreement, however, not with a Corinthian claim but with a Corinthian protest. "What of food in the market," the Corinthians seem to have objected, and Paul concedes the permissibility of this food. Given the serious difficulties this permission makes for Paul's position (I have argued), it would seem that this is exactly a straightforward and not carefully thought out concession to the Corinthians.

Paul offers a similar concession to the Corinthian protest concerning invitations to eat with non-believers, but this concession is hedged with his significant qualification. Paul is attempting to strike a compromise with the Corinthians, but this compromise contains nothing with which Paul is unhappy. He has no problem with such eating (except under his qualifying circumstance) so he has given up nothing in this "compromise," but he has imposed a limitation on the Corinthians.

While Paul has offered concessions over Corinthian protests, he offers no compromise over Corinthian claims to justifying knowledge. Rather, he offers only contradiction thinly disguised as qualification.

Corinthians: "We all have knowledge" (8:1).

52 Compare Paul Gooch, "Burden," p. 114.

Paul: "If someone thinks he has come to know, he does not yet know as he ought to know" (8:2).
"But this knowledge is not in everyone" (8:7).

Corinthians: "There is no idol in the world . . . there is no God but one" (8:4).

Paul: "There are many Gods and many Lords" (8:6); there are *daimonia* (10:14-22).

Corinthians: "All things are permissible" (10:23), and perhaps "Food will not commend us to God" (8:8).

Paul: "Not all things bring benefit or build up" (10:23), and, since the "building up" of the wrongful eating of idol-food can destroy partnership with the Lord or destroy a brother, it is hardly permissible.

Paul provides the appearance of affirmation of the Corinthian position—a clear instance of his becoming "all things . . . to all," here not to the weak but to the strong—in order to win them to his position. This affirmation is in appearance only, however, since every Corinthian affirmation of either knowledge or power is denied. Though he makes concessions concerning the market and invitations, Paul offers a very different conception of the dangers of idol-food. This food is dangerous to other Christians (so Paul appeals for protection of the weak) and to the Corinthians themselves (it threatens their own partnership with their Lord). Paul rejects the assessment of the "strong," sees idol-food as dangerous, and urges avoidance of it.[53]

Did Paul eat idol-food?

Paul's extended appeal to his own example in chapter 9 does not appeal explicitly to his practice regarding idol-food. The point of chapter 9 is to show his willingness to follow his own advice to the Corinthians to renounce their power (*exousia*) in the interests of others, and his method is to point to instances of his renunciation of his own rights. Paul here refers to his own eating (9:4), but not—note well—

53 Compare Hurd, *Origin*, p. 133: "Paul's acceptance of the Corinthian position . . . was neither complete or wholehearted. True he did not flatly reject their principles. But neither did he commend them. Rather he set aside the complicated problem of the exact sense in which these slogans were acceptable and attacked on the ground of Christian love the conclusions which the Corinthians had reached." This view is widely shared, but it does not go far enough. Paul does not accept even the principles of the strong. Some share my view: Willis, *Idol Meat*, p. 116, 120; Horsley, "Gnosis," p. 49-51.

the eating of idol-food. Rather he appeals to his practice in abstract terms, and his practice vis-à-vis not weak Christians but outsiders.

This leads to some important questions. Can Paul not appeal to his practice with regard to idol-food because he has eaten it (and thus undermine his advice to the Corinthians), or instead because he does not eat idol-food?[54]

On the one hand, Paul says in 9:22, "I have become all things to all"—to Jews, to those under the law, to the lawless, to the weak—"in order to save by all ways some." Paul identifies himself as apostle to the Gentiles, and he has lived among them. Because of this, and because the Corinthian Christians are surprised at his demands to shun idolaters in his previous letter, it has been argued that Paul has shown no scruple at eating idol-food. On the other hand, Paul urges a distinctly different view on the Corinthians concerning the reality and potential harm of *daimonia*, and even if Paul has attempted to save in all ways he has remained not lawless toward God and within the law of Christ (9:21).

Any application of Paul's rhetoric in 9:19-23 to his practice in concrete social situations is doubtful simply because he is vague. It is not at all clear what being "under the law," or "lawless," or "not without the law of God," or "within the law of Christ," or "weak" might mean in terms of behaviour. Paul's rhetoric has dragged him along again (still on the leash of his point, that he has renounced his own freedom for the good of his brothers), but even if that rhetoric reveals much of his Paul's willingness to accommodate the expectations of others (compare 10:31-11:1) it cannot be taken as a description of his missionary practice in concrete social terms.

---

54 Hurd says Paul ate idol-food (*Origin*, p. 128-30; 147-48). Oscar Broneer is convinced that Paul would have accepted invitations to dine in a temple ("Corinth: Centre of St. Paul's Missionary Work," p. 96). Barrett implies Paul ate idol-food ("Things Sacrificed," p. 50). Others suggest more diffidently that Paul's variable practice may have been one of the causes of the Corinthians' queries (Fee, "*Eidôlothyta* ," p. 181; Ehrhardt, *Framework*, p. 278). In contrast, Tomson suggests that Paul in no way condoned idol-food (*Paul and the Jewish Law*, p. 185). It is surprising how few commentators ask the specific question whether Paul ate idol-food. For example, in his extended discussion of Paul's *praxis* on the basis of 9:19-23, Weiss does not touch the issue of whether Paul ate idol-food (*1 Kor*, p. 242-46). A similar unconcern is shown in other discussions of 9:19-23: see Chadwick, "'All Things to all Men' (1 Cor 9:22)," *New Testament Studies* 1 (1954-55):261-75; Bornkamm, "The Missionary Stance of Paul in 1 Corinthians 9 and in Acts" in *Studies in Luke-Acts*, ed. Leander E. Keck and J. Louis Martyn (Philadelphia: Fortress Press, 1980), p. 194-207; Conzelmann, *1 Cor*, p. 159-61; and Richardson, "Pauline Inconsistency: 1 Corinthians 9:19-23 and Galatians 2:11-14," *New Testament Studies*, 26 (1980): 347-62). This is one more indication of how little the concrete issue addressed by 1 Cor 8-10 is of interest to many scholars.

In my view Paul does not refer to his practice concerning idol-food in 1 Corinthians 9 because he avoided food that had even the most tenuous connection with idolatrous rite. There is no direct evidence concerning whether Paul ate idol-food. The best indirect evidence is Paul's position concerning idol-food. He thinks it dangerous, thinks it will threaten partnership with his Lord, and recommends that the Corinthian Christians not eat it. This makes it unlikely that he himself ate it. The second sort of indirect evidence is the lack of Paul's appeal to his practice concerning idol-food in chapter 9, particularly when it would have strengthened his case to appeal to his own practice. If Paul had eaten idol-food it would help to establish his credibility (he wants to show as much solidarity with the Corinthians as possible) and also help to support the legitimacy of his demand of the Corinthians.[55] This argument from silence[56] is evidence—tenuous evidence to be sure, but better than speculation—that Paul did not eat in any context connected to idolatrous rite.[57]

The roots of Paul's position

The final question is: why did Paul urge avoidance of idol-food?

The roots of Paul's position are not hard to uncover. Paul here affirms a given of Judaism.[58] Idol-food for Paul was tied intimately to

---

55 Compare 1 Cor 14:18—"I thank God that I speak in tongues more than you all, but"—where Paul uses exactly this technique.

56 Hurd draws an exactly opposite inference from the silence of chapter 9 concerning Paul's practice vis-à-vis idol-food: as part of his argument that Paul's own position is similar to that of the Corinthians, Hurd notes that Paul "does not claim never to have eaten . . . idol meat" (*Origin*, p. 147). I am convinced that the purpose of chapter 9 and the structure of Paul's argument in chapter 8 would make it to Paul's advantage to point to his eating of idol-food, had he eaten it.

57 It might be counter-argued that other evidence in 1 Cor suggests Paul would have eaten idol-food: 8:13, where Paul says he will abstain from meat, and 9:19-22, where Paul's rhetoric could be taken to mean that he became just like those he was with in order to win them. I would respond that 8:13 supports my conclusion, since it shows that it is more likely that Paul abstained to protect others. In 9:19-22 we have a notable and most interesting instance of Paul's rhetoric, from which no conclusions can be drawn concerning his social practice. Just as Paul did not actually become a slave, and did not live outside any law (as he hastens to assure his readers in verse 21b), so his claim that he became "all things" cannot be taken to mean that he participated in idolatrous eating.

58 It is impractical here to enter into adiscussion of the significance of idolatry in the various forms of Judaism extant in Paul's time, or to establish the centrality of the avoidance of idolatry to the faith of many Jews, especially given the non-controversial character of this claim (see, for example, Menachem Stern, *Greek and Latin Authors on Jews and Judaism*, 2 vols. [Jerusalem: Israel Academy of Sciences and

his consciousness as a Jew, and the partnership with other Gods and Lords represented or threatened by idol-food was deeply unacceptable to Paul (and, not incidentally, to other Jewish Christians[59]). Paul was not troubled by abandoning circumcision as the mark of the covenant or by abandoning the requirement of *kashrut*,[60] but he would not abandon the covenantal demand set out in the Torah for exclusive allegiance to the one Lord.[61] He wanted his Gentile converts to express

---

Humanities, 1980], for evidence of the centrality of Jewish monotheism in the perception of Jews by outsiders). Peter Tomson provides a survey of Rabbinic *halakha* and other Jewish sources concerning avoidance of idolatry, concluding that the "prohibition of idolatry for Jews was axiomatic," and that Paul's *halakha* in 1 Cor 8-10 is rooted in this prohibition (*Paul and the Law*, p. 154). It must be noted, however, that Paul had other options as a Jew than unequivocal rejection of any intercourse with other Gods. A major focus of studies of Judaism in the Hellenistic and Greco-Roman periods is the extent to which Jewish groups were influenced by and accepting of the dominant Hellenistic culture, and many Jews did not feel bound by a vigilant and socially exclusive avoidance of connection with other Gods. See Victor Tcherikover, *Hellenistic Civilization and the Jews*, trans. S. Appelbaum (New York: Atheneum, 1959), and Martin Hengel, *Judaism and Hellenism. Studies in their Encounter in Palestine during the Early Hellenistic Period*, 2 vols., trans. John Bowden (London: SCM Press, 1974) [translated from *Judentum und Hellenismus*, Tübingen: J. C. B. Mohr, 1969]. That other Jews chose different responses than Paul reinforces my conclusion that Paul's insistence on the avoidance of idol-food stands close to his religious centre.

59 The clearest evidence of other Jewish Christians concerned with idolatry at the time of Paul is the Apostolic Decree. Hurd's thesis is that 1 Cor 8-10 is historically linked to the Decree, and represents Paul's attempt to recover from Corinthian criticism over his attempted imposition of the Decree. I address this thesis at length below in Appendix 1. I agree with Lake's assessment of Paul's views: "To abstain from idolatry in any form . . . was not a concession" on the part of Paul to those urging some aspects of the Law on Gentiles, but was a fundamental requirement of conversion (*Epistles*, p. 30-33, in a discussion concerning the Apostolic Decree).

60 *Kashrut* refers to the set of food purity requirements followed by many Jews, including—depending on which form of Judaism is in question—avoidance of types of food (for example, pork, shellfish), butchering that removes all blood, purity of vessels and utensils, and requirements of tithing. Because in the example of the cultus of Demeter and Kore a proscription of things offered to idols would often mean the proscription of pork, it might be tempting to suspect that forbidding idol-food was a way of keeping this important aspect of *kashrut*. Such a suspicion is not warranted by evidence of Paul's practice elsewhere (Rom 14; Gal 2). Further, animals other than pigs were sacrificed also to Demeter (Brumfield, *Attic Festivals*, p. 61: ewes and lambs were sacrificed in the Proerosia; see above in chap. 1 concerning votives of many different animals). Even more significantly, grains and fruits were offered to Demeter and eaten as sacred.

61 Compare 1 Thess 1:9: "what a welcome we had among you, and how you turned to God from idols, to serve a living and true God."

obedience to that demand through the careful avoidance of idolatrous rites, and hence, the avoidance of any food with even a tenuous link to idolatry. In short, Paul's objection to the Corinthian Christians' view of idol-food stems not from his concern over the consciousness of the weak but from his own consciousness and his own knowledge,[62] which in turn were conditioned by his Judaism.[63]

---

62 This runs counter to many scholarly conclusions that 1 Cor 8-10 shows one more instance of Paul's rejection of Torah. In general, questions of *kashrut* and questions of food connected to idolatry are not distinguished by scholars. For a typical example of this confusion, see Gordon J. Wenham, "The Theology of Unclean Food," *Evangelical Quarterly*, 53 (1981): 14. Leander Keck and E. P. Sanders are the only scholars of whom I am aware to put forward anything close to the view I argue here. Keck claims that idol-food was a Jewish problem imposed on a Gentile Christian community in Corinth. He concludes that Paul in no way radicalized the law; rather, Paul asked Gentiles to abandon polytheism and their participation in religious cults, and to adopt in their place "elements of an ethos deeply influenced by Judaism and the Scripture" ("Ethos and Ethics in the New Testament," in *Essays in Morality and Ethics*, ed. James Gaffney [New York: Paulist Press, 1980], p. 36). In this, I am in substantial agreement with Keck. Keck goes on, however, to affirm an older view that Paul mediates in some way between a strongly Jewish Christianity and the Gentile Christianity of his communities: "Corinthians regarded him as too conservative and the Jerusalem Christians as too radical" ("Ethos," p. 36). I find Keck's terms "conservative" and "radical" to be unhelpful and misleading, and I do not see Paul mediating here. In Sanders's arguments against the scholarly consensus over Paul's "abandonment" of the law, he claims that in 1 Cor 8 "Paul tries to bring even the prohibition against idolatry under the rubric 'love thy neighbour.' This was not entirely satisfactory, as his further argument in 1 Cor 10 shows. His handling of sexual practices and idolatry (including here 'food offered to idols') indicates both his deeply held Jewish convictions and his struggle to reformulate Jewish prohibitions in terms of Christian principles" (*Paul, the Law, and the Jewish people* [Philadelphia: Fortress Press, 1983], p. 103-104).

63 I do not mean to imply any distinction between Paul's "Christianity" and "Judaism." Such a distinction is anachronistic, and would not be recognized by Paul, or affirmed if it were postulated to him. The question of the relationship to Judaism and other Jews of Paul's discussion of idol-food has been a central feature of commentary on these chapters, though it must be stressed that other commentators reach different conclusions than mine. Paul makes explicit reference to Jews in 9:20 and in his summary at 10:32 (in my view, representing only an attempt to move to a very general level of discussion), but this leads to questions of whether Jews were parties to the dispute in Corinth, or indirect parties, in that Paul had to take the views of Jews elsewhere into account. I address such arguments below in Appendix 1.

8

What effect would Paul's proposed solution to the problem of idol-food have on the Corinthians?

Introduction

A properly objective social-historical reconstruction offers equal attention to all parties to the events of which evidence is provided. An historical investigation of the issue of idol-food in Paul's group in Corinth, then, should not stop with an account of Paul's position. It should be asked (1) what can be learned of the Corinthians' further response to Paul's response to them, (2) whether Paul changed his views concerning idol-food after 1 Corinthians, (3) what effect 1 Corinthians 8-10 had on other early Christian responses to the issue of idol-food, and (4) whether my analysis of 1 Corinthians 8-10 is of any value in understanding other early Christian responses.

My remaining chapters address the effects of Paul's advice on the Corinthians (chap. 8), the Corinthians' likely response to 1 Corinthians 8-10 (chap. 9), Paul's later views (chap. 10), and other early Christian responses to idol-food (chap. 11). Chap. 12 summarizes my conclusions and offers some "last words" reflecting on the significance of idol-food vis-à-vis the social meaning of early Christianity and the relationship between Christianity and Judaism in the first centuries of the common era.

Determining the effect on the Corinthians of Paul's proposed solutions to the problems he perceives involves two questions: first, what was the Corinthian response to Paul's solutions, and second, what would have been the effect of the solutions if they were carried out. In reality, of course, these cannot be separated: whether Paul's solutions were carried out depended on whether the Corinthians accepted them as solutions, and whether they accepted them as solutions depended on both the beliefs and attitudes of the Corinthians and on the probable social effect of those solutions. If Paul's solutions violated Corinthian beliefs and attitudes and if Paul's influence over the Corinthians was not strong enough, then his exhortations would not be carried out. If the social consequences of his solutions created only more serious problems, then again they would likely not be carried out.

This complex interplay of Corinthian attitude and social effect is not directly accessible to us. To attempt answers to the questions posed here is to move beyond the evidence of 1 Corinthians into speculation, but this speculation will be informed by some evidence from Paul's letters and evidence external to Paul's letters presented in chapters 1-3.

This speculation is begun with a pragmatic (and counter-factual) separation between a discussion of the likely effects of Paul's solutions if carried out, and a discussion of the likely Corinthian response to Paul's proposed solutions. In this chapter it is asked what effects a faithful attempt to carry out Paul's exhortation concerning idol-food might have had on Corinthian Christians. (The likely Corinthian response is addressed in chap. 9.) I have set out evidence above concerning the ubiquity and social importance of meals involving religious rites in the society of the Corinthian Christians, and on this basis I argue that the effects of abstinence from idol-food would be significant social restrictions. I am not alone in my earlier assessment of the social significance of religious meals. With Willis and other commentators,[1] I assert that refusing to consume food tainted in any way with religious rite would require (in Paul's words—1 Cor 5:10) "going out of the world."[2]

Determining the concrete social effects of avoiding idol-food demands analysis tied specifically to the evidence presented in chapters 1-3. What follows explores the social effects of not eating idol-food in the concrete contexts to which Paul refers: the marketplace, the table of *daimonia* and eating in temples and in the homes of others.

---

1 To question the concrete social effects of Paul's advice is by no means common or routine among scholars—yet another indication of their lack of interest in Paul's historical context. Several commentators do claim, however, that the effects of the avoidance of idol-food would be significantly restrictive: Willis, *Idol Meat*, p. 63; Ehrhardt, *Framework*, p. 280-82; Lake, *Epistles*, p. 149 (Avoidance would "certainly hinder social intercourse to an enormous extent"); Theissen, "Strong and the Weak," p. 125-32; and Weiss, *1 Kor*, p. 211-12. Hurd takes an independent and opposite view: Paul's advice to the Corinthians would have altered their behaviour minimally, if at all, since the situations in which he prohibits idol-food are hypothetical and counter-factual (*Origin*, p. 129, n. 2; p. 148).

2 Compare Willis, *Idol Meat*, p. 236.

Food at market

In the first place—first because least problematic—it is very likely that Paul's demands would have no effect on purchases at the market. There is no evidence that the Corinthians hesitated to buy food in the market because of its potential or known religious history (it seems that the Corinthian "question" behind 10:25 was a protest against avoidance of such food) and Paul's second letter (1 Cor) made no demand that they change their habits or restrict their behaviour in this context.[3]

The table of *daimonia*

Paul's instructions concerning the table of *daimonia* are as unequivocal as his instruction concerning the market, but opposite: the Corinthian Christians were in no way to participate in these meals.

The investigation of the cultus of Demeter and Kore (chap. 1) showed a clear instance of an active cult in Paul's Corinth, in which it was entirely likely that eating of the sort proscribed by Paul in 1 Corinthians was carried out on an extensive basis. The number of dining rooms and the popularity of the cult make it likely that Christians had opportunities to participate in such dinners. If they wished to follow Paul's instructions, they would have to decline invitations to such meals and accept whatever social repercussions flowed from such a refusal. The significance of such repercussions cannot be determined precisely,[4] but it is clear that Paul's prohibition of the table of *daimonia* would carry some restriction of the social intercourse of the Corinthians.

Eating in an idol's temple

With eating "in an idol's temple" (*en eidôleiôi*, 8:10), the problem arises—at least on the face of the text[5]—when a weak Christian learns of the practice. Would Corinthian Christians have eaten in temples without any consciousness that eating in such a context threatened their allegiance to their Lord? It might be argued that Christians—even Corinthian Christians—would not have been found "in an idol's temple": the hypothetical example is Paul's appeal to the most obvious and damaging instance of eating he can imagine, and, like the rest of Paul's hypothetical argument, may not reflect what is occurring in Corinth. If this is so, Paul's prohibition of eating in an idol's temple would not be felt a burden by the Corinthians nor alter their practice.

---

3 See Hurd's discussion (*Origin*, p. 148-49).

4 Chap. 3, concerning the social importance of meals, is relevant here in assessing the social consequences of not sharing meals.

5 I have argued above that 8:9-13 does not contain all of Paul's objection to eating in temples, nor its basis.

It has more often been argued that Corinthian Christians were eating in temples and that Paul's prohibition of it (in chapter 10 more than chapter 8) was an entirely appropriate Christian response to this abuse of spiritual power (*exousia*).

I am unhappy with both these arguments, for the same reason: they do not rest on a good understanding of the character of meals taken in temples—of their relationship to the cults of the temples, or of their social function in the wider context of Corinthian society. Without this understanding one cannot judge whether Christians were likely to have participated in some such meals, or whether they could have participated without compromising allegiance to their Christ, even in Paul's view.

It is not clear from 1 Corinthians 8:1-11:1 whether Paul assumed that meals "in an idol's temple" were equivalent to sharing the table of demons. This assumption must be questioned in a social-historical reconstruction. The dining rooms near the Asklepieion in Corinth and the cultus of Asklepios provide good evidence to suggest that such non-cultic or merely nominally cultic eating *was* possible "in an idol's temple."[6] It is entirely possible, then, that some Corinthian Christians did eat in what might be considered an idol's temple without any consciousness (at least until Paul's first letter had arrived) that they had compromised their faithfulness to Christ.

If Paul's instructions in chapter 8 concerning eating in a temple were taken at face value, it might be argued that its social effect on the Corinthians would be minimal. The only problem, on this view, would be whether a weak Christian saw the strong one eating at a temple, and this might not be a real problem: the improbability of the weak Christian's learning of the practice would be multiplied by the improbability of his very existence.[7]

6 The sanctuary of Demeter and Kore gives similar but less compelling evidence of the possibility of non-sacred meals eaten in a sanctuary. It is certain that meals sacred to the Goddess were eaten in this sanctuary during festivals, and thus idol-food could be eaten, which in Paul's view, established partnership with a *daimonion*. The sheer number of dining rooms found in the sanctuary, however, the evidence of their frequent use and their location on the least sacred terrace of the sanctuary all suggest at least the possibility that they served the purpose of meeting places for shared meals. These meals might include a nominal offering of thanksgiving to Demeter, the giver of the food, but—for a Corinthian Christian who wished to argue so—they might not be considered cultic meals. To make such a claim, however, would require more direct evidence than that of the number and location of the dining rooms. See above, chap. 1.

7 Hurd, *Origin*, p. 148-49.

Some difficulties, however, impede the ready acceptance of this conclusion. First, given the evidence of the many meals conducted in temples, it is less certain what eating "in an idol's temple" involved than this first view would suggest.[8] Further, in the light of 10:14-22 it is not clear that Paul conveys all that he intends in this example in chapter 8.

It was argued above that Paul's seeming acceptance of eating "in an idol's temple" (unless it affected the weak, of course) was due not to his conviction that such eating was acceptable but to his technique of persuasion. His true view is that sharing the table of *daimonia* breaks partnership with Christ. If the Corinthians understood that eating "in an idol's temple" was equivalent to sharing the table of demons, their course of action on Paul's advice would be clear: they would not eat in temples because it was wrong do so, and, as a happy side-effect, no weak Christians would fall.

Paul's second letter (1 Cor) would have posed two difficulties, then, to the Corinthians wishing to be obedient to him over the question of eating "in an idol's temple." First, they would now have to consider the weak, and second, they would have to consider whether eating "in an idol's temple" was partnership (*koinônia*) with *daimonia.*

First, what of the consideration of the weak? Paul's position concerning the weak and eating in temples is different from that found in 10:27-29—there someone had to raise the problem explicitly, but here someone may be destroyed by the simple awareness that idol-food was eaten in a temple. Paul's appeal concerning the weak, however, is hypothetical. If eating in temples carried any real benefit, it is unlikely that the Corinthians would have to alter their practice out of consideration for someone neither they nor Paul knew.

The second consideration—whether eating "in an idol's temple" constituted partnership with other Gods and other Lords—would carry much more weight for the Christian attempting to follow Paul's instructions faithfully. Such a person would link Paul's prohibitions in chapter 10 with his disapproval (on other grounds) of eating in temples, especially if such meals—as would be highly likely—carried religious rites. Where, before 1 Corinthians, a Corinthian Christian might have passed off such rites as nominal and insignificant, after 1 Corinthians 10, such a meal might well be seen as unacceptable participation at another God's table.

8 Murphy-O'Connor, in his assessment of the implications of the indeterminate religious character of the dining rooms of Lerna, suggests several situations that might give difficulty to the "weak" (*St. Paul's Corinth*, p. 164-65); see my discussion above in chap. 2. Recall also MacMullen's arguments that many communal meals took place in banqueting facilities in temples (*Paganism*, p. 34-42).

On the basis of evidence set out in chapters 1-3, it is certain that the consequences of avoiding meals in temples would be a perceptible restriction, and very likely an onerous restriction, on the social intercourse of the Christian.

Eating with non-believers: Invitations

Problems in assessing the social effects of Paul's position begin with the circumstances set out in 10:27-29—with invitations to eat with non-believers. To comply with Paul's advice, the Corinthians would have one of two choices: either they could take some risk that someone would point out food with a religious history and thus risk the consequent awkward, embarrassing and offensive refusal to eat, or they could avoid such risk and decline invitations to share food with anyone who might serve idol-food. Whether such a risk was substantial or remote would greatly affect the willingness of the Corinthian Christians to accept invitations, but the extent of this risk would itself be dependent on how Paul's exhortation was interpreted.

It is often argued that the "someone" Paul imagines pointing out the sacred character of the food (10:28) is a weak Christian.[9] This reading of 10:27-29 minimizes the ambiguity of the circumstances where Paul's prohibition would apply, and means that the scene I have just set would not result in a refusal to eat by the Corinthian Christian. In the first place it is entirely uncertain whether there *were* weak Christians in Corinth, and in the second place it is extremely unlikely that such weak Christians (if there were any) would be met at the house of a non-believer where idol-food was likely to be served, since those believing such food harmful would be unlikely to accept such an invitation. A Christian eating with non-believers would have no reason to expect another Christian to raise problems of consciousness. On this straightforward reading of 10:27-29, then, Paul's exhortation would have had no significant effect on the social interactions of the Corinthians.

A fundamental difficulty arises at this juncture, however, since Paul's letter does not allow this degree of certainty over the identity of the "someone."[10] Though Paul is not specific concerning this person's identity, his instruction is explicit: if anyone makes known that the

9 See chap. 7 for citations. It might still be argued that the *tis* of 10:28, while most likely in Paul's *view* a weak Christian, remains in Paul's *text* indeterminate, and this indeterminateness might lead to conscientious followers of Paul not eating in the scene I have sketched. See further, immediately below.

10 Commentators' continued disagreement over the identity of the one who calls attention to the sacred food in 10:28-29 is a good indication of the text's lack of specificity.

food served is sacred (*hierothyton*), then it must not be eaten for the sake of the one making it known and for his consciousness. The indeterminate "someone" might give rise to a serious uncertainty concerning the extent of the circumstances to which the prohibition applies. What if the host were to say as the meal was brought to table, "Ah! a fine pig offered today, a votive offered in thanks for my recent success! Come and enjoy!"—a direct and unequivocal statement that "This is sacred food." Would the Christian wishing to conform to Paul's position be required not to eat? My survey of Greco-Roman literary sources concerning the social uses of sacred food supports very strongly the conclusion that such occasions would occur. A Christian wishing to avoid any shared meal where there was an indication of the sacred history of the food, or the open use of food in rites before or during the meal, would have to decline all invitations but those from friends who knew of and respected his or her desire to avoid such food and/or rites.

Problems

A fundamental difficulty raised by 1 Corinthians for obedient Corinthians—a difficulty not noticed by any commentator of whom I am aware—is that the Corinthians might have difficulty determining the boundaries of practice acceptable to Paul.[11]

Paul is very clear that participatory consumption of a meal sacred to another God is idolatry and carries judgment. Paul is imprecise, however, concerning what constitutes participation in the cup and table of *daimonia*, and this might have led to genuine uncertainty among Corinthian Christians. Food with a sacred past was acceptable (if it were simply for sale in the market), but what of food with a sacred present? If the meal resembled strongly the Christians' Lord's meal (*kyriakon deipnon*)—if it was a conscious collective act of worship or thanksgiving or allegiance—then the obedient Corinthians could not participate. But some meals and some practices at meals bore a problematic resemblance to a Lord's meal. What of a meal "in an idol's temple" that was not celebratory of the God of the temple but was rather a simple meal shared with friends, with a merely token part of the menu offered to that God either by the Christian's friends or the

11 Commentators on 1 Cor 8-10 sometimes note the difficulties of uncovering the specific occasion or occasions Paul addresses in these chapters. See, for example, Willis's account of the exegetical possibilities and history of opinion over 10:27-28—over the identity of the host, the identity of the indeterminate person (*tis*) identifying the food as sacred, and the motivation of the players in the scene (Willis, *Idol Meat*, p. 240-43). They do not, however, discuss possible problems of interpretation the Corinthians themselves might have had.

cult officials? Such a meal would be much like that described in 10:27-29 (and thus permissible), with the difference that its consumption in a temple and the offering in the presence of the believer might make it the table of *daimonia* (and thus impermissible). What of a meal that began with a simple libation poured to the God, or even a simple prayer or thanksgiving to the God?

These meals would not fit clearly into the categories suggested by 1 Corinthians. They are not ritual meals expressing allegiance to the cult of the God, but neither are they simple consumption of food with a sacred past, since the meal has been sanctified by its context and by the rites, however nominal, performed during it. This uncertainty over the characteristics of a meal necessary to establish partnership with *daimonia* might lead to significant limits on the social intercourse of Corinthian Christians. Not only would obedient Christians have to shun the idolatry of eating "in an idol's temple" but they would have to shun also any meal tainted by even nominal rites similar to those I have suggested, wherever it was consumed.

The avoidance of idol-food in such common contexts would in turn impose significant and extensive limitations on the social behaviour of Christians. As Paul recognizes, the Corinthians could not leave the world in order to avoid sexual immorality (5:10), but they could not employ prostitutes and were required (if unable to restrain themselves) to keep to one spouse (6:15-7:40); just so, they could not avoid contact with idolaters, but were required to share no idolatrous table with them. To avoid even nominally tainted meals would require an awkward and uncomfortable distance not from strangers (such as prostitutes) but from family, friends and associates.

This conclusion rests, of course, on the condition that obedient Christians would adopt a broad interpretation of "sharing the table of demons," that would exclude participation in these ambiguous meals. The broader the interpretation of this demand, the more restrictive its social effect on Christians. How likely is it that Paul's demand would be understood in this broad sense?

There are two distinct ways to approach this question. First, how strictly would Paul himself apply the demand not to share table with *daimonia*? Second, what was the likely understanding of this demand by a Christian wishing to be obedient to Paul? (How the Corinthians actually responded is explored in chap. 9.)

Nothing in 1 Corinthians 8:1-11:1 gives clear evidence of how Paul would understand participation in meals of ambiguous religious character. On the one hand, Paul says in 9:22, "I have become all things to all"—to Jews, to those under the law, to the lawless, to the weak—"in order to save, by all ways, some." Paul identifies himself as apostle to Gentiles. He has "won" Gentiles, and has lived among them. Because of this, and because the Corinthian Christians are surprised at his demands to shun idolaters in his previous letter, it has been argued that Paul has shown no scruple at eating idol-food. On the other hand, Paul urges a distinctly different view on the Corinthians concerning the reality and potential harm of *daimonia*, and even if Paul has attempted to save all in all ways (9:22), he has remained not lawless toward God and within the law of Christ (9:21).

Any application of Paul's rhetoric in 9:19-23 to his practice in concrete social situations is doubtful simply because he is vague. It is not at all clear what being "under the law" or "lawless" or "not without the law of God" or "within the law of Christ" or "weak" might mean in concrete terms. Paul's rhetoric has dragged him along again (still on the leash of his point—that Paul has renounced his own freedom for the good of his brothers), but even if that rhetoric reveals much of Paul's willingness to accommodate the expectations of others (compare 10:31-11:1), it cannot be taken as a description of his missionary practice in concrete social terms.

Paul might well have preached to Gentiles, and won them, and eaten with them, without ever sharing a meal of ambiguous religious character. To proclaim is not to share a table; to eat food from the market is not to eat food of which a portion is offered to another God at the meal; to eat with Gentile brothers is not necessarily to eat in their non-believing households. I find nothing in 1 Corinthians 8:1-11:1 to support the probability that Paul participated in any meal that could be construed on a broad interpretation to be the table of other Gods.[12] On the contrary, since Paul urges the Corinthians to beware of participation in the table of *daimonia*, and since the eating of which he approves explicitly does *not* include meals of the ambiguous character under discussion, I suspect that Paul would not participate in meals of even a marginally religious character.

Paul himself would hold a broad interpretation of the demand to shun the table of *daimonia*. This runs perhaps against a common perception of Paul—Paul the strong to the strong, Paul the destroyer of godless superstition, Paul the liberator from the external restraints of law—but, none the less, it is the conclusion supported by the evidence.

The obedient Corinthian Christian would also adopt an interpretation of Paul's demand to avoid the table of *daimonia* that prohibited participation in ambiguous cases. A narrower interpretation could be

---

12 The remainder of Paul's letters must also be taken as evidence of his practice of eating among Gentiles. Nothing in the remainder of the Pauline corpus can support the claim that Paul would have participated in meals where offerings or libations or thanksgivings to other Gods were carried out.

reached, but my hypothetical Christian here wishes to be obedient to Paul. Paul has urged that a Christian should not eat if someone indicates the sacred history of the food, and he has pointed to the serious potential harm of eating "in an idol's temple." These exhortations, together with his elaborate warning against contagion from idolatry, would dispose such a Christian to avoid any possible participation in the table of *daimonia*.

Conclusions

The effect of Paul's proposed solution to the problem of idol-food would be felt strongly by Corinthian Christians. They would have no difficulty in obtaining food for their own use. But they would experience difficulty in accepting invitations from non-believers, since they would have to know beforehand the character of the meal—not so much because of the consciousness of a hypothetical "someone" over the food on the menu, but because of their own consciousness of participation at the table of *daimonia*. If a meal was accompanied by any rite sacred to another God, whether that meal was in a temple, at the homes of friends or relatives, or in their own households, obedient Christians would refuse to eat.

This conclusion supports a significant corollary. If there were no weak Christians in Corinth when Paul wrote 1 Corinthians, then there were weak Christians in Corinth after 1 Corinthians had been received—weak not because of intimacy with idols, but because of an anxious eagerness not to violate partnership with their Lord. That Paul's arguments tend to create the weak for whose benefit he writes is further evidence that Paul intends not to protect the interests of the weak and allow maximum freedom to the strong but rather to protect the strong—the Corinthian Christians—from what he believes to be the dangerous contagion of idolatry.

9

What was the Corinthian response to Paul's proposed solution to the problem of idol-food?

With this chapter we come to the final stage of the exchange between Paul and the Christians in Corinth over the issue of idol-food. Now that Paul has had his say, it can be asked how the Corinthians might have responded to 1 Corinthians. Regrettably, there is no direct evidence of the Corinthian response, so any reconstruction of it must remain consciously speculative. Some evidence controls this speculation. Traces of the attitudes and beliefs of the Corinthians before they received Paul's second letter (1 Cor) can be recovered from the fragments of their letter to Paul in 1 Corinthians. Also, Paul's extant later letters to Corinth (2 Cor) give glimpses of the relationship between Paul and the group in Corinth after 1 Corinthians had been received.[1] This evidence is not extensive or straightforward, but it will support some conclusions concerning the likely response of the Corinthians.

1 There is one other possible source of evidence concerning the Corinthian response to Paul's position: Rom 14:1-15:13, where Paul addresses differences over food. Paul wrote to the Romans some time after 1 Cor, so it could be argued that Romans will likely reveal his experience and reflection since the writing of 1 Cor, and thus reflect indirectly the reaction of the Corinthians to his earlier approach to the issue. This evidence is highly problematic: (1) the sequence of the letter fragments in 2 Cor and the letter to Rome is uncertain, so it is unclear whether an eruption of Corinthian discontent over Paul's position (if such occurred) was known to Paul before he wrote the group(s) in Rome; (2) it is not certain that even if Paul knew the Corinthians had rejected his position he would alter it; and (3) this section in Romans addresses a significantly different problem than that of food offered to idols (I will argue this fully below). Rom 14:1-15:13 cannot be read, then, as evidence of the Corinthians' response to Paul's position or as as a refinement of Paul's thinking about idol-food.

Corinthian attitudes and beliefs in 1 Corinthians

Earlier it was concluded that 1 Corinthians 6:12; 8:1,4,8,10 (perhaps); and 10:23 contain quotations or allusions to the Corinthians' letter to Paul. It was also concluded that at every point Paul had demanded serious alterations of the Corinthian position concerning idol-food: there *are* other Gods; eating idol-food *can* make us lacking before God; all things are *not* permissible. Paul's disagreement is carefully presented as agreement augmented by new considerations, but it may be assumed that the Corinthian Christians were as little fooled as we.

Consequently, the Corinthians would not be entirely pleased with Paul's response. They are already annoyed with Paul over what they see as unreasonable restrictions. Because Paul contradicts their claims and the position Paul urges in 1 Corinthians would result in similar (softened, perhaps, but still significant) restrictions, it is most likely that the Corinthians responded negatively to Paul's response.

The evidence of 2 Corinthians

This likelihood is strengthened by the evidence of Paul's later letters to the Corinthians collected under the canonical title of "Paul's Second Letter to the Corinthians."[2] Whether or not disagreements over idol-food played any significant role between Paul and the Corinthians, 2 Corinthians shows that after 1 Corinthians the Corinthians alternated between strained obedience and overt hostility to Paul, and that Paul never gained complete confidence in their obedience or affection.

The hostility and ugly charges behind 2 Corinthians 10-13 are obvious. It is sometimes claimed, however, that 2 Corinthians 1:1-2:13/7:5-16 is a letter (broken by the redactional interpolation of 2:14-7:4) which shows Paul's confidence restored and the Corinthians' obedience complete.[3]

I find this view unpersuasive. The section of the letter from 2:14-7:4 is not an interpolation into its context,[4] so 1:1-7:16 must be

---

2 The strong likelihood that 2 Cor is a redacted collection of letters has led to extensive debate over alternative reconstructions. Formative arguments may be found in Weiss, *The History of Primitive Christianity* (New York: Wilson-Erickson, Inc., 1937), p. 348-54; Schmithals, *Gnosticism*, p. 96-110; G. Bornkamm, "The History of the Origin of the So-called Second Letter to the Corinthians," *New Testament Studies*, 8 (1961-62): 180-86; D. Georgi, "Corinthians, Paul's Second Letter to the," *Interpreter's Dictionary of the Bible*, Supplementary Volume (Nashville: Abingdon Press, 1976), p. 183-84; and R. A. Batey, "Paul's Interaction with the Corinthians," *Journal of Biblical Literature*, 84 (1965): 139-46.

3 Schmithals, *Gnosticism*, p. 99.

4 2 Cor 2:14 anticipates the joyful news of Titus, returned to in 7:5; the use of the terms "confidence" and "comfort" in 7:4 leads clearly into Paul's point in 7:5-16 (see especially vv.6,7,13,16).

read as one letter.[5] The surface tone of this letter is indeed a relieved affirmation of the obedience of the Corinthian Christians. There remains a strong undertone, however, of defensiveness[6] and appeal,[7] which only underlines Paul's relief at the Corinthians' response to his visit and harsh letter testing their obedience.[8] Paul's too often repeated and too effusive affirmations of the Corinthians' obedience[9] also function as an appeal to them, and underline Paul's relief and the depth of his uncertainty. Even if Paul's rejoicing over his reconciliation with the Corinthians is taken as the central message of 2 Corinthians 1-7 (and not, though I think it more likely to be the central message, his appeal to them[10]), still it is clear that this reconciliation follows a serious conflict and remains fragile. Neither 2 Corinthians 10-13 nor 2 Corinthians 1-7, then, is witness to an unproblematic and amiable acceptance of Paul among the Corinthian Christians after the writing of 1 Corinthians.[11]

There is no direct evidence, however, that tensions between Paul and the Corinthians after 1 Corinthians involved the problem of idol-food. The concrete occasion(s) of the difficulties were known to both Paul and the Corinthians but remain opaque to us—a frustration common to all eavesdroppers—but seem to have centred on challenges to Paul himself. The issue in 2 Corinthians 10-13 is Paul's effectiveness and authority over the group,[12] and even his integrity.[13] This personal

---

5 I leave aside the problems of 2 Cor 6:14-7:1 and 2 Cor 8 and 9.

6 In, for example, 2 Cor 1:12-14,17; 1:23-2:9; 2:17-3:1; 4:2-5; 5:11-12; 6:3,8-10; 7:8.

7 For example, 2 Cor 1:12-14; 5:20-7:4 (excluding 6:14-7:1) begins with an appeal to be reconciled to God but is entirely an appeal to be reconciled to Paul.

8 2 Cor 2:3,4,9; 7:8,12. This harsh letter is certainly not 1 Cor, because it does not meet Paul's description of the letter in question, and because this identification does not fit a reconstruction of Paul's visits to Corinth. 2 Cor 10-13 does meet the description of the harsh letter, and is often identified as such. I conclude on the basis of 2 Cor 12:16-18 that 2 Cor 10-13 follows 2 Cor 1-9, but the issue of the place of 2 Cor 10-13 is not important for my present purpose.

9 2 Cor 7:4,7,11,14-16.

10 The defensive tone of this section was perceived by Weiss, and afforded sufficient weight by him that he hypothesized that 2:14-chapter 7 was part of the severe letter referred to in 2 Cor 2:4 (*Primitive Christianity*, p. 348).

11 This conclusion is shared by R. A. Batey: "The Church in Corinth was left by Paul in division and rebellion" ("Paul's Interaction," p. 145). Batey also concludes that 2 Cor 10-13 comes last in the extant correspondence of Paul to the Corinthians.

12 See especially 2 Cor 10:10,14-15 and 11:1-12:13.

13 2 Cor 12:16.

attack is echoed also in 2 Corinthians 1-7.[14] There is little indication, however, of what concrete problems or disagreements gave rise to these challenges to Paul,[15] and there is not even a hint in 2 Corinthians that Paul and the Corinthians continue to disagree over questions of idolatry or idolatrous eating.

None the less, some tantalizing associations between Paul's language in 2 Corinthians and the issue of idol-food in 1 Corinthians 8:1-11:1 may be drawn. Three times in 2 Corinthians 1-7 Paul uses the term *syneidêsis* ("consciousness"), and each time as part of a polemical self-commendation (1:12; 4:2; 5:11). He also refers polemically to not putting obstacles in anyone's way (6:3). He reminds the Corinthians that his power (*exousia*)—unlike that of the false apostles—was given him by his Lord for building up (*eis oikodomên*) and not for destroying (10:8; 13:10). He also protests that he does not restrict the Corinthians (6:12) or "lord it over their faith" (1:24 RSV). Given the likely Corinthian objections to 1 Corinthians 8:1-11:1, these passages take on significant colouring. These passages, however, might be accounted for without any reference to 1 Corinthians 8:1-11:1, so the connections with Paul's stance concerning idol-food remain only tantalizing possibilities.

Less easy to dismiss, however, is Paul's constant ironic reference to his weakness in 2 Corinthians 10-13. The weakness with which Paul has been charged—("His letters are . . . strong but his presence in the flesh is weak" 10:10)—seems at first unconnected with the sort of weakness at issue in 1 Corinthians 8:1-11:1, but a more thorough exploration of 2 Corinthians 10-13 shows that the charge is more complex than ineffective physical presence. Paul's discourse too is rejected with contempt (10:10). Since Paul himself associates discourse with knowledge (*gnôsis*, 11:6) and ironically stoops to foolishness

---

14 2 Cor 2:1-10; 3:1; 4:2; 5:12; 6:3-10; 7:2.

15 The immediate problem behind 2 Cor 10-13 was an incursion of "false apostles" (10:13-16; 11:4), but problems between Paul and the Corinthians may be suspected. First, the Corinthians were clearly receptive to these other "servants of Christ." They have qualities which attract the Corinthians: they exercise their *exousia* (11:20); they are proud of their speech and authoritative presence (10:10); where Paul is weak, they are strong (10:10; 11:21; 12:10). The Corinthians have preferred these apostles over Paul, and the Corinthians found Paul "not what [they] wished" (12:20). Second, Paul attacks not only the other apostles but the Corinthians. He aims his biting irony at the Corinthians (11:19; 12:13); he might no longer approve of them (12:20). Second Cor 1-7 also reinforces this conclusion: the pain of the visit and letter has passed between Paul and a member of the Corinthian community (2:1-11) and it is to the Corinthians that Paul's appeal for reconciliation is directed (5:20-7:4).

(11:16,19,21; 12:11), Paul's knowledge or ability to make sense of things has been attacked also. Paul is constrained to boast of his ecstatic visions (12:1-6) and his "signs and wonders and mighty works" (12:12), and accounts for the weakness of his body as a Satan-sent and Lord-approved check on his elation (12:7-10). Finally, Paul is attacked because he did not demand that the Corinthian group provide money or goods for his needs (11:7-11; 12:13,16), and this too is connected to his weakness, both by association with other charges and by 11:20-21: "You endure it if someone . . . eats you up [*katesthiei*], if someone takes possession of you. . . . In disgrace I say that we were weak."[16]

Paul's weaknesses are polemical reflections of Corinthian strengths. The Corinthians have knowledge and pride themselves on their spiritual "power" (*exousia*) both in speech and deed; they have welcomed other apostles who excel in these. This knowledge and power grounds the Corinthian attitude toward idol-food, which Paul challenges with his appeal to the interests of the weak. Paul rejects the knowledge of the Corinthians and urges a weakening of their *exousia* so that they do not become infected with idolatry. Paul's aggressive celebration of his weaknesses in 10-13 may well reflect, therefore, a Corinthian charge that Paul himself is weak like those Christians he describes whose consciousness is polluted by lifeless images and hollow rites.

It is very likely, then, that the Corinthians turned Paul's arguments about idol-food against him. Paul lacked knowledge and abrogated their rightful *exousia*, and as a result they charged Paul himself with weakness and welcomed other apostles more confident of their strength.[17]

This reconstruction from 2 Corinthians must remain speculative, because there is no explicit reference in 2 Corinthians to idolatry or idol-food. It is hazardous to deduce concrete occasions from associated concepts. None the less, the evidence of 2 Corinthians provides an intriguing glimpse of the possible developments, otherwise inaccessible to us, between the writing of 1 Corinthians and the letters collected in 2 Corinthians.

---

16 The connections between Paul's weakness and money are stressed by Ronald Hock (*The Social Context of Paul's Ministry: Tentmaking and Apostleship* [Philadelphia: Fortress Press, 1980], p. 59-60). Hock argues that Paul's weakness of 1 Cor 4 and 2 Corinthians derives from the appropriation of a Socratic-Cynic *topos*, in which the true philosopher is contrasted with the privileged and powerful Sophists, or false philosophers. Paul's weakness derives in part from his plying of a trade, without power, pride or privilege.

17 The link between the weak of 1 Cor 8-10 and the Corinthians' charge of weakness reflected in 2 Cor is not postulated by any other commentator of whom I am aware. Victor Furnish does not cite any such hypothesis (*2 Corinthians*, Anchor Bible, vol. 32A [Garden City, NJ: Doubleday, 1984], p. 476-78).

Conclusions

The attitudes and beliefs of the Corinthian Christians revealed in their letter to Paul and the suggestive association of issues between 1 Corinthians 8:1-11:1 and 2 Corinthians make it very likely that the Corinthians found Paul's response to their first objections equally objectionable. There is no evidence of whether or not the Corinthian objections were motivated by the undesirable restrictive social effects of Paul's position. Rather, the slim data would suggest that the conflict was cast in terms of spiritual *exousia* and Christian knowledge. This reconstruction of the Corinthian response to 1 Corinthians 8:1-11:1 is based on inference carefully controlled by indirect evidence, so the reconstruction of the Corinthian response stands on a less secure footing than the reconstruction either of the origin of the problem of idol-food or Paul's position concerning idol-food.

10

Paul's position after 1 Corinthians

Paul's subsequent letters to the Corinthian Christians do not give us any indication of whether Paul's views changed concerning the use of idol-food or the avoidance of situations where it was served, but this does not exhaust the possible evidence concerning this question. Paul's other extant letters might reveal something of relevance to this question, especially Paul's advice to the Romans over differences in convictions over food in Romans 14-15. Galatians, too, makes references to disputes over eating, so it might be—depending on one's view of the placing of Galatians in the sequence of Paul's letters—further evidence of Paul's position concerning idol-food.

Romans

Following Paul's sweeping vision in Romans 9-11 of the role of the Gentiles in the salvation of all God's people and his own apocalyptic role in that salvation drama (11:13-15), Paul turns to a series of paraenetic instructions. Included in these are instructions concerning food and abstinence from food (Rom 14:1-15:6).

The passage in Romans shows some clear links to Paul's discussion of food offered to idols in 1 Corinthians. Prime among these is the designation of Christians who eat certain foods as strong and those who refrain as weak (14:1; 15:2). Equally significant is the theme of Paul's advice: the strong ought to refrain from making food the cause of their brothers' falling, and ought to have their behaviour governed by love (14:13-21). There is a significant overlap in vocabulary: note *skandalon* (14:13), *oikodomên* (15:2), and the description of the harmed brother as one for whom Christ died (14:15).

These links have drawn the attention of several scholars, and it is common to find in discussions of 1 Corinthians 8-10 allusions to this section in Romans. It is also common to find no critical or sustained comparison of the passages in the two letters. Rather, it is assumed or suggested that this passage in Romans is further evidence that (1) Paul agreed with the Christian strong, and (2) urged the primacy of love over knowledge.[1]

These links between Romans and 1 Corinthians at first sight undermine my claims that Paul's appeal to protection of the weak in 1 Corinthians was at best only one element of his persuasive tactics and that his central concern was to warn against idolatry. My conclusions are difficult to reconcile with the explicit and sustained focus of Romans 14-15 on the theme of accommodation of the weak. More significantly, Paul explicitly identifies himself as among the strong in Romans—"We who are strong[2] ought to bear with the weaknesses of those not strong" (15:1)—and makes a clear and sustained distinction between food, which is harmless, and the impact of eating on others, which can be dangerous. Concerning eating per se, Paul makes explicit that neither the views of the strong nor of the weak were superior to the other:

> Let not him who eats despise him who abstains, and let not him who abstains pass judgment on him who eats (14:3). . . . He also who eats, eats in honour of the Lord, since he gives thanks to God; while he who abstains, abstains in honour of the Lord and gives thanks to God (14:6). . . . The faith that you have, keep between yourself and God; happy is he who has no reason to judge himself for what he approves (14:22).

In Romans Paul has no concern whatever with the food itself or any danger inherent in it; the sole danger lies in causing a brother to stumble or fall. This attitude contrasts sharply with Paul's serious warnings in 1 Corinthians 8 and 10, where, along with his call to heed dangers to others, Paul warns explicitly of dangers to the strong themselves (10:1-22).

Romans 14-15, then, presents at first reading either a serious challenge to my earlier reading of 1 Corinthians 8-10 or a clear indication that Paul's views concerning the dangers of eating changed between

---

1 Robert Karris provides an extensive analysis and concludes that Romans "repeats, rephrases and echoes" the arguments of 1 Cor 8-10 and that Romans is a "theoretical development of the thoroughly actual treatment" of 1 Cor ("Rom 14:1-15:13 and the Occasion of Romans," *Catholic Biblical Quarterly*, 35 [1973]: 163-69). See also Horsley, "Consciousness," p. 588; Weiss, *1 Kor*, p. 230; R. Bultmann, *Primitive Christianity in its Contemporary Setting*, trans. R. H. Fuller (New York: New American Library, 1956), p. 206; Klauck, *Herrenmahl*, p. 281-83; Robertson and Plummer, *1 Cor*, p. 194; and Wenham, "Theology of Unclean Food," p. 14.

2 Paul's inclusion in the strong is reinforced by the syntax of the sentence: *opheilomen de hêmeis hoi dynatoi* (Rom 15:1). Paul's self-identification as among the strong is given an interesting twist when compared to 2 Cor 10-13, especially if my hunch is correct that the Corinthians accused Paul of being weak over idol-food.

1 Corinthians 8-10 and Romans 14-15. A close reading of Romans 14-15, however, will reveal telling differences between it and 1 Corinthians 8-10, sufficiently telling differences that it must be concluded that the similarities between the passages lie only on the surface.

The central difference is that Romans 14-15 does not anywhere address idol-food.[3] The matters under contention by the strong and weak[4] are whether to eat meat or only vegetables (14:2) or to regard certain days as of special status (14:5). It might be argued that these matters do concern idol-food or idolatrous rites—the weak might abstain from meat because it had possibilities of idolatrous taint—but the development of the issues in the passage shows clearly that Paul here addresses not idol-food but *kashrut*. This is shown by (1) the repeated references to the vocabulary of purity, and (2) Paul's even-handedness over the motivations of both strong and weak.

In Romans 14 the issue over food concerns not the context in which it is eaten, nor its sacred history, but whether it is ritually pure: "I know and am persuaded in the Lord Jesus that nothing is unclean (*koinon*) in itself (14:14). . . . Everything is indeed clean" (*panta men kathara*, 14:20). This vocabulary falls naturally and uncontroversially into the arena of disputes over whether the laws of *kashrut* were still valid,[5] and would not be connected, but for 1 Corinthians 8-10, with the problem of food offered to idols.[6]

This conclusion is reinforced by Paul's even-handedness over the views of the strong and the weak. Even if Paul saw no harm in participation in a meal where rites sacred to other Gods occurred, it is not credible that he would call such eating "in honour of the Lord" (Rom 14:6), and not likely that he would find such participation to be of

---

3 It is surprising that some scholars never notice this basic fact, even when comparing directly Rom 14-15 with 1 Cor 8-10. Karris, for example, does not comment on the lack of reference to idol-food ("Rom 14:1-15:13").

4 More accurately, the matters Paul presumes to be under contention. Whether Paul had specific information concerning a dispute over food among Christians in Rome is uncertain and the subject of debate. See Karris for an analysis of the issues; he concludes that it is wrong to read a specific occasion into Paul's general paraenesis in Romans ("Rom 14:1-15:13," p. 161), and that the strong and the weak are not ethnic communities but individuals (p. 172).

5 Compare the identical vocabulary in the account of Peter's vision of the animals descending in a sheet, and his instructions to eat them (Acts 10:13-15). Here the context makes explicit that the issue is ritual purity and not idolatry.

6 Note too that the other (putative) dispute in Rom 14 concerns not food but days which are esteemed or not (14:5-6). The most persuasive reading of this is that it refers to the Sabbath ("He who observes the day observes in honour of the Lord" vs. 6), and this in turn reinforces the conclusion that the issue over food in these chapters is the continued observance of the law over ritual purity of food.

exactly the same religious validity as abstinence from such. Paul's careful even-handedness in Romans concerning the religious meaning of both eating and abstinence, then, is also evidence that here Paul addresses not the issue of idol-food but *kashrut*.[7]

Galatians

Galatians is the only other extant letter of Paul to address issues of food explicitly. Is it possible that it too might provide some evidence of Paul's position concerning idol-food after the writing of 1 Corinthians?[8]

Concrete details over the nature of the conflict alluded to in Galatians 2:11-14 are thin in the extreme. Paul indicates only that Cephas ate with Gentiles until persons from James came (2:12), and that Paul confronted Cephas with the argument that Cephas, a Jew, lived like a Gentile so he should not compel Gentiles to live like Jews (2:14). These details are not enough evidence on which to reconstruct the contexts or menus of the eating in dispute.

The context of the passage supports the hypothesis that here Paul, and presumably Cephas, were concerned not with idol-food but with *kashrut*. The central theme of Paul's complaint in Galatians is that Gen-

---

7 Compare von Soden: "here [in Rom 14-15] the viewpoint of idolatry is not even considered; it is a question rather of ritualistic asceticism" ("Sakrament," Meeks's translation, p. 265). Barrett notes that "there is no definite indication in Rom 14;15 that . . . idolatry is in mind" but adds that there is also no definite indication that Paul is concerned with Judaism ("Things Sacrificed," p. 42). Tomson concludes that "Paul's plea appears to have been for willingness on the part of Gentile Christians to make allowances for basic Jewish food laws" such as the forbidding of unclean animals, meat improperly slaughtered or meat prepared with milk (*Paul and the Jewish Law*, p. 244). Other scholars note the lack of reference to idol-food in Romans 14-15, but maintain, in varying degrees of tentativeness, a connection with 1 Cor 8-10: Kirsopp Lake, *Epistles*, p. 382; Paul Gooch, "Burden," p. 111-12. Early Christians made an explicit contrast between *kashrut* and idolatry like that I postulate for Paul: see *Didache* 6.3; Novatian, *On Jewish Meats* 7; and Origen, *Contra Celsum*, 8.29-30 (see below in chap. 11).

8 The place of Galatians in the sequence of Paul's letters is notoriously difficult, primarily because it cannot be adequately placed in the sequence of Paul's collection tour around Asia Minor and Achaia. Whether Galatians was written before or after 1 Cor is not necessary to determine in this context, since, as I will argue, Galatians provides no additional evidence for the questions which are addressed here. For discussions of chronology see Hurd, *Origin*, p. 12-41; Gerd Luedemann, *Paul, Apostle to the Gentiles: Studies in Chronology*, trans. F. S. Jones (Philadelphia: Fortress Press, 1984); and Robert Jewett, *A Chronology of Paul's Life* (Philadelphia: Fortress Press, 1979). Luedemann stands in the alternative tradition Hurd carries from John Knox; Jewett exemplifies the more conventional (and seriously flawed) approach.

tile Christians were not bound by the law's demands over circumcision and, presumably, not bound by the law's dietary restrictions. The issue that Paul disputed with Cephas—eating with Gentiles—more likely concerned *kashrut* than idol-food, because for Paul even those bound under the Spirit and not under the law could not be found in idolatry: "the works of the flesh are plain: fornication, impurity, licentiousness, idolatry. . . . I warn you, as I warned you before, that those who do such things shall not inherit the kingdom of God" (Gal 5:19; 5:21).

There is no specific evidence in Galatians either to support or to undermine my reading of 1 Corinthians 8-10, or to indicate any change of Paul's position concerning food offered to idols.

Conclusions

Neither Romans nor Galatians offers any evidence of whether Paul's views concerning idol-food changed after the writing of 1 Corinthians. These letters also do not provide any additional evidence concerning the motivation of Paul's position in 1 Cor 8-10, or help to determine the central convictions out of which his position grew.

11

Other early Christian practice concerning idol-food

How did other early Christians deal with the matter of food offered to idols? It is a relief that, after the tenuous evidence adduced concerning the Corinthians' response to Paul's advice concerning idol-food, the evidence concerning other early Christian views is anything but tenuous: the extant voices of other Christians in the first three centuries are virtually unanimous in their condemnation of the eating of idol-food.[1] Indications from outside the Christian community confirm the abstinence of Christians from food which had been sacrificed.

Sources

Early Christians within the institutional developments which survived as Christianity rejected any consumption of idol-food. The evidence supporting this claim is so straightforward that little more than a list is needed to establish this conclusion.[2]

1 The exceptions are echoes of Christian Gnostics found in polemics against them by the Fathers, or other groups outside what became orthodoxy. Both Irenaeus and Justin indicate clearly that Christians outside their communities (Marcionites, Valentinians, Basilidians) ate idol-food openly: see Irenaeus, *Against Heresies*, in *The Ante-Nicene Fathers*, vol. 1, *The Apostolic Fathers-Justin Martyr-Irenaeus*, ed. A. Roberts and J. Donaldson (Edinburgh: T. & T. Clark, 1885), 1.6, and especially Justin, *Dialogue with Trypho*, in ibid., vol. 2, 35. Justin spares no invective towards these, whom he calls ravening wolves in sheep's clothing.

2 The sources which follow have been noted, and sometimes discussed, by Barrett ("Things Sacrificed"), Ehrhardt (*Framework*), and Brunt ("Ignored"). Their conclusions over the significance of these references are noted below.

New Testament references to idol-food

The three versions of the Apostolic Decree setting out the limits of the law on Gentile Christians in Acts 15 and 21 are the most often discussed evidence in commentary on 1 Corinthians. In the first version of the Decree abstinence from idol-food is implicit, and in the second and third versions, explicit:

> to abstain from the pollutions of idols and from unchastity and from what is strangled and from blood (Acts 15:20).
>
> that you abstain from what has been sacrificed to idols [*eidôlothytôn*] and from blood and from what is strangled and from unchastity. If you keep yourselves from these, you will do well (Acts 15:29).
>
> They should abstain from what has been sacrificed to idols [*eidôlothytôn*] and from blood and from what is strangled and from unchastity (Acts 21:25).

Other evidence in the New Testament is less often noted, but equally significant: Revelation 2:14, to the church in Pergamum:

> But I have a few things against you: you have some there who hold the teaching of Balaam,[3] who taught Balak to put a stumbling block before the sons of Israel, that they might eat food sacrificed to idols and practise immorality [*phagein eidôlothuta kai porneusai*].

Revelation 2:19-20, to the church in Thyatira:

> I know your works, your love and your patient endurance, and that your latter works exceed your first. But I have this against you, that you tolerate the woman Jezebel, who calls herself a prophetess and is teaching and beguiling my servants to practise immorality and to eat food sacrificed to idols.

Non-canonical references to idol-food

Non-canonical evidence is as follows:

Didache:[4]

> For if you can bear the whole yoke of the Lord, you will be perfect, but if you cannot, do what you can. And concerning food, bear what you can, but keep strictly from food which is offered to idols, for it is the worship of dead gods.

---

3 On the basis of this reference, Barrett develops an argument also linking Rev 2:14, Jude 11, and 2 Pet 2:15 to the forbidden consumption of idol-food ("Things Sacrificed," p. 41-42).

4 *Didache* 6.3, trans. Kirsopp Lake, in *The Apostolic Fathers*, vol. 1, Loeb Classical Library, 1912, p. 318-19. This source's clear distinction between *kashrut* and abstention from idol-food is notable, especially since the former is presented as desirable but not essential and the latter as unequivocally prohibited.

Justin, *Dialogue with Trypho*:[5]

> Those of the Gentiles who know God, the Maker of all things through Jesus the crucified . . . abide every torture and vengeance even to the extremity of death, rather than worship idols, or eat meat offered to idols.

Irenaeus, *Against Heresies*:[6]

> The "most perfect" among them addict themselves without fear to all those kinds of forbidden deeds of which the Scriptures assure us that "they who do such things shall not inherit the kingdom of God." For instance, they make no scruple about eating meats offered in sacrifice to idols, imagining that they can in this way attract no defilement. Then, again, at every heathen festival celebrated in honour of the idols, these men are the first to assemble.[7]

Clement of Alexandria quotes 1 Corinthians 10:25 and affirms that food can be bought in the marketplace[8]

> with the exception of things mentioned in the Catholic epistle of all the apostles . . . which is written in the Acts of the Apostles, and conveyed to the faithful by the hands of Paul himself. For they intimated "that they must of necessity abstain from things offered to idols, and from blood, and from things strangled."

Novatian, in *On Jewish meats*, argues on allegorical and typological grounds that the Jewish laws of purity are superseded, and that Chris-

---

5 *Dialogue with Trypho* 34, in *Corpus apologetarum Christianorum saeculi secundi*, vol. 2, *Justini philosophi et marturis. Opera quae feruntur omnia*, t. 1, pt. 2, *Opera indubitata. Dialogus cum Tryphone Iudaeo*, ed. Johannes C. T. Otto (Wiesbaden: Sändig, 1969 [first published 1877]), p. 116; translation from *The Ante-Nicene Fathers*, 1:212.

6 *Against Heresies* 1.6.3, in *Sancti Irenaei. Libros quinque adversus haereses*, t. 1, ed. W. Wigan Harvey (Cambridge: Typis Academicis, 1852), p. 55; translation from *The Ante-Nicene Fathers*, 1:324.

7 It is significant that Irenaeus distinguishes between eating idol-food and attendance at pagan rites. Though no certain conclusion may be derived concerning the extent of Irenaeus's disapproval of eating idol-food from the way in which he lists it, it is still interesting to note that the evil of eating idol-food stands at the head of an impressive list of heretical vices (attendance at pagan festivals, attendance at spectacles, and sexual sins).

8 *Stromata* 4.15, in *Clemens Alexandrinus*, 2 Band, *Stromata. Buch. 1-6*, herausgegeben von Otto Stählin, in 3 Auflage neu herausgegeben von Ludwig Früchtel (Berlin: Akademie Verlag, 1960); translation from *The Ante-Nicene Fathers. Translations of the Writings of the Fathers Down to A.D. 325*, vol. 2, *Fathers of the Second Century*, ed. A. Roberts and J. Donaldson (Buffalo: Christian Literature Publishing Co., 1885), p. 427.

tians need not avoid unclean meats. He concludes, however, with a warning:[9]

> We must be warned lest any should think that liberty is permitted to that degree that even he may approach to what has been offered to idols. For, as far as pertains to God's creation, every creature is clean. But when it has been offered to demons, it has been polluted. . . . And when this creature is taken for food, it nourishes the person who so takes it for the demon and not for God.

Novatian clearly distinguishes between *kashrut* and the avoidance of idols, and evaluates them differently. After rejecting Jewish understanding of Scripture and practice over *kashrut* he then commends their avoidance of idol-food: "as rightly do the Jews also."[10]

Non-Christian references to Christians and idol-food

The same conclusion concerning consistent avoidance of idol-food by early Christians also emerges from non-Christian sources.

Lucian, in *The Death of Peregrinus*, provides a view of a Christian community taken with the charlatan philosopher Peregrinus, and in the end, if Lucian is correct concerning his shameless consumption of that community's resources, taken by him. Lucian indicates the reason for the Christians' final rejection of Peregrinus:[11]

> For a time he [Peregrinus] battened himself thus; but then, after he had transgressed in some way even against them—he was seen, I think, eating some of the food that is forbidden them—they no longer accepted him.

This is not an explicit reference to idol-food and could give rise to a number of alternative interpretations, but other non-Christian sources support the interpretation that this forbidden food was idol-food. Pliny the Younger's letter to Trajan concerning what to do with those accused of Christianity is explicit, as is Celsus's criticism of the dietary practices of Christians. Pliny:[12]

> It is not only the towns, but villages and rural districts too which are infected through contact with this wretched cult. I think though that it is still possible for it to be checked and directed to better ends, for there is no doubt that [after Pliny's prosecutions] people have begun to throng the temples which had been almost entirely

9 *On Jewish meats* 7, in ibid., 5:650.

10 *On Jewish meats* 7, in ibid., 5:650. Origen makes exactly the same distinction: Christians have rejected abstention from particular animals, but will not participate in idolatry through the eating of idol-food (*Contra Celsum*, 8.29-30).

11 Lucian, *The Death of Peregrinus*, 16, in *Lucian*, Loeb Classical Library (1919), 5:19.

12 *Letter* 10.96, in Radice, *Letters of the Younger Pliny*, p. 294-95).

> deserted for a long time; the sacred rites which had been allowed to lapse are being performed again, and flesh of sacrificial victims is on sale everywhere, though up till recently scarcely anyone could be found to buy it.[13]

Celsus (from Origen, *Contra Celsum*):[14]

> If they [the Christians] follow a custom of their fathers when they abstain from particular sacrificial victims, surely they ought to abstain from the food of all animals—such is the view taken by Pythagoras. . . . But if, as they say, they abstain to avoid feasting with daemons [*mê sunesthôntai daimosi*], I congratulate them on their wisdom, because they are slowly coming to understand that they are always associating with daemons [*sunestioi daimonôn*]. They take pains to avoid this only at the time when they see a victim being sacrificed. But whenever they eat food, and drink wine, and taste fruits, and drink even water itself, and breathe even the very air, are they not receiving each of these from certain daemons, among whom the administration of each of these has been divided?

Conclusions

What many scholars take to be the centre of Paul's argument concerning idol-food—that idol-food should be avoided for the sake of others—did not become a standard approach to the question in the early Christian communities.[15] "Orthodox" sources—to use the anachronism consciously—are unanimous in their condemnation of Christians who ate idol-food. Where there was not agreement, the issue seems to have brooked no compromise: the criticisms in "orthodox" sources of Christians who did eat idol-food suggest that instead of curbing their *exousia* in the interests of their Christian siblings these apostates encouraged others to eat.

The "orthodox" view of idol-food is disparaged by commentators. The church, Barrett concludes, "could see no way of excluding idolatry that did not include rigid abstention from heathen food and heathen dinner parties. . . . The church as a whole retreated into a narrow religious shell. Jewish Christianity (in this matter) triumphed, though

13 Even idol-food sold in markets was apparently avoided by Christians in Bithynia and Pontus in Pliny's time, though idol-food sold in markets is Paul's one unequivocal allowance (1 Cor 10:25). This is a stark indication of the extent to which Paul's attempted accommodation of the Corinthians' position was disregarded (see further discussion immediately below).

14 Origen, quoting Celsus, in *Contra Celsum*, 8.28 (*Origene. Contra Celse*, t. 4 [livres 7 et 8]); translation by Henry Chadwick, *Contra Celsum*, p. 471-72).

15 Keck captures the essence of other early Christian views in Asia Minor: in the matter of idol-food, "Paul was flatly repudiated" ("Ethos," p. 37).

Jewish Christians became less important in the church."[16] John Brunt's assessment is similarly unflattering of early Christians: Paul's arguments concerning idol-food were rejected, ignored, or misunderstood.[17] Other early Christian views are disparaged because they are incoherent with Paul's position and unreflective of Paul's ethical approach.[18]

It is useful to quote Brunt's conclusion, in order to refute both his and Barrett's understanding of the relationship between 1 Corinthians 8-10 and later Christian views. Brunt concludes:[19]

> It may well be that a very important reason for the early church's misunderstanding of Paul's approach was the level of principled, ethical thought in Paul's discussion, where the specific question of idol meat is transcended by the consideration of love's responsibility. When one considers the degree to which most early Christian discussion of this and other ethical questions focus merely on whether the act itself is right or wrong, it is not hard to grasp why Paul's level of thinking would be misunderstood.

Brunt's and Barrett's assessment begins from the view that early Christians misunderstood Paul.[20] It follows from my reconstruction, however, that—despite Paul's attempts to accommodate the strong in Corinth, and despite the wishes of those who look for a principled Paul bravely rejecting narrow, religiously conditioned rules—Paul stood firmly within the "orthodox" position concerning idol-food.

The extant sources outside Paul's letters concerning the Christian use or avoidance of idol-food support my social-historical reconstruction. They also support some important wider conclusions concerning the importance of idol-food in earliest Christianity.

The unanimity of the "orthodox" sources support my reading of 1 Corinthians 8-10. I have argued that Paul's position at root was that idol-food was dangerous and was to be avoided, and these other

---

16 Barrett, "Things Sacrificed," p. 56.

17 This is the thesis of Brunt's article on idol-food; see especially his conclusions ("Rejected," p. 120-22).

18 Richardson, for example, sees that where Paul concluded that Christ was the end of the law, apostolic Christianity in the matter of idol-food made "the safer but much less satisfactory assertion that Christianity embraces a new Law" (*Israel*, p. 199).

19 Brunt, "Rejected," p. 121.

20 Brunt also postulates another reason for the church's failure to follow Paul concerning idol-food: the "continuing influence of the Apostolic Decree." Brunt finds this influence "somewhat baffling, especially in light of the widespread rejection of Jewish food laws in general" (ibid., p. 121)—a bafflement I have attempted to dispel with a distinction between *kashrut* and idolatry. This distinction is blatant in the Decree itself.

sources take that view explicitly.[21] They also support the distinction I have urged between food which is impure and food offered to idols. For many Jews, both were unclean; for "orthodox" Christians and for Paul, impure food was not forbidden but food offered to idols was.

Wherever one group of Christians opposed to the eating of idol-food is confronted with the less restricted practice of other Christians, the sources reflect the divisive nature of the resulting conflict. I would argue not that this makes a divided community in Paul's Corinth more likely, but that this conflict shows the un-workableness of Paul's attempted accommodation of the "orthodox" view of idol-food. Paul's views were unacceptable to the sensibilities of the strong, who stand in some likely genetic relation to later Gnostics and Gnostic Christians opposed by Irenaeus; similarly, his attempted accommodations of the strong were probably not accepted by the other "orthodox" early Christian writers I have quoted. Due to the impracticality of avoidance of idol-food and the detrimental social effects of avoidance, no middle ground could be held for long. The accommodation Paul attempts probably did not work in Corinth, and there is no evidence that it worked elsewhere.

Idol-food became for earliest Christianity a marker of the limits of community. The perceptible social liabilities of avoidance of idol-food and the social and religious precedents of the avoidance of idol-food in Judaism both contribute to this significance of food as a marker of community.

---

21 The existence of a consensus urging avoidance of idol-food gives such a reading of Paul a surface credibility (so that Baur, for example, can claim that Paul's arguments concerning the avoidance of tables of demons became the standard early Christian view [*Paul*, 2:140]). On the other hand, other Christians *did* eat idol-food, presumably on justifications similar to those employed by the Corinthians (and, on some views, affirmed by Paul), and Paul might well be seen as on the trajectory leading to the views of those whom the "orthodox" sources criticize. Klauck argues explicitly that Paul's position concerning idol-food in 1 Cor 8/10:23-11:1 gave the Gnostics opposed by Irenaeus and Justin their justification for eating idol-food (*Herrenmahl*, p. 244). See also Elaine Pagels, *The Gnostic Paul. Gnostic Exegesis of the Pauline Letters* (Philadelphia: Fortress Press, 1975), for an extended discussion of Valentinian interpretation of Paul (Pagels does not discuss 1 Cor 8-10 at any length, however, noting only these passages of Irenaeus and Justin as indications of Valentinian exegesis of these verses).

12

Conclusions

Summary

What was idol-food? It could be many kinds of food, hallowed in many different contexts by differing rites. Idol-food included but was not limited to meat.

For whom was idol-food a problem? It was a problem for Paul, and he in turn urged it as a problem on the Corinthian Christians.

What was Paul's position concerning idol-food? He urged the Corinthian Christians to avoid it. While Paul abandoned the requirements of the law concerning circumcision and *kashrut*, Paul did not abandon the covenantal demand for exclusive allegiance to Yahweh, expressed concretely through the avoidance of even the most tenuous participation in idolatrous rites.

What effect would Paul's demands have on the Corinthians? Since idol-food was found in many contexts, and especially at events marking important social occasions, to avoid idol-food faithfully in the way Paul suggests would have carried significant social liabilities for Christians.

What was the Corinthian Christians' response to Paul? Very likely they rejected his advice, and his advice contributed to the rift between Paul and that group.

Did Paul's position concerning idol-food change? Not in any way of which there is evidence.

What of other early Christian views of idol-food? Evidence of other early Christian views reflects the conflict between Paul and the Corinthian Christians. Christians outside "orthodox" groups continued to eat idol-food, and "orthodox" Christians avoided it entirely. The accommodating position Paul attempts (avoidance in consideration of the weak) was not consistent with Paul's convictions, and was unworkable.

Last words

These conclusions and their supporting arguments are useful in their own right, but this investigation also illuminates in a significant way the social meaning of Christianity in its earliest period.

One fundamental question perennially addressed by scholars of earliest Christianity is the nature of its change from a sect within the group of sects constituting Judaism before the fall of Jerusalem in 70 C.E. to a sect that, in the West at least, was almost entirely ethnically Gentile and increasingly distinct from Judaism. This investigation is relevant to this question, and provides a perspective on that change which is not shared by many scholars of the New Testament.

Paul, in the standard view, is not taken with fear of demons and is unwilling to import the misled legalism of Judaism's rules concerning such ethically neutral matters as food into his own religious system which has so clearly abandoned allegiance to the law. The religious agenda of this standard view of Paul is both entirely familiar and increasingly untenable, due to the work especially of E. P. Sanders but also of many others addressing the question of anti-Judaism in earliest Christianity.[1] Though Paul certainly abandons allegiance to the Torah concerning circumcision and *kashrut*, the pattern of his religion remains that of Judaism: God offers salvation (for Paul, "in" Christ), but the offer must be met with open allegiance and faith, expressed through obedience.[2]

My conclusions also significantly undermine the standard view of Paul's and early Christianity's disengagement from Judaism. Paul's position concerning idol-food shows the limits of Paul's own consciousness (*syneidêis*). His consciousness was in this regard, as in others, entirely shaped by his Judaism. Paul's demand that any idolatry be avoided comes straight out of his covenantal religion: "Shall we provoke the Lord to jealousy?" Paul asks (1 Cor 10:22), and answers that Christians can in no way undermine their allegiance to Christ through dubious connections to other Gods and other Lords. Paul's "liberalism" thus may extend to *kashrut* and to circumcision, but it extends no

---

1 E. P. Sanders, *Paul and Palestinian Judaism*, and *Paul, the Law, and the Jewish People*. For other Canadian views, see *Anti-Judaism in Early Christianity*, vol. 1, *Paul and the Gospels*, ed. Peter Richardson, and vol. 2, *Separation and Polemic*, ed. Stephen G. Wilson (Waterloo, ON: Wilfrid Laurier University Press, 1986); B. E. Meyer and E. P. Sanders, eds., *Jewish and Christian Self-definition in the First Three Centuries*, vol. 1, *The Shaping of Christianity in the Second and Third Centuries*, vol. 2, *Aspects of Judaism in the Greco-Roman Period*, vol. 3, *Self-definition in the Greco-Roman Period* (Philadelphia: Fortress Press, 1980-82).

2 This is not the place to argue this view thoroughly, but see, for a clear example of this pattern even in a context of supposed abandonment of the law, Gal 5:13-25.

further, and does not abandon Judaism's conception of the relationship between God and his people.

Nor is Paul's avoidance of idolatry unique in earliest Christianity. Virtually every other early "orthodox" Christian source that addresses the issue of idol-food urges abstinence from it. As a result Paul—however much (particularly Protestant) scholars dislike it—stands with the uniform views of these other early "orthodox" Christian sources. This is hardly surprising since it was early Christians who preserved Paul's discussion of idol-food, including those Christians on the institutional and theological trajectory which came to be orthodox Christianity. Thus the earliest Christian positions over idol-food show the religious and conceptual continuity between earliest Christianity and other sects of Judaism.

The issue of idol-food also shows strong social similarities between early Christian groups and groups of Jews in the Diaspora. Jews were everywhere known, it would seem from the many references concerning Jews and Judaism in Greco-Roman literature, for their rejection of all Gods but their own, circumcision, keeping of the Sabbath, abstinence from pork, their original expulsion from Egypt due to their infectious diseases, and (last in interest to us but not least in the volume of references) the asphalt and salinity of the Dead Sea.[3]

Jews were also considered xenophobic and misanthropic, directly as a result of their practices over food. This perception, however, did not arise over *kashrut*. The Jews' abstinence from pork was usually considered just another ethnic oddness: for example, Sextus Empiricus says that "a Jew or Egyptian priest would prefer to die instantly rather than eat pork, while to taste mutton is reckoned an abomination in the eyes of a Libyan, and Syrians think the same about pigeons, and others about cattle."[4] The perception of misanthropy arose because Jews did

---

3 Extant references in Greco-Roman literature are collected, translated and annotated in Menahem Stern, *Greek and Latin Authors on Jews and Judaism*. References in the following are to Stern. Concerning circumcision and the Sabbath, Petronius is notable (1:443-44), as well as Juvenal (2:103), Seneca (1:431), Plutarch (1:549) and Tacitus (2:25). Concerning the Jews' expulsion from Egypt, see Josephus's *Contra Apionem* (1:394) and Lysimachus (1:384). Concerning Jews' avoidance of pork, see, for example, Josephus's *Contra Apionem* (1:415), Seneca (1:434), Erotianus (1:446), Epictetus (1:542), Plutarch (1:554, 566), Sextus Empiricus (2:159), and Celsus (2:285). Stern's volumes are well cross-referenced, so the interested reader can use the citations I provide to find others in the volumes.

4 Cited by Stern, *Greek and Latin Authors*, 2:159. Plutarch (1:554) and Celsus (2:285) make similar comparisons between Jewish dietary exclusions and those of other ethnic groups.

not engage in normal social intercourse, and in particular did not eat with those outside their group:[5]

> The Jews are extremely loyal toward one another, and always ready to show compassion, but toward every other people they feel only hate and enmity. They sit apart at meals and sleep apart, and, although as a race they are prone to lust, they abstain from intercourse with foreign women. . . . Those who are converted to their ways follow the same practice, and the earliest lesson they receive is to despise the gods, to disown their country, and to regard their parents, children and brothers as of little account (Tacitus, *Historiae*).
>
> The Jews had made their hatred of mankind into a tradition, and on this account had introduced utterly outlandish laws: not to break bread with any other race [*to mê deni allôi ethnei trapêzês koinônein*], nor to show them any good will at all (Diodorus, *Bibliotheca historica*).

Josephus alludes to a similar charge (*mê den koinô nein*) in *Contra Apionem*.[6]

This distinction between menu (*kashrut*) and social intercourse was probably blurred—it was the Jews' abstinence from ritually impure and idolatrous food that made them unwilling to eat in other contexts—but the distinction is significant: the refusal of early Christians to eat food tainted by idolatry would have the same negative social consequences as Jews' refusal to share tables on related grounds, with the result that the social meaning of early Christianity was as closely linked to Judaism as its pattern of religion and its concepts. It is hardly surprising to find visited on Christians the same calumny, focussing on exclusive eating practices, as that directed toward the Jews—the charge of cannibalism.[7]

The effect of Christians' avoidance of idol-food would have been social isolation, like that of Jews but without the protection of a licit religion or a venerable history which was respected (to varying degrees). In his assessment of third- and fourth-century sources concerning idol-food and Christians, Ehrhardt concludes that "the prohibition of the consumption of such meat not only separated the Chris-

---

5 Tacitus, *Historiae* 5.1-2, trans. C. H. Moore (cited by Stern, *Greek and Latin Authors*, 2:26); Diodorus, *Bibliotheca historica* 34.1.2, trans. F. R. Walton (cited by Stern, *Greek and Latin Authors*, 1:182-83).

6 Josephus, *Contra Apionem* 2.258 (Stern, *Greek and Latin Authors*, 1:155-56).

7 Directed against Christians: see Justin, *Dialogue with Trypho* 10 (similar citations are collected by David Ayerst and A. S. T. Fisher in *Records of Christianity*, vol. 1, *In the Roman Empire* [Oxford: Basil Blackwell, 1971], p. 45, 58, 74-80). Directed against Jews: Josephus, *Contra Apionem*, 91-96 (cited by Stern, *Greek and Roman Authors*, 1:410-13; see Stern's references to similar charges).

tians from their pagan neighbours, and made them outcasts, but it also made them very conspicuous," and that as a result it was no accident that official persecutions of Christians from the middle of the third century on made explicit provision for the compulsory eating of sacrificial food.[8]

My investigation traces some of the reasons for and the nature of the widespread prohibition of the eating of sacrificial food in earliest Christianity. The ubiquitous use of sacrificed food in Greco-Roman social contexts sat ill with Christians' inherited understanding of the nature of their covenant with their God. As with the Jews, the avoidance of idol-food helped to maintain the cohesiveness of their community, but also set limits on their intercourse which attracted criticism and provided a focus for persecution.[9] In stark contrast to the assessment of many modern scholars, who see idol-food per se as a historical curiosity of interest only because it allowed Paul to develop religious and ethical principles, the problem of idol-food stood close to the centre of the earliest Christians' allegiance to their faith. Against Paul's social context—both the use of idol-food in Greco-Roman social intercourse, and the use of food to define the limits of Jewish communities—Paul stands with other early Christians in seeing idol-food as a threat to partnership (*koinônia*) with his Lord.

---

8 Ehrhardt, *Framework*, p. 286. Barrett agrees, with notable comments: the church "could see no way of excluding idolatry that did not include rigid abstention from heathen food and heathen dinner parties. . . . The church as a whole retreated into a narrow religious shell. Jewish Christianity (in this matter) triumphed, though Jewish Christians became less important in the church." ("Things Sacrificed," p. 56). Ramsay MacMullen reaches similar conclusions concerning the social isolation of early Christians, based on the exclusive character of their meetings and their unwillingness to marry outside the group. MacMullen does not consider the matter of food (*Christianizing the Roman Empire, A.D. 100-400* [New Haven: University Press, 1984], p. 103-104).

9 Idol-food not only marked the limits of intercourse with non-Christians, but also with Christians aligned with other Christian or Gnostic groups, as shown by the citations from Justin and Irenaeus above in chap. 11.

Appendix 1

Different views of Paul's position concerning idol-food

The position I put forward in the chapters above is not shared by earlier commentators, though a few support elements of my reconstruction. Gordon Fee argues explicitly that the centre of Paul's response to the Corinthians is to warn them against idolatry. In Fee's view Paul's demand to avoid the table of *daimonia* in 10:14-22 is not a digression but "in fact the main point, to which the whole argument of 8:1-10:13 has been leading."[1] But Fee also claims, in contrast to my position, that Paul accepts the *gnôsis* of the strong.[2] Richard Horsley argues that Paul saw demons as real, and participation in cultic meals as dangerous to the Corinthians.[3] Peter Tomson agrees that Paul prohibits consumption of (some) idol-food, based on the axiomatic rejection of idolatry by Jews, and that Paul's permission to eat food sold in the marketplace is not consistent with his instructions in other contexts.[4] Wayne Meeks recognizes the relevance of the distinction between avoidance of impurity and idolatry, and agrees that Paul "persists in using traditional Jewish paraenesis . . . against idolatry." Meeks concludes, however, that the centre of Paul's concern is *not* idolatry and the dangers of idol-food, but instead the community: Paul wants to "build up" the community and not divide it over questions of food.[5]

---

1 Fee, "*Eidôlothyta,*" p. 179; compare Fee, "2 Cor 6:14-7:1," p. 156-61.

2 Fee, "2 Cor 6:14-7:1," p. 152.

3 Horsley, "Gnosis," p. 49-50.

4 Tomson, *Paul and the Law*, p. 154, 203-20.

5 Wayne Meeks, " 'Since then you would need to go out of the world': Group Boundaries in Pauline Christianity," in *Critical History and Biblical Faith: New Testament Perspectives*, College Theological Society Annual Publication Series, ed. Thomas J. Ryan (Ann Arbor, MI: Edward Brothers, 1979), p. 15-16. Meeks shares a standard view: the problem emerges from competing views within the

No other commentator of whom I am aware has argued as I do that Paul's position vis-à-vis idol-food was at root conditioned by Paul's own consciousness (*syneidêsis*) and his authentic fear of the dangers idol-food held for the Corinthian Christians.[6]

The alternative readings of Paul's underlying convictions concerning idol-food by other commentators should be set out, and my differences with those views explained. In this appendix I present the views of several scholars, who each present extensive and reasoned socio-historical reconstructions of 1 Corinthians 8-10 that conflict directly with my own. I will attempt to present a fair account of their views and show why their reconstructions of the situation in Corinth and Paul's position are unpersuasive. I will discuss in turn the reconstructions of Johannes Weiss, John Coolidge Hurd, C. K. Barrett, Gerd Theissen, Jerome Murphy-O'Connor, and Wendell Lee Willis.

J. Weiss

Johannes Weiss's discussion of 1 Corinthians 8:1-11:1, published in 1910, stands as a classic whose insights shaped much of the subsequent debate over these chapters.[7] Weiss is always lucid and often challenging; his reconstruction, both directly and through its subsequent development in the commentary of others, is largely the reconstruction over against which mine has been developed.

Weiss states that there were two groups in the Christian community at Corinth. The strong ate idol-food, even in the temples of other Gods, because they did not wish to relinquish family and social connections. They were in the majority among the Corinthian Christians. Their attitudes ranged from naïveté to bravado, and some of the strong made the eating of idol-food a deliberate test of their religious authority.[8] The weak, on the other hand, were "stuck" in their fear of demons, and believed that consumption of such food put them in a deadly material connection with supernatural beings.[9]

Corinthian group, and Paul attempts to balance between the legitimate concerns and arguments of both factions in order to foster the solidarity of the group. He presents a synthesis of the views of Weiss and Barrett on the one hand and Theissen on the other (see Meeks, *Moral world*, p. 134-36; "And rose up to play," p. 73-75).

6 Leander Keck ("Ethos," p. 36) and E. P. Sanders (*Paul, the Law, and the Jewish People*, p. 103-104) put forward views which are closely akin, but these views are not developed from a close reading of 1 Cor 8-10.

7 Johannes Weiss, *1 Kor.*

8 Ibid., p. 211-12. That the strong ate in temples is again affirmed in Weiss's exegesis of 8:10 (ibid., p. 229).

9 Ibid., p. 211.

In Weiss's reconstruction, Paul writes because of the conflict between these groups, but his response as found in 1 Corinthians is twofold. First, in 10:1-22 Paul takes a rigorous stand against idolatry, demanding that the Corinthians flee any connection with demons (as in 5:10 and 6:18); here Paul takes the same stance as the weak, influenced by his inherited Jewish sensibilities. In contrast, Paul's other response to the Corinthians found in chapter 8 and in 10:23-11:1 abandons his materialistic and superstitious fear of demons and regards eating itself as *adiaphoron*—morally indifferent. Paul adopts the stance of the strong, both in principle and in the more superficial aspects of their understanding of the eating of food. Where Paul withdraws from the position of the strong in this second response he does so not on the basis that eating posed a moral or religious danger, but because the weaker members would take offence.[10]

Weiss concludes from the tensions between these responses that Paul could not have taken these opposing views in the same letter. Paul at first took the position of the weak, urging the avoidance of all connection with idolatry. This advice led to the sundering of important social contacts for many of the Corinthians, with the result that they complained—as reflected in 5:10—that they would have to "go out of the world" to do as Paul said. The strong, then, either did not break off eating or resumed it, and attempted to justify their behaviour with the slogans Paul quotes in chapter 8 and 10:23-11:1. This put Paul in a difficult position, since he could neither condone the effects of their eating on the weak nor disagree with the correct principles which they forwarded in their slogans. As a result, in chapter 8 and 10:23-11:1 Paul attempts to slant the argument away from *gnôsis* towards the love he believes more fundamental.[11] The passage urging avoidance of idolatry in 10:1-22 belongs, then, Weiss concludes, to the previous letter referred to in 1 Corinthians 5:9-13. The passages

10 Ibid., p. 212, 264.

11 Ibid., p. 213; carefully developed in his exegesis of 8:1-13 in (ibid., p. 214-18; 227-30). Weiss's reconstruction has become the standard view of the concrete social setting of the issue of idol-food in Corinth and Paul's attitude toward it and the Corinthians. This basic structure is assumed by virtually every commentator—with variants, to be sure, but these variants still share a generic view of the origin of the conflict and Paul's stance between the two groups. Representative arguments that Paul affirmed the knowledge of the strong but urged consideration for the weak can be found as follows: Barrett [with qualifications; see discussion below]; Brunt, "Ignored," p. 115; Ehrhardt, *Framework*, p. 277; Fee, "2 Cor 6:14-7:1," p. 152; Paul Gooch, "Burden," p. 111; Manson, "Corinthian Correspondence (1)," p. 200; Meyer, *1 Cor*, p. 235-36; Murphy-O'Connor, "Freedom," p. 557-60; Schmithals, *Gnosticism*, p. 227-28.

reflecting agreement with the principles of the strong in chapter 8 and 10:23-11:1 show Paul's later (and presumably better) position on the matter.[12]

The partition of the canonical 1 Corinthians into fragments reflecting an evolution of Paul's position is at the heart of Weiss's reconstruction. It allows Weiss to present a strong Paul, liberated in the end from his superstitious Jewish fears over the dangers of connection to idols through tainted food.[13]

This partition of the letter, however, is an unsound foundation for Weiss's reconstruction and vitiates his main conclusions. Hurd presents extensive arguments against a partition of 1 Corinthians 8-10: (1) There is no textual evidence that 1 Corinthians 8-10 circulated in an arrangement other than its canonical form. (2) Supporters of partition have not argued that the two sections (10:1-22 and 8:1-13/10:23-11:1) are so different that Paul could not have written both. If Paul could vary this much between letters, why not between sections of letters? (3) The differences in content and attitude among the sections have been exaggerated (Paul does *not* wholeheartedly agree with the strong in chapter 8, and he does not reach different conclusions over the permissibility of eating idol-food in the different sections).[14]

Hurd's arguments against partition can be supported directly by tensions in Weiss's own exegesis of the passages. For example, his exegesis of 8:5-6 runs across the grain of his overarching hypothesis that Paul agreed with the *gnôsis* of the strong. Weiss struggles eloquently with the conflicting phrases of the verses that dismiss then affirm the reality of other Gods.[15] Weiss's conclusion concerning what he calls these *haarscharf* distinctions in Paul's text is that Paul, in contrast to the

---

12 Weiss, *1 Kor*, p. 212, 213.

13 This depiction of Weiss's view is blunt but accurate: see, for example, *1 Kor*, p. 264, where Weiss concludes that Paul's extraordinary liberal view of the harmlessness of food seen in 10:23 and 10:26, standing in stark contrast to the earlier fear of demons seen in 10:1-22, is all the more remarkable in a "former Jew." This designation of Paul is one that Paul would not even recognize let alone accept (Rom 9:3, especially in its context; 2 Cor 11:22; Phil 3:4-6).

14 Hurd (*Origin*, p. 131-41) addresses in detail the integrity of 1 Cor 8:1-11:1. The points I note above are only a sample of those which Hurd argues. In my view, he conclusively establishes the integrity of the idol-food passages in their canonical form.

15 Weiss, *1 Kor*, p. 220: The designation of other Gods as *legomenoi* ("so-called") in 8:5a accords with the dismissal of their reality by the strong, but the *hôsper* of the next phrase ("*as indeed* there are many gods and lords" [RSV]) reaffirms their reality; the position of *eisin* in 8:5b stresses the reality of the Gods, but the *all' hymin* of 8:6 retracts that reality again.

superficial enlightenment of the strong, affirms the existence of other Gods and the reality of the relations of non-Christians to their Gods. The accent of the verses remains, Weiss recognizes, on the claim of verse 5 that there are many Gods.[16] This conclusion brings 8:5-6 into clear resonance with 10:14-22, and undercuts his view of an enlightened Paul agreeing with the principles of the strong after a false start in the previous letter.

Similarly, Weiss's comments on 8:13 are also strikingly at odds with his overarching reconstruction. Of Paul's claim that he will renounce food if it causes his brother to fall, Weiss says, "In this [Paul] demands of the gnostics . . . a complete abandonment of *eidôlothyton*, and therefore again comes in the end to the demands of 10:1-22 [in his previous letter], even if from different motives." Paul has changed only the reason for abstaining from idol-food—from fear of demons to regard for the weak—and Weiss wonders whether Paul here defends only the rights of the weak, without a word to say to them.[17]

Finally, much of Weiss's reconstruction seems motivated by an implicit anti-Judaism. Weiss constantly links the warnings against demons in chapter 10 with what he calls the "superstitions" and fearfulness of Judaism, and he is clearly more comfortable with the "enlightened" Paul he reconstructs from chapter 8 and 10:23-11:1. This anti-Judaism is perhaps at its most blatant in Weiss's description of Paul's "fear" of demons in 10:14-22 as Jewish superstition, and his designation of Paul as a "former Jew."[18]

Weiss's religious agenda and its working out in an insupportable partition theory makes his seminal and often repeated reconstruction untenable.[19]

---

16 Ibid., p. 211.

17 Ibid., p. 231 (translation mine).

18 Ibid., p. 264.

19 The reconstruction of H.-J. Klauck is an extensive re-working of Weiss's hypothesis. Klauck's reconstruction avoids many of the flaws I have identified in that of Weiss, but it retains its basic structure on the premise of a similar partition theory (*Herrenmahl*, p. 272, 282-84). Klauck moderates both Weiss's anti-Judaism and his account of the stark difference in Paul's positions in the two letters: in Klauck's view, Paul's underlying assessment of the impermissibility of participating in cultic meals remains unchanged, but between 10:1-22 and 8:1-13/10:23-11:1 Paul changes only his assessment of the relevance of his analogies in 10:1-22. In his second assessment of idol-food, Paul in essence agrees with the strong that the analogy with the Lord's meal was inappropriate, and shifts his objections to possible harm to the weak (ibid., p. 284).

J. C. Hurd

The many similarities between my reading of 1 Corinthians 8-10 and that of J. C. Hurd[20] have already been acknowledged. Hurd's challenging reading of the letter has persuaded me in significant respects: (1) the unity of the Corinthian position concerning the permissibility of idol-food, (2) the hypothetical character of Paul's appeal to the weak, and (3) the origin of the problem of idol-food not in intra-community disagreement but in Paul's earlier advice concerning idolatry.

There is, however, an important difference between my reconstruction and Hurd's that centres on Paul's motivation in prohibiting idolatrous eating. I have argued that Paul's position comes out of his own conviction about the limits of behaviour required to maintain partnership with his Lord, and that his conviction in this, as in every other matter of central significance to him, is strongly conditioned by his religious view of the world as a Jew. For this reason it is not surprising to find Paul setting the limits of community by food. In contrast, Hurd's central hypothesis is that Paul's position concerning idol-food comes out of an uncomfortable compromise struck by Paul, in which Paul agreed to impose the Apostolic Decree on his churches in order to legitimize his mission to the Gentiles in the eyes of the leadership of the church in Jerusalem. Hurd argues that 1 Corinthians was the third stage of a dialogue which began with Paul's attempt in his previous letter (alluded to in 1 Cor 5:9) to impose the conditions of the Apostolic Decree (Acts 15) on the Corinthians.[21] Since Paul had not taught these prohibitions in his first visit to Corinth the Corinthians were understandably taken aback at Paul's inconsistency. They sent a letter requesting clarification, to which in turn 1 Corinthians is the response. The challenging nature of Hurd's hypothesis has impeded careful consideration of it, and too often Hurd's work is simply dismissed, without justification.[22]

---

20 Hurd, *Origin*. *Origin* was republished with a new foreword in 1983 by Mercer University Press (Macon, GA).

21 Hurd was not the first to suggest this hypothesis—as early as 1910 Weiss saw the possible connection between the Apostolic Council and Paul's position vis-à-vis idol-food in Paul's earlier letter (*1 Kor*, p. 213)—but, unlike Weiss, Hurd develops the hypothesis extensively. Ehrhardt also suggests that Paul urged adherence to the Decree on behalf of the weak, but Ehrhardt's analysis is undeveloped and uncritical (*Framework*, p. 277). Though Barrett explicitly rejects Hurd's reconstruction, he reintroduces elements of it himself: probably, Barrett claims, the "Jewish-Christian orthopraxy of the [Apostolic] Decree was introduced to Corinth under the aegis of Peter" ("Things Sacrificed," p. 49-50).

22 Rejections of Hurd's hypothesis usually follow Weiss's earlier arguments: the Acts account of the Council is simply wrong, since Paul would have had to implement

The weak link of Hurd's reconstruction is that there is no explicit evidence of the Apostolic Decree on the surface of the text of 1 Corinthians. The themes which link 1 Corinthians to the Apostolic Decree—*porneia*, idol-food—are themes found everywhere in earliest Christianity, and thus do not themselves require a direct connection with the Decree.[23] Hurd infers a link between 1 Corinthians and the Apostolic Decree: because Paul is clarifying an earlier instruction concerning idol-food (among other things) and the Corinthians were unopposed to eating idol-food and complained to Paul about his instructions, he infers that Paul had changed his position from his first visit and that the Apostolic Decree lay behind Paul's changed position. The farther one moves from the letter itself into the stages of dialogue preceding it, the more the reconstruction depends on inference rather than evidence, and thus becomes more tenuous. Hurd acknowledges this explicitly.[24]

This weakness in Hurd's reconstruction is met, specifically with respect to idol-food, with a corresponding strength in my alternative reconstruction. My reconstruction does not postulate Paul's uncomfortable compromise with hidden actors in Jerusalem, but rather takes the more straightforward view that Paul's position concerning idol-food is his own. On the other hand, the strength of Hurd's reconstruction is that it does account—where mine has not until now—for the obvious need for Paul to clarify his positions in 1 Corinthians. Hurd argues cogently that Paul was attempting to back-pedal, so to speak, out of the position in which his previous letter had placed him: Paul had been misunderstood (so he would have the Corinthians think, at least); the Corinthians' questions are more objections from a consistent point of view; and Paul does his best to appear to agree with Corinthians' objections. From this evidence Hurd argues that the Corinthians' objections and Paul's clarifications derive from Paul's inconsistency between his first contact with the Corinthians and his previous letter. This is a marked strength of Hurd's reconstruction, and admittedly it raises difficulties for my own. This challenge becomes stronger when Hurd adds the claim that Paul himself held views concerning idol-food similar to those argued by the Corinthians in their response to the pre-

---

such an agreement in Corinth, and the Corinthians seem to know nothing of the Decree and Paul does not acknowledge it (*1 Kor*, p. 213). Hurd counters exactly these objections, but scholars continue to dismiss Hurd's views. See, for example, Barrett's and Murphy-O'Connor's treatment of *Origin of 1 Corinthians* (discussed below); Klauck, *Herrenmahl*, p. 279-80.

23 See chap. 11 above, where the significance of other early Christian views of idol-food is explored.

24 See especially Hurd's preface to the 1983 reprinting of *Origin*, p. xxi.

vious letter, and that the Corinthians were in effect echoing Paul's first teaching on the matter. Not only that, but Hurd argues explicitly that Paul ate idol-food.[25]

The essence of Paul's task in 1 Corinthians 8-10, I agree, is clarification and defence of his views against Corinthian objections; Paul's previous letter, in the Corinthians' view, went much too far in demands which would have taken the Corinthians out of any contact with outsiders. The previous letter could have been perceived by the Corinthians as a marked change in Paul's earlier position. I am not convinced, however, that the previous letter represented a real change in Paul's position, motivated by external pressure on him and running against both his earlier practice in Corinth and his own views. I have presented my reasons for concluding that Paul's true view of idol-food is that its connection with idolatry makes it dangerous. I would add the following arguments against Hurd's view.

Chapter 9 of 1 Corinthians provides some tenuous evidence that Paul did not eat idol-food. Paul's lack of reference to his practice concerning idol-food is all the more striking in that if he had eaten idol-food it would help to establish his credibility (he wants to show as much solidarity with the Corinthians as possible) and to support the legitimacy of his demand.[26]

Why the Corinthians perceived new and onerous demands in Paul's previous letter may be explained by Paul's missionary techniques. Paul indicates his willingness to accommodate the sensitivities of others in order to win them (9:19-23), and—as chapters 8-10 show—Paul is more concerned with persuasion than consistency. I am not suggesting that Paul originally ate idol-food but that he simply did not raise the issue, in keeping with his over-riding desire to win his hearers and not frighten them off with demands which they might not understand and to which they would object.

The reconstruction I offer here is captured in a wonderfully acute portrait of parents' attempts to introduce for the first time to their young child the social requirements of membership in the family:

---

25 *Origin*, p. 128-30, 147-48. Hurd's arguments are as follows: (1) Paul does not attack directly the Corinthians' position, or the principles which underlie them; (2) Paul's own defence of his actions does not include any claim that he did not eat idol-food; (3) Paul limits the conduct of the Corinthians "only slightly, if at all." My different conclusions concerning whether Paul limits the conduct of the Corinthians, whether Paul disagreed with the Corinthians and whether Paul ate idol-food have been set out above.

26 See my more extended discussion in chap. 7 above. Hurd draws the opposite conclusion from the silence of 1 Cor 9 concerning idol-food: Paul "does not claim never to have eaten . . . idol meat" (*Origin*, p. 147).

> The missionaries have arrived. . . . They smuggled themselves in as infatuated parents, of course. They nurtured him, made themselves indispensable to him, lured him into discovery of their fascinating world, and after a decent interval they come forth with salesmen's smiles to promote higher civilization.[27]

I do not mean to disparage either Paul's methods or motives. Paul truly sees himself in the role of father to his converts.[28] I do suggest that Paul introduced a more rigorous set of demands concerning sexual behaviour and the avoidance of idolatry only after a "decent interval" from the Corinthians' new allegiance to Paul's Lord. Thus abstinence (both from idol-food and from sexual relations) is indeed Paul's own request of them in the previous letter, introduced when he was more confident of their acceptance of these (wrongly confident, it turned out).

The merits of Hurd's views and my own could be decided properly only with better evidence. Paul's motivation in the writing of the previous letter lies in events buried well behind the text. Whether Hurd's views or my own are accepted depends on the persuasiveness of the broad reconstruction in which the available evidence is placed.

C. K. Barrett

Charles Kingsley Barrett presents an attractive view of a masterly Paul who considers the needs of recently converted Gentiles, the religious sensitivities of Jewish Christians and the demands of libertine gnostic Gentile Christians, and develops a carefully balanced response to each in a complex position concerning idol-food and idolatry.[29]

Barrett is aware of the importance of Paul's appeals to the dangers to the Christian weak in eating idol-food, but he does not consider this the heart of Paul's position. Instead, the origin and focus of the issue in Corinth is a conflict between Jewish Christians in Corinth who urge abstinence from idol-food and Gentile Christians in Corinth who eat with impunity on the basis of a "rationalistic"—that is, stressing knowledge—belief in the non-existence of idols.

Barrett does not provide extensive arguments for the existence of Jewish Christians in Corinth urging such abstinence. It is enough for him that (1) there is evidence that Jewish Christians elsewhere urged

---

27 Selma H. Fraiberg, *The Magic Years* (New York: Charles Scribner's Sons, 1959), p. 62. This is an articulate, amusing and most telling analysis of early childhood, a classic from the psychoanalytical school.

28 Paul asserts this explicitly in 1 Cor 4:14,15. Compare 1 Cor 3:1-2,5; 1 Thess 2:7; 2 Cor 11:2.

29 C. K. Barrett, "Things Sacrificed;" and *The First Epistle to the Corinthians*, Black's New Testament Commentaries (London: Adam and Charles Black, 1968).

avoidance of idol-food (citing Acts 15 and the Apostolic Decree, and general Jewish practice),[30] (2) there was a "Petrine party" in Corinth (citing 1 Cor 1:12),[31] and (3) that the conflict over idol-food in chapters 8-10 is best explained by this hypothesis.[32]

Barrett's understanding of Paul's position depends on the presence of Jewish Christians. He sees Paul's view as an "attitude of extraordinary liberalism," countering a Jewish Christian position demanding separation from outsiders and retreat to a "Christian ghetto."[33] The heart of Paul's position is that he *permits* the eating of idol-food (10:25,27): Paul is "nowhere more un-Jewish" than in his instructions not to raise scruples over food in the market, and Paul's intention is that social contact with outsiders, "which almost certainly would involve eating *eidôlothyta* [idol-food]," should remain possible.[34]

---

30 "Things Sacrificed," p. 49.

31 The view that the conflict over idol-food in Corinth was sparked by a Petrine party is as old, in modern scholarly debate, as F. C. Baur (*Paul*, 1: 260). Though Barrett does not accept in total scholarly arguments proposing a Petrine party in Corinth, still he finds it probable that "an attempt [was made], by or at least under the *aegis* of Peter, to introduce into the Church at Corinth the Jewish Christian orthopraxy of the [Apostolic] Decree" ("Things Sacrificed," p. 53). See also Barrett's "Cephas and Corinth," in *Abraham unser Vater. Festschrift für Otto Michel* (Leiden: E. J. Brill, 1963).

32 Compare Peter Richardson, "On the Absence of 'anti-Judaism' in 1 Corinthians," in *Anti-Judaism in Early Christianity*, vol. 1, *Paul and the Gospels* (Waterloo, ON: Wilfrid Laurier University Press, 1986), p. 59-74. Richardson sees the roots of the conflict in intra-community Jewish-Gentile conflict, and sees Paul as attempting to mediate that conflict (as irenically as possible, hence the absence of anti-Judaism). Richardson argues the likely presence of Jews in Corinth (citing explicit references to Jews in 1:18-25, 9:19-23, and 10:32) and a Jewish mission there (carried on by Paul, Peter, Apollos, Prisca and Aquila, Sosthenes and others [2 Cor 10]) (p. 63-64). He argues that food is often the *locus* of Jew-Gentile conflicts in early Christianity, and that idol-food is such a *locus* in Corinth (ibid., p. 69-71). Richardson's reconstruction can be challenged, as follows: the evidence he cites proves only the presence of Jewish apostles, and the predominance of Jewish matters in Paul's mind (p. 63-64); he pays insufficient attention to the focus of 1 Cor 8-11 on idol-food rather than *kashrut*, and thus collapses other situations into this one without warrant (p. 69); and he pays insufficient attention to Paul's position *against* eating (p. 60, 73). J. Massingberd Ford presents an extreme version of this hypothesis: she argues that the Christians in Corinth followed the religious and social divisions of rabbinic Judaism. The weak are "Pharisaic Christians," opposed to "*'am ha-aretz* Christians" without their extreme scruples ("'Hast Thou Tithed Thy Meal?' and 'Is Thy Child Kosher?'" *Journal of Theological Studies* n.s., 17 [1966]: 75-76).

33 Barrett, "Things Sacrificed," p. 50.

34 Ibid., p. 47. Barrett here cites in support Paul's correction of his previous letter in

Barrett asserts that Paul's liberalism "brought him into at least equally uncomfortable alliance with Christian 'gnostics.'" Just as Paul argues against Jewish Christian fears of infection, he must also argue against Gentile Christian over-confidence. Where the strong asserted the straightforward non-existence of idols—a view Barrett labels "rationalistic"—Paul holds to the reality of demons, and their ability to harm even the strong if they participated in idolatrous rites.[35]

Barrett's Paul keeps a fine balance in the interests of all his followers in Corinth: "In Corinth . . . Paul had to walk the tightrope between the legalism of Jewish Christianity and the false liberalism of gnostic rationalism. That he was able to do this is one of the clearest marks of his greatness."[36]

As appealing as Barrett's Paul is—and the basic outlines of Barrett's position are often found in other assessments of Paul[37]—the evidence of 1 Corinthians does not support this portrait of Paul. There are three major weaknesses in Barrett's position.

First, Barrett's hypothesis that Jewish Christians in Corinth were the spur to the conflict there over idol-food is not warranted by our evidence. Conflict between Jewish and Gentile Christians in Corinth is seen nowhere in the Corinthian correspondence[38]—apart from the conflict, of course, between Paul and the Corinthians.[39] The oft-cited

---

1 Cor 5: if Paul has made a volte face from that letter, Barrett argues, it is in a liberal direction.

35 Ibid., p. 52, 54.

36 Ibid., p. 55.

37 For example, in that of Murphy-O'Connor discussed immediately below. Von Soden also presents a view with a very similar structure: the underlying theme of "Sakrament und Ethik" is that Paul steers between Jewish legalism (God will reward the avoidance of tainted food) and Hellenistic super-naturalism (God is coerced by the sacred rite), and instead puts forward a truly sacramental view: the rites are efficacious (1 Cor 10), but an ethical response is also required (1 Cor 8). Again, this is true of the positions of Meeks (described briefly above) and Theissen (see below). As far as I am aware, every positive evaluation of Paul's treatment of the issue of idol-food hinges in some way or another on a view of Paul mediating opposing views and/or persons.

38 This assertion holds true even for 2 Cor. Even though Paul boasts that his Jewish credentials meet those of the super-apostles he opposes, the issues are not law or circumcision or diet but—as nearly as can be recovered—an attempt to undermine Paul's authority.

39 In fairness it should be made explicit that in one sense at least my own view is simply a variant of the explanation Barrett develops. I too propose that the conflict over idol-food centres on Jewish-Gentile conflict, but suggest instead—to draw it in very broad strokes—that Paul is the Jew, and the Corinthians the Gentiles. In this sense I have appropriated much of the general justification of Barrett

"parties" of Peter, Apollos and Paul in 1:12 are not evidence of a Jew/Gentile division in the community, contrary to uncritical readings of the passage. Even if this reference is evidence of parties,[40]—and this is doubtful—it is not evidence of Jewish and Gentile parties, since (1) all three of these apostles are Jewish and associated with both Jews and Gentiles, and (2) there is no authentic indication in 1 Corinthians of the positions or views of these "parties" sufficient to attach Jews to one and Gentiles to another.

Barrett's perception of a Jewish/Gentile conflict in Corinth derives not from a clear reading of 1 Corinthians but from a mistaken generalization of this conflict known elsewhere in earliest Christianity. This generalization prevents attention to the very specific context of one small community in one Greco-Roman city. It also inverts proper historical method, since evidence of specific contexts should be primary, and generalizations built from close observation of specific situations.[41]

A second weakness of Barrett's view is closely related to the first. He assumes a Jewish Christian group in Corinth but he appears unaware of one element of his reading of chapter 8 which is in tension with this assumption. Barrett's conclusion concerning the identity of the weak in chapter 8 is unequivocal: because the weak have always eaten idol-food as sacred to another God and are in recent acquaintance with idolatry, the weak must be Gentiles.[42] But if Jews have the scruples, why should Paul appeal to possible harm to Gentiles? If the Gentile weak are the problem to which Paul appeals, how can Barrett maintain that the problem originates with Jewish Christians urging social withdrawal?

The final weakness of Barrett's analysis is his reading of Paul's views on the reality of demons. Where Barrett presents a Paul balancing between Jewish legalism and Gentile libertinism, my reading pres-

---

and others for their reconstruction of the potential cultural and religious conflicts over food between Jewish Christians and Gentiles, but I have rejected their specific claims concerning the role of Paul in that conflict.

40 The other indications of conflict between groups in Corinth do not fit a pattern of "parties": in chapter 8 there are Paul's hypothetical weak and in chapter 11 there are the richer and poorer.

41 A similar too ready generalization underlies much commentary concerning Paul's "opponents" in 2 Cor and Philippians, which reads conflicts over circumcision and Torah in Galatians into the scant evidence of these other letters. These issues do not emerge from 2 Cor. While the "dogs" of Phil 3:2 certainly teach circumcision, these verses do not offer solid evidence that such opponents were in Philippi: Paul may here be offering final advice, in anticipation of his possible inability—despite his confidence of the contrary—to return to the Philippians (Phil 1:19-26).

42 Barrett, *1 Cor*, p. 194-95.

ents a Paul worried over idolatry. Barrett's reading of 8:5-6 betrays a reluctance to admit that Paul believed that demons existed and—as in chapter 10 also—could harm. "On the whole," Barrett admits, Paul agrees with the strong Corinthians concerning the non-reality of other Gods, but his position "is not so simple as Corinthian rationalism suggests, and monotheism needs a firmer foundation than rationalism and the simple denial of spiritual existences can supply."[43] In his commentary on 8:5-6 Barrett attempts to describe the complexity of Paul's view:

> It would exaggerate in one direction to suppose that he denied the existence of beings neither truly God nor human, but it would exaggerate in the other direction if we were to take his *there are* [8:5] to affirm the reality of beings mentioned. . . . The drive of his argument is towards the assertion that, whatever other spiritual or demonic beings there may be, *for us* there is only one whom we recognize as God [emphasis Barrett's].

Barrett has Paul neither denying nor affirming the reality of demons; Paul "appears to express no definite opinion on the subject."[44]

While I can understand Barrett's motive for this reading of 8:5—he sees Paul balancing between opposing views—I cannot make sense of the reading itself. It violates the sense deriving from its context: Paul sets out a Corinthian position (here, "an idol has no existence") and, as elsewhere, corrects it: there is only one true God, but there are many beings called Gods and Lords. The wider context of chapter 10, as Barrett himself is aware, shows clearly that Paul expects harm not only to the weak but also to the strong from *koinônia* at a demon's table.[45]

While Barrett's Paul is a masterful and compassionate mediator between opposing religious views of the world, this Paul belongs more to Barrett's idealism than to the text of 1 Corinthians. The Paul I find there is not a mediator between views, but a persuader trying to win the Corinthians to a different view of idol-food than that which they hold.

---

43 Barrett, "Things Sacrificed," p. 55.

44 Barrett, *1 Cor*, p. 192.

45 Ibid., Barrett's commentary on 10:20: "the effect of sacrifice lies . . . in personal relations [with demons], and the consequences that flow from them. . . . Paul believed in the reality of an unseen spirit-world, and idolatry . . . meant that man, engaged in spiritual act . . . was brought into intimate relation with the lower, and evil, spiritual powers" (*1 Cor*, p. 237). Barrett's direct admission of Paul's belief in the reality of demons here sits ill with Barrett's ambivalence over the meaning of 8:5-6 (*1 Cor*, p. 192).

G. Theissen

Gerd Theissen's three articles concerning the Corinthian Christian community[46] apply sociological analysis to 1 Corinthians.[47] Theissen grounds his arguments concerning the social context of the Corinthian community in a survey of Greco-Roman literary sources. His reconstruction is a stimulating alternative to those of earlier commentators.

The community of Christian converts in Corinth, in Theissen's reconstruction, was a socially diverse group, informally dominated by leaders from the privileged upper classes who were outnumbered by the majority from the lower classes.[48] Theissen stresses the significance of the social stratification of the Corinthian Christian community in the causes and working-out of the problems Paul addresses, and in particular the problems over idol-food[49] and the Lord's meal.[50]

Theissen finds the source of the conflict over idol-food in the differential impact of the eating of sacrificed food on the different strata of the community. Based on his brief survey of Greco-Roman sources concerning idol-meat and the differences in diet between the rich and the poor, Theissen hypothesizes that Christians from the upper social strata would have eaten meat used in cultic contexts as a matter of

---

46 Theissen's articles concerning 1 Cor are translated and collected by John H. Schütz in *The Social Setting of Pauline Christianity. Essays on Corinth by Gerd Theissen* (Philadelphia: Fortress Press, 1982), as follows: "Social Integration and Sacramental Activity: An Analysis of 1 Cor. 11:17-34," p. 145-74 (translation of "Soziale Integration und sakramentales Handeln: Eine Analyse von 1 Cor. 11:17-34," *Novum Testamentum*, 16 [1974]: 179-206); "Social Stratification in the Corinthian Community: A Contribution to the Sociology of Early Hellenistic Christianity," p. 69-120 (translation of "Soziale Schichtung in der korinthischen Gemeinde: Ein Beitrag zur Soziologie des hellenistischen Urchristentums," *Zeitschrift für die neutestamentliche Wissenschaft und die Kunde der älteren Kirche*, 65 [1974]: 232-72); "The Strong and the Weak in Corinth: A Sociological Analysis of a Theological Quarrel," p. 121-44 (translation of "Die Starken und Schwachen in Korinth: Soziologische Analyse eines theologischen Streites," *Evangelische Theologie*, 35 [1975]: 155-72).

47 Theissen's work is exemplary of the merits of applying sociological questions and theories to historical data, but also exemplary of the pitfalls of cross-disciplinary approaches. I will argue that Theissen draws from an insufficient sample of the historical data concerning the social context of idol-food, and that this makes his conclusions invalid.

48 This is argued most extensively in "Social Stratification." Theissen draws on evidence concerning the identity and social roles of known persons from the Corinthian Christian group, the indications of the wealth of the group's leaders, and from Paul's descriptions of the group in 1 Cor.

49 In "Strong and Weak."

50 In "Social Integration."

course in their daily social interactions. Their business and social dealings would have been adversely affected by avoiding such food.[51] In contrast, the poorer Christians—the "weak"—had very few occasions on which to eat meat which had been sacrificed (the poor could not afford meat at all),[52] and those occasions were explicitly linked to religious festivals (primarily the free distribution of sacrificed meat at public festivals).[53] Hence the strong saw no harm in eating idol-meat and considerable harm in avoiding it, while the weak saw religious danger in eating idol-meat. Theissen also draws connections between the strong's more likely access to education and their arguments appealing to knowledge in defence of the eating of idol-food.[54] Like many other commentators Theissen interprets 1 Corinthians 8-10 as Paul's attempt to mediate between the groups of strong and weak Christians.[55]

Theissen makes an assumption that seems both unconscious and uncontroversial but flaws his conclusions seriously. He assumes that idol-food refers exclusively to meat. Theissen's conclusions concerning the different attitudes toward idol-food between the strong and the weak depend on the different use of meat in the daily social intercourse of the rich and poor.

The identification of meat and idol-food is too narrow. All kinds of food, whether derived from animals or not, could be and were sanctified (or polluted, depending on one's point of view) by ritual acts of thanksgiving or consecration. This makes it possible that even the simplest meal might become idol-food (for example, grain porridge hallowed by rites sacred to the Two Goddesses).[56]

Further, the stark difference in the social use of food (whether sacred or not) between social classes in Greco-Roman society which Theissen argues is not borne out by the Greco-Roman literary and archaeological evidence.[57] The bulk of this evidence derives from the upper classes of that society, but what evidence there is of the lower classes shows social and religious uses of food virtually identical in structure, only on a different scale. The humble used the sanctuary of Demeter and Kore extensively, and probably its dining rooms; the lower class carried away (along with its laughable pretensions) sacrificed

---

51 "Strong and Weak," p. 130-32.

52 Ibid., p. 125-28. It is interesting to note a proto-typical version of this argument in Barrett, "Things Sacrificed," p. 48-49.

53 "Strong and Weak," p. 128.

54 Ibid., p. 137-38.

55 Ibid., p. 138-39. Klauck concurs with Theissen's account of the nature of the groups and the source of their conflict (*Herrenmahl*, p. 246-47).

56 This is argued more fully above, in chap. 5.

57 This evidence is set out in chaps. 1, 2 and 3, above.

chicken (instead of beef) from the Asklepieion; the poor clients needed to angle for invitations for social advancement more than the wealthy; weddings of the humble involved sacrifice just as those of the rich.

Because Theissen mistakenly identifies idol-food with meat and draws an unjustified contrast in the social uses of food between classes in Greco-Roman society, his reconstruction is unpersuasive. One aspect of Theissen's claims is true: the social intercourse of the rich would be more affected by avoidance of idol-food, and their social goals more seriously hampered than those of the poor. This addresses the differential effect of Paul's position, however, and does not address the cause of the dispute or problem. The central premise of Theissen's reconstruction—that the rich would eat idol-food but the poor would not—is not supported by a thorough reading of the evidence from outside 1 Corinthians.

J. Murphy-O'Connor

Jerome Murphy-O'Connor's articles on 1 Corinithians 8-10 provide a reconstruction of the position of the "strong"[58] Corinthians and Paul's response to them.[59] He perceives Paul as a masterful mediator between the strong and the weak, akin to the view of C. K. Barrett, but does not affirm Barrett's interpretation of the ethnic roots of the conflict.

Murphy-O'Connor argues that: (1) the Corinthian slogans of 8:1,4 and 8 were arguments developed by the strong against weak Christians, who were Gentile converts still troubled by irrational fears over the powers of non-existent demons and who objected to the practices of the strong; (2) Paul agreed with the strong's assessment of the nature of idol-food and its harmlessness, but countered the strong's cold rationalism with a sensitive assessment of social and moral reality (the reality of the weak's fear of demons and the potential harm in their eating) and called for behaviour reflecting the priority of Christian love over knowledge.[60]

Murphy-O'Connor argues not only that the conflict over idol-food in Corinth was between the strong and the weak, but that the weak had taken an aggressive stance towards the strong. The strong did

58 This designation is adopted by Murphy-O'Connor, with explicit recognition that its basis is not in Paul's letters but on an obvious contrast with those Paul calls the weak.

59 J. Murphy-O'Connor, "1 Cor 8:6: Cosmology or Soteriology?" *Revue biblique*, 85 (1978): 253-67; "Corinthian Slogans in 1 Cor 6:12-20," *Catholic Biblical Quarterly*, 40 (1978): 391-96; "Freedom or the Ghetto (1 Cor 8:1-13; 10:23-11:1)," *Revue biblique*, 85 (1978): 543-74; "Food and Spiritual Gifts in 1 Cor 8:8," *Catholic Biblical Quarterly*, 41 (1979): 292-98.

60 This is set out most fully in "Freedom or the Ghetto."

not need the monotheistic arguments over the harmlessness of idol-food reflected by the slogans, since for them sins of the body were irrelevant (citing 1 Cor 6:12-20, where it is clear that the strong argued that all things were lawful, that food was a matter of indifference, and possibly even that sexual relations were a matter of indifference). The strong themselves felt no need to justify the eating of idol-food.[61] Their defence of their behaviour was necessary only to counter criticism from the weak, who were Gentile Christians "whose intellectual conviction that there was only one God had not been fully assimilated emotionally," and who, when they had followed the example of the strong and eaten idol-food, had experienced the pain of conscience. The weak assumed the strong felt similar pain, and as a result criticized them.[62] The strong's arguments from monotheistic principles were developed to persuade the weak to adopt a view of idol-food consistent with basic principles of their faith.[63]

This summary is sufficient to demonstrate how dependent Murphy-O'Connor's reconstruction is on the assumption that there was a party of weak Christians in Corinth. Hurd's arguments and my own that the conflict over idol-food centred on Paul and the Corinthians rather than on factions within the Corinthian group attack the foundation of Murphy-O'Connor's position. Murphy-O'Connor is aware of Hurd's position, but, like Barrett, chooses simply to dismiss it,[64] even to the extent of stating baldly that "no evidence contradicts the traditional opinion that there were two groups within the Corinthian church." This is simply incorrect.

The second plank in Murphy-O'Connor's reconstruction is the claim that Paul agreed with the strong's assessment of the harmlessness of idol-food per se but countered their correct but coldly rational knowledge about idol-food with a call to love. Paul shows a broader and deeper appreciation of the social and moral realities of both the strong and weak; he recognizes that the strong are correct on the level of "objective truth" over the non-reality of demons and its implications for the harmlessness of sacrificed food, but also recognizes the "subjective existence" of demons for the weak and the harm that eat-

---

61 "Freedom," p. 547. His arguments that the strong believed that the body was morally indifferent are developed in "Corinthian Slogans in 1 Cor 6:12-20."

62 "Freedom," p. 554-56.

63 Ibid., p. 548.

64 Ibid., p. 544. Murphy-O'Connor points only to Hurd's conclusions that Paul disagreed with the Corinthians throughout 1 Cor 8-10 but in the end allowed them to continue their current practice concerning idol-food. Hurd's conclusion does indeed ring strange, but Hurd has carefully established it on a close reading of the text and fit it into a larger reconstructed context.

ing condemned by conscience could effect. Murphy-O'Connor thus provides a stirring picture of Paul as a subtle and effective conciliator, urging the primacy of love.[65]

This reconstruction is deeply flawed by the omission of any consideration of 1 Corinthians 10:1-22. Murphy-O'Connor's article, as its subtitle makes clear, is explicitly a discussion of only 1 Corinthians 8:1-13 and 10:23-11:1, but this is no defence, since he purports to analyze Paul's true position vis-à-vis idol-food. His claim that Paul agreed with the objective content of the strong Corinthians' knowledge cannot be made without consideration of Paul's warnings against the dangers of participation at the table of demons, especially when the opening references to the Israelites in chapter 10 make it abundantly clear that Paul's warnings are directed towards those confident in their standing in the community—the strong. An exegesis of 1 Corinthians 8:1-13 and 10:23-11:1, no matter how persuasive, will not provide an adequate account of Paul's views about idol-food and Paul's assessment of the position of the Corinthian Christians.

W. L. Willis

The last competing reading of 1 Corinthians 8-10 to be addressed is Wendel Lee Willis's *Idol Meat in Corinth: The Pauline Argument in 1 Corinthians 8 and 10.* Willis's analysis of the social importance of meals involving religious rites and the motivation of the Corinthian Christians in desiring not to be excluded from these is very similar to my own. My disagreement with Willis centres not on his analysis of the social importance of idol-food, but on its religious significance. Willis's different conclusion regarding the religious significance of cultic meals leads to a different analysis of Paul's position concerning idol-food.

Willis's central thesis argues against a "sacramental" understanding of Greco-Roman cultic meals, and, by extension, a similar understanding concerning partnership at the table of *daimonia* in 1 Corinthians 10. I have placed the term sacramental in quotation marks because Willis adopts a technical sense of sacramental: food rites as a magical or quasi-magical consumption of the God, and power (or however its effect is conceived) taken up in the food by its consumer. Accordingly, his assessment of the significance of Greco-Roman meals for the understanding of 1 Corinthians 8-10 is dominated by one agenda: to determine whether an earlier scholarly understanding of the "sacramental" nature of Greco-Roman meals is correct.

65 "Freedom," p. 556-74.

Willis focusses on this question both because he sees this understanding of Greco-Roman religious meals dominating religious scholarship earlier in this century,[66] and also because this understanding of Greco-Roman meals often lies behind still current interpretations of 1 Corinthians 8-10, and in particular 10:16-22, where Paul warns against the table of *daimonia.* Willis argues against the perception of inconsistency between Paul's "sacramental" understanding of pagan meals in chapter 10 and a more "enlightened" non-sacramental view in chapter 8.[67] Because Willis defends the consistency of Paul's views, he is concerned to establish an alternative understanding of Greco-Roman religious meals in support of his reading of chapter 10.

This alternative understanding of the religious significance of Greco-Roman meals is termed by him a social interpretation. Religious meals on this view do not denote theophagy, or even participation of the God in the meal through his or her allotted portion on the God's table or through sacrifice. Rather, meals at the table of *daimonia* are little more than social occasions pure and simple, with participation—*koinônia*—not of the God but only of the partakers of the meal: "while due regard was given the deity and a portion allotted to him, the focus is on the social relationship among the worshippers. The deity is more an observer than a participant."[68]

To demonstrate the validity of this view, Willis presents diverse literary evidence in support of his alternative "social" interpretation. He focusses on three sorts of evidence: (1) meals held by the many and varied associations or clubs prevalent in all periods of Greco-Roman society, (2) cult regulations, and (3) literary remains which indicate various sorts of misconduct at ritual meals (misconduct whose unifying theme is the disregard of the religious significance of the meal in favour of filling the belly as full, and as crudely as possible).[69] He concludes from these sources that there is no clear evidence for a "sacramental" view of religious meals but there is positive evidence for an understanding of cult meals as social occasions pure and simple. He also concludes that since these meals held no "sacramental" significance, Paul's objections to them are *not* on the basis that they effect partnership with demons.

Willis's position is seriously flawed in its stress on the social purpose of religious meals and in its account of the reasons for Paul's

---

66 Willis cites F. Cumont, E. R. Goodenough, H. Lietzmann, J. A. MacCulloch, A. D. Nock, and M. J. Vermaseren as holding some variant of a "sacramental" view of Greco-Roman cultic meals. See references in Willis, *Idol Meat,* p. 18, 33.

67 *Idol Meat,* p. 48.

68 Ibid., p. 20.

69 Ibid., p. 47-61.

opposition to partnership at the table of *daimonia*. As Willis argues, many meals involving religious rites in Greco-Roman society had a social character. This conclusion is supported both by the sources Willis surveys and by my analysis of a wider range of sources more specific to Paul's period. Willis's inference from this conclusion—that social intercourse was the primary purpose and effect of cultic meals—is not, however, sensible. There is no necessity that occasions of "good company, good food and good fun"[70] not be at the same time deeply religious occasions. Willis is aware of the fineness of the distinction he proposes between the religious function of these meals and their social function (he states that the difference is one of "focus" of the participants[71]). His distinction is too fine, and not warranted by the evidence.

Willis's sources are unrepresentative, in that they concern social abuse of religious events. He refers to cult regulations (whose purpose was to set limits on behaviour and sanctions), satirical accounts of parasites at cultic tables, and earnest lamentations on the lack of true devotion at cultic meals. Though Willis is sensitive to the difficulties of using satire as social description,[72] he is surprisingly ready to dismiss authentic religious expression in meals involving rites.

Willis's reconstruction is further weakened by his analysis of Paul's opposition to participation in cultic meals in 10:16-22. The skeleton of his argument is this. Partnership (*koinôni*) at table should be understood as fellowship *with others*.[73] Paul's argument makes partnership with demons parallel to partnership with the Lord in both Jewish and Christian worship. No Jewish sources support a view of sacrifice as theophagy, so Paul's reference to partnership with *daimonia* should not be understood in a "sacramental" sense. The focus of the passage is not on the *daimonia* but rather on the table and cup, so the problem is less *daimonia* and more the partnership with others in idolatry.[74] Paul's warning against partnership at the table of demons, then, does not reflect a fear of contagion but rather reflects Paul's desire to have the Corinthians avoid fellowship with idolaters. This reading makes chapter 10 more consistent with Paul's warnings against idol-food in chapter 8 on the basis of its effect on the weak rather than its nature as food.[75]

---

70 Ibid., p. 63. This is Willis's description of the meaning of cultic meals.

71 Ibid., p. 48.

72 Ibid., p. 59.

73 Ibid, p. 191. This point is made at length earlier in an extended discussion of Greco-Roman literary evidence (ibid., p. 21-61).

74 Ibid., p. 191.

75 Ibid., p. 184-88; 191; 215-19.

My critique of this view can be stated simply. Paul believes in the reality of *daimonia*—not just in some social reality in that new adherents to the group will be led again into old, pagan ways, but in the concrete reality of other Gods and other Lords (8:5). Paul's parallel treatment of the Lord's table and the table of *daimonia* shows that he perceives real religious effect in these meals, and finds participation in them to be dangerous to the Corinthians.

Willis offers no plausible reason why, if both Paul and the Corinthians find no religious significance in these meals, Paul would forbid participation at the table of *daimonia*. The explanation left to Willis is that Paul, though at heart holding as liberal a view concerning idol-food as the Corinthians, forbids such participation to protect the weak. But this is no adequate explanation. Paul does not mention the weak or consideration for others in 10:16-22; it is no accident that commentators, including Willis, have long grappled with the tension between 10:16-22 and chapter 8. If all that Paul were concerned with was the other, then Paul would presumably permit participation at the table of *daimonia* as long as no one objects or is threatened, or Paul would agree with the strong that the weak should be educated about the harmlessness of the food. But, of course, this is not what Paul permits.

Willis infers incorrectly from the social purposes of cultic meals that their nature was not sufficiently religious to threaten Paul or the Corinthian Christians of robust knowledge.[76] He develops a flawed view both of the religious nature of meals involving rites and, in turn, of the reasons for Paul's opposition to partnership at the table of *daimonia*.

Conclusions

The scholarly consensus, broadly stated, is that Paul addressed a divided community in Corinth and mediated between parties to a conflict there, and that Paul's basic position was to see food itself as a matter of indifference and to urge restrictions for the sake of others. The scholarly consensus on both these issues—that Paul addresses a divided community, and rejects a so-called superstitious fear of idol-food as vigorously as the strong—is ill-founded and mistaken.

---

76 See, for example: "It was probably not regarded [by Corinthian Christians] as pagan worship to participate in the various 'socials' held in temple precincts" (*Idol Meat*, p. 63).

Appendix 2

Aristides, Oration *49*

When he had also made this experiment, he permitted me to drink as much as I wished, and made some sort of joke, to the effect that they are foolish men who are rich in material goods and do not dare to use them freely. And this book which I mentioned seemed to be Antisthenes' *On Use*. It pertained to wine, and there were certain tokens of Dionysus as well. I became so accustomed to it that, although the god granted it, I deviated but slightly in the measure of my drinking. And in some way, I longed for the stewardship of those times.

For a long time I abstained from all living things, except chicken, and all greens, except wild ones and lettuce. Indeed, I even abstained from all sweetmeats. Once he commanded me to use only one food, and I used chicken, I, for whom even this order was difficult. And we endured some of these things without bathing and with phlebotomies [blood-lettings] and enemas, and some, as each circumstance might be. For six years I have also abstained from all fish. I do not know how long from pork. Again when he allowed it, I used both. Then, in turn, I was kept from some things, and used some, according to each particular circumstance. Indeed, he has kept me completely from fish sauce, for he said it was not safe for my head, and least of all for my teeth. He gave me remedies for my teeth. First there was: burn the tooth of a lion, and grinding it up, use it as a dentifrice. Second: clean your teeth with that famous ointment, sap of silphium. After this, pepper, which he added for warmth. After all these things, came Indian nard, this also as a dentifrice. And these are dreams which have recently appeared.

I have been kept from beef in this way. I dreamed that an oracle had fallen to Zosimus, "and that he would live as long as the cow in the field lived." And then I said to him: "Do you know what the oracle means? It commands you to abstain from beef." Zosimus was said, in addition to the cold from which he died, to have been harmed also by touching some beef from a sacrifice. There was, as is likely, much nicety and care about not even secretly touching it with the tip of my finger.[1]

---

1 Source: P. Aelius Aristides, *Oration* 49 (*Sacred Tales* 3), 1.32-37, in *The Complete Works*, trans. Charles A. Behr (Leiden: E. J. Brill, 1981), 2:314.

Bibliography

Primary Sources

Achilles Tatius. *The Adventures of Leucippe and Clitophon.* Trans. S. Gaselee. Loeb Classical Library. 1917.

Aristides, P. Aelius. *The Complete Works.* Trans. Charles A. Behr. 2 vols. Leiden: E. J. Brill, 1981.

Aristophanes. *Plays 2.* Trans. Patrick Dickinson. Oxford: Oxford University Press, 1970.

Catullus. *Odi et Amo. The Complete Poetry of Catullus.* Trans. Roy A. Swanson. Indianapolis: Bobbs-Merill, 1959.

———. *The Poems.* Ed. Kenneth Quinn. 2nd ed. London: Macmillan, 1973.

———. *The Poems of Catullus.* Trans. Peter Whigham. Harmondsworth, Middlesex: Penguin, 1966.

Cicero. In Brook, Dorothy, ed. *Private Letters Pagan and Christian.* London: Ernest Benn, 1929.

———. *Letters to Atticus.* Trans. E. O. Winstedt. 3 vols. Loeb Classical Library. 1912-1918.

———. *The Letters to his Friends.* Trans. Glynn Williams. 3 vols. Loeb Classical Library. 1927-1929.

Clement of Alexandria. *Clemens Alexandrinus.* 2 Band. *Stromata. Buch. 1-6.* Herausgegeben von Otto Stählin, in 3 Auflage neu herausgegeben von Ludwig Früchtel. Berlin: Akademie Verlag, 1960.

———. *The Stromata, or Miscellanies.* In *The Ante-Nicene Fathers. Translations of the Writings of the Fathers Down to A.D. 325.* Vol. 2, *Fathers of the Second Century.* Ed. A. Roberts and J. Donaldson. Buffalo: Christian Literature Publishing, 1885.

Didache. In *The Apostolic Fathers.* Vol. 1. Trans. Kirsopp Lake. Loeb Classical Library. 1912.

Dio Chrysostom. *The Hunters of Euboea.* In *Three Greek Romances.* Trans. Moses Hadas, 173-89. Garden City, NJ: Doubleday, 1953.

Epictetus. *The Discourses as Reported by Arrian, the Manual [Encheiridion] and Fragments.* Trans. W. A. Olddfather. 2 vols. Loeb Classical Library. 1925.

Herodas (also cited as Herondas). *Mimiambi*. Ed. I. C. Cunningham. Oxford: Clarendon, 1971.

Herondas (also cited as Herodas). *The Mimes of Herondas*. Trans. Guy Davenport. San Francisco: Grey Fox Press, 1981.

Homeric Hymn to Demeter. Trans. Hugh G. Evelyn-White. In *Hesiod, the Homeric Hymns and Homerica*. Ed. E. H. Warmington. Loeb Classical Library. 1970.

Horace. *The Odes of Horace with Five Prefacing Epodes*. Trans. Margaret Ralston Gest. Ed. M. M. H. Thrall. Kutztown, PA: Kutztown Publishing, 1973.

________. *Satires and Epistles*. Trans. Niall Rudd. Harmondsworth, Middlesex: Penguin, 1979.

Hunt, A. S., and C. C. Edgar. *Select Papyri*. Vol. 1, *Non-Literary Papyri. Private Affairs*. Vol. 2, *Non-Literary Papyri. Public Documents*. Loeb Classical Library. 1954.

Irenaeus. *Sancti Irenaei. Libros quinque adversus haereses*. Tome 1. Ed. W. Wigan Harvey. Cambridge: Typis Academicis, 1852.

________. *Against Heresies*. In *The Ante-Nicene Fathers*. Vol. 1, *The Apostolic Fathers—Justin Martyr-Irenaeus*. Ed. A. Roberts and J. Donaldson. Edinburgh: T. & T. Clark, 1885. Reprinted: Grand Rapids: Eerdmans, 1967.

Justin Martyr. *Corpus apologetarum Christianorem saeculi secundi*. Vol. 2, *Justini philosophi et marturis. Opera quae feruntur omnia*. Tome 1, part 2, *Opera indubitata. Dialogus cum Tryphone Iudaeo*. Ed. Johannes C. T. Otto. Wiesbaden: Sändig, 1969 (first published 1877).

________. *Dialogue with Trypho*. In *The Ante-Nicene Fathers*. Vol. 2, *The Apostolic Fathers-Justin Martyr-Irenaeus*. Ed. A. Roberts and J. Donaldson. Edinburgh: T. & T. Clark, 1885. Reprinted: Grand Rapids: Eerdmans, 1967.

Juvenal. *Juvenal and Persius*. Rev. ed. Trans. G. G. Ramsay. Loeb Classical Library. 1940.

________. *Satires*. Trans. Charles Plumb. London: Panther, 1968.

________. *Sixteen Satires upon the Ancient Harlot*. Trans. Steven Robinson. Manchester: Carcanet New Press, 1983.

Longus. *Daphnis and Chloe*. In *Three Greek Romances*. Trans. Moses Hadas, 17-100. Garden City, NJ: Doubleday, 1953.

________. *The Story of Daphnis and Chloe. A Greek Pastoral by Longus*. Ed. and trans. W. D. Lowe. New York: Arno Press, 1979.

Lucian of Samosata. *Lucian*. Trans. A. M. Harmon. 8 vols. Loeb Classical Library. 1919-1925.

________. *Satirical Sketches*. Trans. Paul Turner. Harmondsworth, Middlesex: Penguin, 1961.

Lucius Apuleius. *Apuleius. The Golden Ass, being the Metamorphoses of Lucius Apuleius*. Trans. W. Adlington, rev. S. Gaselee. Loeb Classical Library. 1915.

———. *The Golden Ass (Metamorphoses)*. Trans. Robert Graves. Harmondsworth, Middlesex: Penguin, 1950.

Malherbe, Abraham J. *The Cynic Epistles. A Study Edition*. Society of Biblical Literature Sources for Biblical Study, no. 12. Missoula, MT: Scholars Press, 1977.

Minucius Felix. *Octavius*. Trans. Gerald H. Rendall. Loeb Classical Library. 1931.

Musonius Rufus. *Discourses*. Ed. and trans. Cora E. Lutz, 3-147. Yale Classical Studies 10. New Haven: Yale University Press, 1947.

Novatian. *On Jewish Meats*. In *The Ante-Nicene Fathers. Translations of the Writings of the Fathers Down to A.D. 325*. Vol. 5, *Fathers of the Third Century*. Ed. A. Roberts and J. Donaldson. Buffalo: Christian Literature Publishing, 1886.

Origen. *Contra Celsum*. Trans. Henry Chadwick. Cambridge: Cambridge University Press, 1953. Reprinted with corrections, 1965.

———. *Origène. Contra Celse*. t. 4 (livres 7 et 8). Introduction, texte critique, traduction et notes par Marcel Borret. Sources chrétiennes, no. 150. Paris: Les éditions du Cerf, 1969.

Pausanius. *Description of Greece*. Trans. W. H. S. Jones and H. A. Omerod. 5 vols. Loeb Classical Library. 1918-1935.

———. *Guide to Greece*. Trans. Peter Levi. 2 vols. Harmondsworth, Middlesex: Penguin Books, 1971.

Persius. *Juvenal and Persius*. Rev. ed. Trans. G. G. Ramsay. Loeb Classical Library. 1940.

———. *Satires*. Trans. Niall Rudd. Harmondsworth, Middlesex: Penguin, 1979.

Petronius. *The Cena Trimalchionis of Petronius*. Ed. W. B. Sedgwick. 2nd ed. Oxford: Clarendon, 1950.

———. *Satyricon*. Trans. Paul Dinnage. London: Syracuse & Calder, 1953.

———. *Satyricon*. Trans. Michael Heseltine. Loeb Classical Library. 1930.

Philostratus. *Life of Apollonius*. Trans. C. P. Jones. Harmondsworth, Middlesex: Penguin, 1970.

———. *Philostratus. Lives of the Sophists*. Trans. Wilmer C. Wright. Loeb Classical Library. 1952.

Plautus. *Plautus*. Trans. Paul Nixon. 5 vols. Loeb Classical Library. 1916-1930.

———. *Roman Comedies*. Ed. George E. Duckworth. New York: Random House, 1942.

Pliny. *The Letters of the Younger Pliny*. Trans. Betty Radice. Harmondsworth, Middlesex: Penguin, 1963.

———. *Pliny. Letters*. Trans. William Melmoth. 2 vols. Loeb Classical Library. 1915.

Plutarch. *Lives of the Noble Greeks*. Ed. Edmund Fuller. New York: Dell, 1968.

———. *Lives*. Trans. Bernadotte Perrin. 11 vols. Loeb Classical Library. 1914-1926.

_______. *Convivial Questions* (612C-748D of the *Moralia*). In *Moralia*, vol. 8, trans. P. A. Clement and H. B. Hoffleit; Vol. 9, trans. E. A. Linear and F. H. Sandbach. Loeb Classical Library. 1969.

Seneca. *Ad Lucilium epistulae morales.* Trans. Richard M. Grummere. 3 vols. Loeb Classical Library. 1925.

_______. *Four Tragedies and Octavia.* Trans. E. F. Watling. Harmondsworth, Middlesex: Penguin, 1966.

_______. *Letters from a Stoic.* Selected and trans. Robin Campbell. Harmondsworth, Middlesex: Penguin, 1969.

Terence. *Roman Comedies.* Ed. George E. Duckworth. New York: Random House, 1942.

_______. *Terence.* Trans. John Sargeaunt. 2 vols. Loeb Classical Library. 1912.

Tertullian. *Apology.* Trans. T. R. Glover. Loeb Classical Library. 1931.

Vitruvius, *On Architecture.* Trans. Frank Granger. 2 vols. Loeb Classical Library. 1931-34.

Xenophon. *An Ephesian Tale.* In *Three Greek Romances.* Trans. Moses Hadas, 101-72. Garden City, NJ: Doubleday, 1953.

_______. *Xenophontis Ephesii Ephesiacorum Libri V: de amoribus Anthiae et Abracomae.* Ed. Antonius D. Papanikolaou. Leipzig: Teubner, 1973.

Commentary and analysis

Arndt, William F., and F. Wilbur Gingrich. *A Greek-English Lexicon of the New Testament and Other Early Christian Literature.* Rev. ed. Chicago: University of Chicago Press, 1954. Translated and adapted from Walter Bauer. *Greichische-Deutsches Wörterbuch zu den Schriften des Neues Testaments und der übrigen urchristliche Literatur.* Berlin: 1949-52.

Ayerst, David, and A. S. T. Fisher. *Records of Christianity.* Vol. 1, *In the Roman Empire.* Oxford: Basil Blackwell, 1971.

Batey, R. A. "Paul's Interactions with the Corinthians." *Journal of Biblical Literature*, 84 (1965): 139-46.

Barrett, C. K. *The First Epistle to the Corinthians.* Black's New Testament Commentaries. London: Adam and Charles Black, 1968.

_______. "Things Sacrificed to Idols." In *Essays on Paul*, 40-59. London: SPCK, 1982. First published in *New Testament Studies*, 11 (1964-65): 138-53.

Baur, Ferdinand Christian. *Paul the Apostle of Jesus Christ. His Life and Work. His Epistles and his Doctrine.* 2nd ed. Trans. and rev. A. Menzies, after a translation of the second German edition by Edward Zeller. 2 vols. London and Edinburgh: Williams and Norgate, 1876. 1st German ed., 1845.

Bianchi, Ugo. *The Greek Mysteries.* Iconography of Religions, Section 17: Greece and Rome. Fascicle 3. Ed. Th. P. van Baaren et al. Leiden: E. J. Brill, 1976.

Bleeker, C. J., ed. *Initiation. Contributions to the Theme of the Study-Conference of the International Association for the History of Religions Held at Strasburg,*

Sept. 17th to 22nd, 1964. Studies in the History of Religions (Supplements to *Nvmen*), 10. Leiden: E. J. Brill, 1965.

Blegen, Carl William, Oscar Broneer, Richard Stillwell, and Alfred Raymond Bellinger. *Corinth: Results of Excavations Conducted by the American School of Classical Studies at Athens.* Vol. 3, Part 1, *Acrocorinth. Excavations in 1926.* Cambridge, MA: Harvard University Press, 1936.

Bookidis, Nancy. "The Sanctuary of Demeter and Kore on Acrocorinth: Preliminary Report 3: 1968." *Hesperia,* 38 (1969): 297-310.

———, and Joan E. Fisher. "The Sanctuary of Demeter and Kore on Acrocorinth: Preliminary Report 4: 1969-1970." *Hesperia,* 41 (1972): 283-331.

———. "The Sanctuary of Demeter and Kore on Acrocorinth: Preliminary Report 5: 1971-1973." *Hesperia,* 43 (1974): 267-307.

Bornkamm, Günther. "The History of the Origin of the So-Called Second Letter to the Corinthians." *New Testament Studies,* 8(1961-62): 258-64.

———. "The Missionary Stance of Paul in 1 Corinthians 9 and in Acts." In *Studies in Luke-Acts.* Ed. Leander E. Keck and J. Louis Martyn, 194-207. Philadelphia: Fortress Press, 1980 (1st ed., 1966).

Broneer, Oscar. "Corinth: Centre of St. Paul's Missionary Work in Greece." *Biblical Archaeologist,* 14 (1951): 78-96.

———. *Corinth: Results of Excavations Conducted by the American School of Classical Studies at Athens.* Vol. 1, Part 4, *The South Stoa and its Roman Successors.* Princeton, NJ: American School of Classical Studies at Athens, 1954.

———. "Paul and the Pagan Cults at Isthmia." *Harvard Theological Review,* 64 (1971): 169-87.

Brumfield, Allaire Chandor. *The Attic Festivals of Demeter and their Relation to the Agricultural Year.* Monographs in Classical Studies. Ed. W. R. Connor. New York: Arno Press, 1981.

Brunt, John C. "Rejected, Ignored, or Misunderstood? The Fate of Paul's Approach to the Problem of Food Offered to Idols in Early Christianity." *New Testament Studies,* 31 (1985): 113-24.

Bultmann, Rudolph. *Primitive Christianity in its Contemporary Setting.* Trans. R. H. Fuller. New York: New American Library, 1956. Translated from *Das Urchristentum in Rahmen der antiken Religionen,* n.p.

Burford, Alison. *The Greek Temple Builders at Epidauros.* Toronto: University of Toronto Press, 1969.

Cadbury, Henry J. "The Macellum of Corinth." *Journal of Biblical Literature,* 53 (1934): 134-41.

Carpenter, Rhys, and Antoine Bon. *Corinth: Results of Excavations Conducted by the American School of Classical Studies at Athens.* Vol. 3, Part 2, *The Defenses of Acrocorinth and the Lower Town.* Cambridge, MA: Harvard University Press, 1936.

Case, Shirley Jackson. *The Social Origins of Christianity*. Chicago: University of Chicago Press, 1923.

Chadwick, Henry. "'All Things to All Men' (1 Cor 9:22)." *New Testament Studies*, 1 (1954-55): 261-75.

Conzelmann, Hans. *A Commentary on the First Epistle to the Corinthians*. Trans. James W. Leitch. Hermeneia. A Critical and Historical Commentary on the Bible, no. 36. Philadelphia: Fortress Press, 1975. Translated from *Der erste brief an die Korinther*. Kritisch-Exegetischer Kommentar über das Neue Testament begrundet von Heinrich August Wilhelm Meyer, Fünfte Abteilung. 11 Auflage. Göttingen: Vandenhoeck & Ruprecht, 1969.

Deissmann, Adolf. *New Light on the New Testament from Records of the Graeco-Roman Period*. Trans. L. R. M. Strachan. Edinburgh: T. & T. Clark, 1908.

Delatte, Armand. *Le cycéon. Breuvage rituel des mystères d'Eleusis*. Collection d'études anciennes publiée sous le patronage de L'Association G. Bude. (Extrait du *Bulletin de l'Academie Royale de Belgique*, Classe de lettres et sciences morales et politique, 5e serie, tome 40, 1954.) Paris: Société d'Édition Les Belles Lettres, 1955.

Deubner, Ludwig August. *Attische Feste*. Berlin: Akademie-Verlag, 1956. Reprint. Berlin: Verlag Heinrich Keller, 1932.

Deubner, Otfried. *Das Asklepieion von Pergamon*. Berlin: Verlag für Kunstwissenschaft, 1938.

Douglas, Mary. "Deciphering a Meal." *Daedalus*, 101 (1972): 61-81.

_______. *Purity and Danger. An Analysis of the Concepts of Pollution and Taboo*. London: Routledge and Kegan Paul, 1966.

Dow, Sterling, and Robert F. Healey, S. J. *A Sacred Calendar of Eleusis*. Harvard Theological Studies, 21. Cambridge: Harvard University Press, 1965.

Edelstein, Emma J., and Ludwig Edelstein. *Asclepius. A Collection and Interpretation of the Testimonies*. 2 vols. Publications of the Institute of the History of Medicine, The Johns Hopkins University. Second series: Texts and Documents. Baltimore: Johns Hopkins Press, 1945.

Ehrhardt, Arnold. "Social Problems in the Early Church. I. The Sunday Joint of the Christian Housewife." Chap. 12 of *The Framework of the New Testament Stories*, 275-90. Manchester: Manchester University Press, 1964.

Enslin, Morton Scott. *Christian Beginnings*. New York: Harper and Brothers, 1938.

Farnell, Lewis Richard. *The Cults of the Greek States*. Vol. 3. Oxford: Clarendon Press, 1907.

Fee, Gordon D. "2 Corinthians 6:14-7:1 and Food Offered to Idols." *New Testament Studies*, 23 (1977): 140-61.

_______. "*Eidôlothyta* Once Again: an Interpretation of 1 Corinthians 8-10." *Biblica*, 16 (1980): 172-97.

Festugière, André-Jean. "Popular Piety: Aelius Aristides and Asclepius." Chap. 6 of *Personal Religion among the Greeks*. Sather Classical Lectures, 26: 85-104. Berkeley: University of California Press, 1954.

Ford, J. Massingberd. "'Hast Thou Tithed thy Meal?' and 'Is thy Child Kosher?'" *Journal of Theological Studies* n.s., 17 (1966): 71-79.

Foucart, Paul. *Les mystères d'Eleusis*. Paris: Auguste Picard. ed. Libraire des Archives Nationales et de la Société de l'École des Chartes, 1914.

Fowler, Harold North, and Richard Stillwell. *Corinth: Results of Excavations Conducted by the American School of Classical Studies at Athens*. Vol. 1, Part 1, *Introduction, Topography, Architecture*. Cambridge, MA: Harvard University Press, 1932.

Furnish, Victor Paul. *2 Corinthians*. Anchor Bible, vol. 32A. Garden City, NJ: Doubleday, 1984.

Gager, John G. *Kingdom and Community. The Social World of Early Christianity*. Ed. J. P. Reeder, Jr., and J. F. Wilson. Prentice-Hall Studies in Religion Series. Englewood Cliffs, NJ: Prentice Hall, 1975.

Georgi, Dieter. "Corinthians, Paul's First Letter to the."; "Corinthians, Paul's Second Letter to the." *Interpreter's Dictionary of the Bible*. Supplementary Volume. Nashville: Abingdon Press, 1976.

Giblin, Charles H. "Three Monotheistic Texts in Paul (1 Cor 8:1-13; Gal 3; Rom 3)." *Catholic Biblical Quarterly*, 37 (1975): 524-47.

Gooch, Paul W., and Peter Richardson. "Accommodation Ethics." *Tyndale Bulletin*, 29 (1978): 90-142.

———. "'Conscience' in 1 Corinthians 8 and 10." *New Testament Studies*, 33 (1987): 244-54.

———. "The Burden of the Weak: 1 Corinthians 8-10." Chap. 5 in *Partial Knowledge. Philosophical Studies in Paul*, 102-23. Notre Dame, IN: University of Notre Dame Press, 1987.

Grant, Robert M. "Dietary Laws among Pythagoreans, Jews, and Christians." *Harvard Theological Review*, 73 (1980): 299-310.

———. *Gods and the One God*. Ed. Wayne A. Meeks. Library of Early Christianity. Philadelphia: Westminster Press, 1986.

Hadas, Moses, trans. *Three Greek Romances*. Garden City, NJ: Doubleday, 1953.

Hengel, Martin. *Judaism and Hellenism. Studies in their Encounter in Palestine During the Early Hellenistic Period*. Trans. John Bowden. 2 vols. London: SCM Press, 1974. Translated from *Judentum und Hellenismus*. Tübingen: J. C. B. Mohr, 1969.

Héring, Jean. *La première épître de Saint Paul aux Corinthiens*. Deuxieme ed., revue. Ed. P. Bonnard et al. Commentaire du Nouveau Testament, 8. Neuchatel: Delachaux et Niestle, 1959.

Hill, Bert Hodge. *Corinth: Results of Excavations Conducted by the American School of Classical Studies at Athens*. Vol. 1, Part 6, *The Springs: Peirene,*

Sacred Spring, Glauke. Princeton, NJ: American School of Classical Studies at Athens, 1964.

Hock, Ronald F. *The Social Context of Paul's Ministry: Tentmaking and Apostleship*. Philadelphia: Fortress Press, 1980.

Horsley, Richard A. "The Background of the Confessional Formula in 1 Cor 8:6." *Zeitschrift für neutestamentliche Wissenschaft*, 69 (1978): 130-35.

_______. "Consciousness and Freedom among the Corinthians: 1 Corinthians 8-10." *Catholic Biblical Quarterly*, 40 (1978): 574-89.

_______. "Gnosis in Corinth: 1 Corinthians 8:1-6." *New Testament Studies*, 27 (1981): 32-51.

_______. "Pneumatikos vs. Psychikos. Distinctions of Spiritual Status among the Corinthians." *Harvard Theological Review*, 69 (1976): 269-88.

Hurd, John Coolidge, Jr. *The Origin of 1 Corinthians*. New York: Seabury Press; London: SPCK, 1965. Reprint. Macon, GA: Mercer University Press, 1983.

Isenberg, M. "The Sale of Sacrificial Meat." *Classical Philology*, 70 (1975): 271-73.

Jevons, F.B. *Introduction to the History of Religion*. 3 vols. n.p. 1896.

Jewett, Robert. *A Chronology of Paul's Life*. Philadelphia: Fortress Press, 1979.

_______. *Paul's Anthropological Terms: A Study in Their Use in Conflict Settings*. Arbeiten zur Geschichte des antiken Judentums und des Urchristentums, 10. Leiden: E. J. Brill, 1971.

Karris, Robert J. "Rom 14:1-15:13 and the Occasion of Romans." *Catholic Biblical Quarterly*, 35 (1973): 155-78.

Keck, Leander E. "Ethos and Ethics in the New Testament." In *Essays in Morality and Ethics*. Ed. James Gaffney, 29-49. New York: Paulist Press, 1980.

Kent, John Harvey. *Corinth: Results of Excavations Conducted by the American School of Classical Studies at Athens*. Vol. 8, Part 3, *The Inscriptions. 1926-1950*. Princeton, NJ: American School of Classical Studies at Athens, 1966.

Kerényi, C. *Asklepios. Archetypal Image of the Physician's Existence*. Trans. Ralph Manheim. Bollingen Series 65. Vol. 3, Archetypal Images in Greek Religion. New York: Pantheon, 1959. Translated from *Der göttliche Arzt: Studien über Asklepios und seine Kultstätten*. Basel: Ciba, 1947; rev. ed., Darmstadt: Wissenshaftliche Buchgesellschaft/HermanGentner Verlag, 1956.

_______. "Voraussetzungen der Einweihung in Eleusis." In *Initiation. Contributions to the Theme of the Study-Conference of the International Association for the History of Religions Held at Strasburg, Sept. 17th to 22nd, 1964*. Studies in the History of Religions (Supplements to *Nvmen*), 10. Ed. C. J. Bleeker, 62-64. Leiden: E. J. Brill, 1965.

Klauck, Hans-Joseph. *Herrenmahl und hellenistischer Kult. Eine religionsgeschichtliche Untersuchung zum ersten Korintherbrief*. Neutestamentliche

Abhandlungen, neue Folge, Band 15. Herausgegeben von J. Gnilka. Münster: Aschendorff, 1982.

Koester, Helmut. *Introduction to the New Testament.* Vol. 1, *History, Culture, and Religion of the Hellenistic Age.* Philadelphia: Fortress Press; Berlin and New York: Walter de Gruyter, 1982. Translated from *Einführung in das Neue Testament,* chaps. 1-6. Berlin: Walter de Gruyter, 1980.

Lake, Kirsopp. *The Earlier Epistles of St. Paul: Their Motive and Origin.* London: Rivingtons, 1911.

Lang, Mabel. *Cure and Cult in Ancient Corinth: A Guide to the Asklepieion.* American Excavations in Old Corinth, Corinth Notes, no. 1. Princeton, NJ: American School of Classical Studies at Athens, 1977.

Liddell, Henry George, and Robert Scott, eds. *A Greek-English Lexicon,* rev. H. L. Jones. 2:1074. Oxford: Clarendon Press, 1940.

Lietzmann, Hans. *An die Korinther I,II.* Handbuch zum Neuen Testament, 9. Tübingen: J. C. B. Mohr (Paul Siebeck), 1931 (1st ed., 1907).

Lobeck, Christian Augustus. *Aglaophanius, sive de theologiae mysticae Graecorum causis.* 3 vols. n.p. 1829.

Luedemann, Gerd. *Paul, Apostle to the Gentiles: Studies in Chronology.* Trans. F. Stanley Jones. Philadelphia: Fortress Press, 1984. Translated from *Paulus, der Heidenapostel.* Forschungen zur Religion und Literatur des Alten und Neuen Testaments, Heft 130. Göttingen: Vandenhoeck & Ruprecht, 1980.

McDonald, William A. "Archaeology and St. Paul's Journeys in Greek Lands. Part 3—Corinth." *Biblical Archaeologist,* 5(1942): 36-48.

MacMullen, Ramsay. *Christianizing the Roman Empire. A.D. 100-400.* New Haven: Yale University Press, 1984.

———. *Enemies of the Roman Order. Treason, Unrest and Alienation in the Empire.* Cambridge, MA: Harvard University Press, 1966.

———. *Paganism in the Roman Empire.* New Haven: Yale University Press, 1981.

———. *Roman Social Relations, 50 B.C. to A.D. 284.* New Haven: Yale University Press, 1974

Malherbe, Abraham J. *Social Aspects of Early Christianity.* 2nd ed., enlarged. Philadelphia: Fortress Press, 1983 (1st ed., 1977).

Malina, Bruce J. "Clean and Unclean: Understanding Rules of Purity." Chap. 6 of *The New Testament World: Insights from Cultural Anthropology,* 122-52. Atlanta: John Knox Press, 1981.

Manson, T. W. "The Corinthian Correspondence (1) (1941)." In *Studies in the Gospels and Epistles.* Ed. Matthew Black, 190-209. Manchester: Manchester University Press, 1962.

Meeks, Wayne A. "'And Rose Up to Play': Midrash and Paraenesis in 1 Corinthians 10:1-22." *Journal for the Study of the New Testament,* 16 (1982): 64-78.

_______. *The First Urban Christians. The Social World of the Apostle Paul.* New Haven and London: Yale University Press, 1983.

_______. *The Moral World of the First Christians.* Ed. Wayne A. Meeks. Library of Early Christianity. Philadelphia: Westminster Press, 1986.

_______. "Review of *Herrenmahl und hellenistischer Kult: Eine religionsgeschichtliche untersuchung zum erster Korinthbrief,* by Hans-Joseph Klauck. NTAbh 15. Münster: Aschendorf, 1982." *Journal of Biblical Literature,* 103 (1984): 663-65.

_______. " 'Since Then You Would Need to Go Out of the World': Group Boundaries in Pauline Christianity." In *Critical History and Biblical Faith: New Testament Perspectives.* Ed. Thomas J. Ryan, 4-29. College Theological Society Annual Publication Series. Ann Arbor, MI: Edward Brothers, 1979.

Mehauden, Maurice. "Le secret central de l'initiation aux mystères d'Eleusis." in *Initiation. Contributions to the Theme of the Study-Conference of the International Association for the History of Religions Held at Strasburg, Sept. 17th to 22nd, 1964.* Studies in the History of Religions (Supplements to *Nvmen*), 10. Ed. C. J. Bleeker, 65-70. Leiden: E. J. Brill, 1965.

Meritt, Benjamin Dean. *Corinth: Results of Excavations Conducted by the American School of Classical Studies at Athens.* Vol. 8, Part 1, *The Greek Inscriptions. 1896-1927.* Cambridge, MA: Harvard University Press, 1931.

Meyer, B. E., and E. P. Sanders, eds. *Jewish and Christian Self-Definition in the First Three Centuries.* Vol. 1, *The Shaping of Christianity in the Second and Third Centuries.* Vol. 2, *Aspects of Judaism in the Greco-Roman Period.* Vol. 3, *Self-Definition in the Greco-Roman Period.* Philadelphia: Fortress Press, 1980-82.

Meyer, Heinrich August Wilhelm. *Critical and Exegetical Handbook to the Epistles to the Corinthians.* Vol. 1, *First Epistle, Chapters 1-13.* Critical and Exegetical Commentary on the New Testament, Parts 5 and 6. Trans. (from the 5th German ed. [1869]) D. Douglas Bannerman. Edinburgh: T. & T. Clark, 1877.

Murphy-O'Connor, Jerome. "1 Cor. 8:6: Cosmology or Soteriology?" *Revue biblique,* 85 (1978): 253-67.

_______. "Corinthian Slogans in 1 Cor. 6:12-20." *Catholic Biblical Quarterly,* 40 (1978): 391-96.

_______. "Food and Spiritual Gifts in 1 Cor. 8:8." *Catholic Biblical Quarterly,* 41 (1979): 292-98.

_______. "Freedom or the Ghetto (1 Cor. 8:1-13; 10:23-11:1)." *Revue biblique,* 85 (1978): 543-74.

_______. *St. Paul's Corinth. Texts and Archaeology.* Good News Studies, vol. 6. Ed. Robert J. Karris. Wilmington, DE: Michael Glazier, 1983.

Mylonas, George E. *Eleusis and the Eleusinian Mysteries.* Princeton: Princeton University Press, 1961.

Nilsson, Martin P. *Greek Folk Religion.* New York: Harper, 1961. Reprint. New York: Columbia University Press, 1940.

Nock, Arthur Darby. *Early Gentile Christianity and its Hellenistic Background.* New York: Harper & Row, 1964.

Orr, William F., and James Arthur Walther. *1 Corinthians.* Anchor Bible, vol. 32. Garden City, NJ: Doubleday, 1976.

Pagels, Elaine H. *The Gnostic Paul. Gnostic Exegesis of the Pauline Letters.* Philadelphia: Fortress Press, 1975.

Pierce, C. A. *Conscience in the New Testament.* Studies in Biblical Theology, no. 15. London: SCM Press, 1955.

Richardson, N. J. ed. *The Homeric Hymn to Demeter.* Oxford: Clarendon Press, 1974.

Richardson, Peter. "'I say, not the Lord': Personal Opinion, Apostolic Authority and the Development of Early Christian Halakah." *Tyndale Bulletin,* 31 (1980): 65-86.

———. *Israel in the Apostolic Church.* Cambridge: Cambridge University Press, 1969.

———. "On the Absence of 'Anti-Judaism' in 1 Corinthians." In *Anti-Judaism in Early Christianity.* Vol. 1, *Paul and the Gospels.* Ed. Peter Richardson, with D. Granskou, 59-74. Studies in Christianity and Judaism, no. 2. Waterloo, ON: Wilfrid Laurier University Press, 1986.

———. "Pauline Inconsistency: 1 Corinthians 9:19-23 and Galatians 2:11-14." *New Testament Studies,* 26 (1980): 347-62.

Riddle, D. W. "Early Christian Hospitality: A Factor in Gospel Transmission." *Journal of Biblical Literature,* 57 (1938): 141-54.

Robertson, Archibald, and Alfred Plummer. *A Critical and Exegetical Commentary on the First Epistle of St. Paul to the Corinthians.* International Critical Commentary. Edinburgh: T. & T. Clark, 1911.

Roebuck, Carl A. *Corinth: Results of Excavations Conducted by the American School of Classical Studies at Athens.* Vol. 14, *The Asklepieion and Lerna.* Princeton, NJ: American School of Classical Studies at Athens, 1951.

Sanders, E. P. *Paul and Palestinian Judaism. A Comparison of Patterns of Religion.* Philadelphia: Fortress Press, 1977.

———. *Paul, the Law, and the Jewish people.* Philadelphia: Fortress Press, 1983.

Schazmann, Paul. *Asklepieion. Baubeschreibung und Baugeschichte, Kos.* Ergebnisse der deutschen Ausgrabungen und Forschungen, 1. Herausgegeben von Rudolf Herzog. Berlin: Heinrich Keller, 1932.

Schmithals, Walter. *Gnosticism in Corinth. An Investigation of the Letters to the Corinthians.* Trans. John E. Steely. Nashville: Abingdon Press, 1971. Translated from *Die Gnosis in Korinth: eine Untersuchung zu den Korintherbriefen.* 2 neubearb. Aufl. Forschungen zur Religion und Literatur des Alten und Neuen Testaments, n.F., Heft 48. Göttingen: Vandenhoeck & Ruprecht, 1965.

Schütz, John H. "Introduction" to Gerd Theissen's *The Social Setting of Pauline Christianity. Essays on Corinth by Gerd Theissen.* Trans. John H. Schütz. Philadelphia: Fortress Press, 1982.

Scranton, Robert L. *Corinth: Results of Excavations Conducted by the American School of Classical Studies at Athens*. Vol. 1, Part 3, *Monuments in the Lower Agora and North of the Archaic Temple*. Princeton, NJ: American School of Classical Studies at Athens, 1951.

Scroggs, Robin. "The Sociological Interpretation of the New Testament: The Present State of Research." *New Testament Studies*, 26 (1979-80): 164-79.

Shear, Theodore Leslie. *Corinth: Results of Excavations Conducted by the American School of Classical Studies at Athens*. Vol. 5, *The Roman Villa*. Cambridge, MA: Harvard University Press, 1930.

Smith, Dennis E. "Meals and Morality in Paul and his World." *Society of Biblical Literature Seminar Papers*, 20: 319-39. Chico, California: Scholars Press, 1981.

Smith, Jonathan Z. "The Social Description of Early Christianity." *Religious Studies Review*, 1 (1975): 19-25.

Stambaugh, John E., and David L. Balch. *The New Testament in its Social Environment*. Ed. Wayne A. Meeks. Library of Early Christianity. Philadelphia: Westminster Press, 1986.

Stern, Menahem. *Greek and Latin Authors on Jews and Judaism*. 2 vols. Jerusalem: Israel Academy of Sciences and Humanities, 1980.

Stillwell, Richard. *Corinth: Results of Excavations Conducted by the American School of Classical Studies at Athens*. Vol. 2, *The Theatre*. Princeton, NJ: American School of Classical Studies at Athens, 1952.

________, Robert L. Scranton, and Sarah Elizabeth Freeman. *Corinth: Results of Excavations Conducted by the American School of Classical Studies at Athens*. Vol. 1, Part 2, *Architecture*. Cambridge, MA: Harvard University Press, 1941.

Stroud, Ronald. "The Sanctuary of Demeter and Kore on Acrocorinth. Preliminary Report 1: 1961-1962." *Hesperia*, 34 (1965): 1-24.

________. "The Sanctuary of Demeter and Kore on Acrocorinth: Preliminary Report 2: 1964-1965." *Hesperia*, 37 (1968): 299-330.

Tannahill, Reay. *Food in History*. New York: Stein and Day, 1973.

Tcherikover, Victor. *Hellenistic Civilization and the Jews*. Trans. S. Appelbaum. New York: Atheneum, 1959.

Theissen, Gerd. "Social Integration and Sacramental Activity: An Analysis of 1 Cor. 11:17-34." In *The Social Setting of Pauline Christianity. Essays on Corinth by Gerd Theissen*. Trans. John H. Schütz, 145-74. Philadelphia: Fortress Press, 1982. Translated from "Soziale Integration und sakramentales Handeln: Eine Analyse von 1 Cor. 11:17-34." *Novum Testamentum*, 16 (1974): 179-206.

________. "Social Stratification in the Corinthian Community: A Contribution to the Sociology of Early Hellenistic Christianity." In *The Social Setting of Pauline Christianity. Essays on Corinth by Gerd Theissen*. Trans.

John H. Schütz, 69-120. Philadelphia: Fortress Press, 1982. Translated from "Soziale Schichtung in der korinthischen Gemeinde: Ein Bietrag zur Soziologie des hellenistischen Urchristentums." *Zeitschrift für die neutestamentliche Wissenschaft und die Kunde der älteren Kirche*, 65 (1974): 232-72.

_______. "The Strong and the Weak in Corinth: A Sociological Analysis of a Theological Quarrel." In *The Social Setting of Pauline Christianity. Essays on Corinth by Gerd Theissen*. Trans. John H. Schütz, 121-44. Philadelphia: Fortress Press, 1982. Translated from "Die Starken und Schwachen in Korinth: Soziologische Analyse eines theologischen Streites." *Evangelische Theologie*, 35 (1975): 155-72.

Thrall, Margaret E. *The First and Second Letters of Paul to the Corinthians*. Cambridge: Cambridge University Press, 1965.

_______. "Pauline Use of *Syneidêsis*. *New Testament Studies*, 14 (1967): 118-25.

_______. "The Problem of 2 Cor 6:14-7:1 in Some Recent Discussion." *New Testament Studies*, 24 (1977): 132-48.

Tomlinson, R. A. *Epidauros*. Archaeological Sites. Ed. Malcolm Todd. London: Granada, 1983.

_______. "Two Buildings in Sanctuaries of Asklepios." *Journal of Hellenic Studies*, 89 (1969): 108-17.

Tomson, Peter J. *Paul and the Jewish Law: Halakha in the Letters of the Apostle to the Gentiles*. Compendium Rerum Iudiacarum ad Novum Testamentum. Section 3, Jewish Traditions in Early Christian Literature, 1. Minneapolis: Fortress Press, 1990.

Travlos, John. "The Asklepieion," In *Pictorial Dictionary of Ancient Athens*, 127-37. New York: Praeger, 1971.

_______. "Spring House of the Asklepieion," In *Pictorial Dictionary of Ancient Athens*, 138-39. New York: Praeger, 1971.

von Soden, Hans Freiherr. "Sakrament und Ethik bei Paulus." In *Urchristentum und Geschichte*, 239-51. Tübingen: J. C. B. Mohr (Paul Siebeck), 1951. A greatly abridged translation is found in Wayne Meeks, ed. *The Writings of St. Paul*. A Norton Critical Edition, 257-68. New York: W. W. Norton, 1972.

Walton, Alice. *The Cult of Asklepios*. Cornell Studies in Classical Philology, no. 3. Ithaca, NY, 1894. Reprint. New York: Johnson Reprint Corporation, 1965.

Weinberg, Saul S. *Corinth: Results of Excavations Conducted by the American School of Classical Studies at Athens*. Vol. 1, Part 5, *The Southeast Building; the Twin Basilicas; the Mosaic House*. Princeton, NJ: American School of Classical Studies at Athens, 1960.

Weiss, Johannes. *Der erste Korinthbrief*. Göttingen: Vandenhoeck & Ruprecht, 1910.

_______. *The History of Primitive Christianity.* Trans. "4 friends" and ed. Frederick C. Grant. New York: Wilson-Erickson, 1937. Translated from *Das Urchristentum.* Göttingen: Vandenhoeck & Ruprecht, 1914.

Welter, Gabriel. *Troizen und Kalaureia.* Berlin: Verlag Gebr. Mann, 1941.

Wenham, Gordon J. "The Theology of Unclean Food." *Evangelical Quarterly,* 53 (1981): 6-15.

West, Allen Brown. *Corinth: Results of Excavations Conducted by the American School of Classical Studies at Athens.* Vol. 8, Part 2, *Latin Inscriptions. 1896-1926.* Cambridge, MA: Harvard University Press, 1931.

Willis, Wendell Lee. *Idol Meat in Corinth. The Pauline Argument in 1 Corinthians 8 and 10.* SBL Dissertation Series, 68. Chico, CA: Scholars Press, 1985.

Wilson, Stephen G. *Anti-Judaism in Early Christianity.* Vol. 2, *Separation and Polemic.* Studies in Christianity and Judaism, no. 2. Waterloo, ON: Wilfrid Laurier University Press, 1986.

Wiseman, James. "Corinth and Rome 1: 228 B.C.-A.D. 267." In *Aufstieg und Niedergang der römischen Welt. Geschichte und Kultur Roms in Spiegel der neueren Forschung.* 2.7 (*Politische Geschichte*). 1. Berlin: Walter de Gruyter, 1979: 438-548.

Index of Subjects and Authors

Please note: This is not an exhaustive index for subjects or authors cited. Authors are cited only where the substance of their arguments is discussed, or where I have disputed their views. Many other briefer citations of authors will be found in the notes to the text. Only extended discussion of subjects is cited; other discussion of subjects listed may be found in the text.

Index of Citations of Ancient Sources

New Testament

Other Sources

SR SUPPLEMENTS

Note: Nos. 1 to 8, 10, 13, 15, 18 and 20 in this series are out of print.

9. ***Developments in Buddhist Thought: Canadian Contributions to Buddhist Studies***
   Edited by Roy C. Amore
   1979 / iv + 196 pp.
11. ***Political Theology in the Canadian Context***
   Edited by Benjamin G. Smillie
   1982 / xii + 260 pp.
12. ***Truth and Compassion: Essays on Judaism and Religion in Memory of Rabbi Dr. Solomon Frank***
   Edited by Howard Joseph, Jack N. Lightstone and Michael D. Oppenheim
   1983 / vi + 217 pp.
14. ***The Moral Mystic***
   James R. Horne
   1983 / x + 134 pp.
16. ***Studies in the Book of Job***
   Edited by Walter E. Aufrecht
   1985 / xii + 76 pp.
17. ***Christ and Modernity: Christian Self-Understanding in a Technological Age***
   David J. Hawkin
   1985 / x + 181 pp.
19. ***Modernity and Religion***
   Edited by William Nicholls
   1987 / vi + 191 pp.

STUDIES IN CHRISTIANITY AND JUDAISM / ÉTUDES SUR LE CHRISTIANISME ET LE JUDAÏSME

Note: No. 1 in this series is out of print.

2. ***Anti-Judaism in Early Christianity***
   Vol. 1, ***Paul and the Gospels***, edited by Peter Richardson with David Granskou
   1986 / x + 232 pp.
   Vol. 2, ***Separation and Polemic***
   Edited by Stephen G. Wilson
   1986 / xii + 185 pp.
3. ***Society, the Sacred, and Scripture in Ancient Judaism: A Sociology of Knowledge***
   Jack N. Lightstone
   1988 / xiv + 126 pp.
4. ***Law in Religious Communities in the Roman Period: The Debate Over*** **Torah** ***and*** **Nomos** ***in Post-Biblical Judaism and Early Christianity***
   Peter Richardson and Stephen Westerholm
   with A. I. Baumgarten, Michael Pettem and Cecilia Wassén
   1991 / x + 164 pp.
5. ***Dangerous Food: 1 Corinthians 8-10 in Its Context***
   Peter D. Gooch
   1993 / xviii + 178 pp.

THE STUDY OF RELIGION IN CANADA / SCIENCES RELIGIEUSES AU CANADA

1. ***Religious Studies in Alberta: A State-of-the-Art Review***
   Ronald W. Neufeldt
   1983 / xiv + 145 pp.
2. ***Les sciences religieuses au Québec depuis 1972***
   Louis Rousseau et Michel Despland
   1988 / 158 p.
3. ***Religious Studies in Ontario: A State-of-the-Art Review***
   Harold Remus, William Closson James and Daniel Fraikin
   1992 / xviii + 422 pp.
4. ***Religious Studies in Manitoba and Saskatchewan: A State-of-the-Art Review***
   John M. Badertscher, Gordon Harland and Roland E. Miller
   1993 / vi + 166 pp.

EDITIONS SR

Note: Nos. 1, 3, 5, 6 and 9 in this series are out of print.

2. ***The Conception of Punishment in Early Indian Literature***
   Terence P. Day
   1982 / iv + 328 pp.
4. ***Le messianisme de Louis Riel***
   Gilles Martel
   1984 / xviii + 483 p.
7. ***L'étude des religions dans les écoles : l'expérience américaine, anglaise et canadienne***
   Fernand Ouellet
   1985 / xvi + 666 p.
8. ***Of God and Maxim Guns: Presbyterianism in Nigeria, 1846-1966***
   Geoffrey Johnston
   1988 / iv + 322 pp.
10. ***Prometheus Rebound: The Irony of Atheism***
    Joseph C. McLelland
    1988 / xvi + 366 pp.
11. ***Competition in Religious Life***
    Jay Newman
    1989 / viii + 237 pp.
12. ***The Huguenots and French Opinion, 1685-1787: The Enlightenment Debate on Toleration***
    Geoffrey Adams
    1991 / xiv + 335 pp.
13. ***Religion in History: The Word, the Idea, the Reality / La religion dans l'histoire : le mot, l'idée, la réalité***
    Edited by / Sous la direction de Michel Despland and/et Gérard Vallée
    1992 / x + 252 pp.
14. ***Sharing Without Reckoning: Imperfect Right and the Norms of Reciprocity***
    Millard Schumaker
    1992 / xiv + 112 pp.
15. ***Love and the Soul: Psychological Interpretations of the Eros and Psyche Myth***
    James Gollnick
    1992 / viii + 174 pp.

COMPARATIVE ETHICS SERIES / COLLECTION D'ÉTHIQUE COMPARÉE

Note: No. 1 in this series is out of print.

2. ***Methodist Education in Peru: Social Gospel, Politics, and American Ideological and Economic Penetration, 1888-1930***
   Rosa del Carmen Bruno-Jofré
   1988 / xiv + 223 pp.
3. ***Prophets, Pastors and Public Choices: Canadian Churches and the Mackenzie Valley Pipeline Debate***
   Roger Hutchinson
   1992 / xiv + 142 pp.

DISSERTATIONS SR

1. ***The Social Setting of the Ministry as Reflected in the Writings of Hermas, Clement and Ignatius***
   Harry O. Maier
   1991 / viii + 230 pp.
2. ***Literature as Pulpit: The Christian Social Activism of Nellie L. McClung***
   Randi R. Warne
   1993 / viii + 236 pp.

Available from / en vente chez :

Wilfrid Laurier University Press

Waterloo, Ontario, Canada N2L 3C5

Published by Wilfrid Laurier University Press for the Canadian Corporation for Studies in Religion/ Corporation Canadienne des Sciences Religieuses